IMPOSSIBLE TO EASY

111 DELICIOUS RECIPES TO HELP YOU PUT GREAT MEALS ON THE TABLE EVERY DAY

ROBERT IRVINE

with Brian O'Reilly

WILLIAM MORROW
An Imprint of HarperCollinsPublishers

HarperCollins books may be purchased for educational, business, or sales promotional use. For information please write: Special Markets Department, HarperCollins Publishers, 10 East 53rd Street, New York, NY 10022.

FIRST EDITION

Designed by Kris Tobiassen

Recipes edited and tested by Virginia O'Reilly

Library of Congress Cataloging-in-Publication Data

Irvine, Robert
  Impossible to easy : 111 delicious recipes to help you put great meals on the table every day / Robert Irvine with Brian O'Reilly.—1st ed.
    p. cm.
  Includes index.
  ISBN 978-0-06-147411-8
  1. Cookery. I. O'Reilly, Brian II. Title.
  TX714.I75 2010
  641.5—dc22

2009040153

---

10 11 12 13 14 WBC/WCF 10 9 8 7 6 5 4 3 2 1

CONTENTS

5. The Importance of Being Protein: Meats and Poultry 124

6. Bounty of the Sea: Fish and Shellfish 166

10. Never Skip Dessert! 253

INTRODUCTION

I've always thought of myself as a student of culinary theory. I started collecting second-hand cookbooks and interpreting and analyzing the photographs contained therein from about the age of eleven, devising my own approaches (though sometimes only in my imagination) for preparing and presenting the dishes they depicted. I've always felt that cooking is largely about creativity and inspiration, not just talented mimicry of other cooks' recipes and favorite tricks of the trade. Whenever I managed any opportunity to cook for people in my youth, whether at sleepaway camp, at school, onboard a school ship, or at home for my family and neighbors, I inevitably added personal touches of my own to old standards, kept or eliminated elements according to my personal preferences, experimented by recombining ingredients and preparations in ways that excited me and that I thought would excite the taste buds of my dining audience (or victims, depending on the success or failure of my latest and greatest innovations).

I've never been attracted to the esoteric in cooking for its own sake. The majority of my preferred methodologies are tried and true. My goal has always been to cajole the most flavor that can possibly be achieved out of my chosen ingredients. I've studied classical French technique. I understand the importance of ambient temperature when creating a terrine, I know how emulsification works in a wide variety of circumstances, and I can fillet a fish and break down a chicken in no time flat. My soufflés rise, my sauces don't break and, on a good day, I can smell a perfect sear or a tainted stock from fifty feet away.

I graduated with honors from the Culinary School of Hard Knocks. My early professional instruction came at the hands of hundreds, if not thousands, of hungry sailors in Her Majesty's Royal Navy at every mealtime. They worked hard, played hard, and came to the table hungry, wanting to eat as much good food as they could get their hands on. They were tough. Yet I've seldom, if ever, run across an audience more appreciative of the special touches that

I learned to bring to some of the typical shipboard fare, whether it be a sprinkling of fresh herbs, a surprisingly tender and flavorful cut of meat, or a dessert that might have unexpectedly reminded them of home. They could be hard to handle when disappointed but purred like kittens when they were well fed. They taught me many valuable lessons, the most important of which is what it takes to get a good hot meal on the table in the real world.

I've traveled extensively and have cooked and eaten a swath through miles and miles of ships' messes, captain's tables on cruise ships, VIP and state dinners in the capitals of the world; in hotels, both modest and fine, large and small; in taverns, restaurants, pubs, and bars of every stripe and description. As I cook and as I sample, I try to pay attention, both to the bad and the good on the plates in front of me.

My experience as the crazed, overstressed, somewhat tyrannical (but lovable!) star of *Dinner: Impossible* has broadened my portfolio even more. Now I know that when you're cooking in an Ice Hotel and you cut into a potato when the temperature around you is eleven degrees Fahrenheit, its high moisture content causes ice crystals to form at the point of the cut, at which point it's best to place it in water in a refrigerator to keep warm. I now have at least half a dozen recipes at my fingertips for venison appetizers, including venison Oscar, venison curry meatballs, venison hot dogs, and venison-stuffed shrimp, and they all serve four thousand. I've learned that the proper application of liquid nitrogen to pureed mango will cause it to look and behave like Cheddar cheese. I know that fresh hogs' ears and trotters need a bit longer than three hours when braised in an iron pot in a blazing hot fireplace before they are perfectly al dente. I can tell you with perfect confidence that frogs' legs are delicious stewed with a little white wine on a cattle range over an open fire, that golf club shafts (with the heads neatly knocked off) make a terrific rotisserie turning device when grilling whole beef tenderloins, that Elvis ate fried peanut butter and banana sandwiches only *once* in a great while (gospel according to Priscilla), and that I will probably never completely and perfectly understand what children like to eat for their dinners.

I know these things because I am a chef. My job demands that I gather information, constantly experiment with cooking methods, preparations, and presentations, and endlessly obsess over the detail of every plate I serve. It's not for everybody.

But *everybody* has to eat, and most everybody either needs to, likes to, or wishes they could cook.

So, cook!

It's not hard to learn the mostly simple skills that can make you a good cook, even if you start without much knowledge at all. You can learn how to make a roux, and from there, how to make great soups, sauces, and stews. You can learn knife skills: how to julienne (cut meat or vegetables into thin strips), chiffonade (cut herbs and leafy vegetables into thin strips), or brunoise (cut vegetables into tiny bits—the French have a different word for everything). Learn the difference between a simmer and a rolling boil, and you can perfect your approach both toward poaching an egg and cooking al dente pasta. Learn how to take whisk in hand and move it briskly in a clockwise motion (come on, how hard can it be?), and you too can make hollandaise and meringue. Then you're already more than halfway to eggs Benedict and lemon meringue pie. And if you're already handy in the kitchen, you know how satisfying it is to broaden your outlook and try new techniques, new flavor combinations, and new recipes.

Learn when to be patient and when to be active in the kitchen:

Patient: Wait an extra minute or two when putting a sear on a piece of fish or meat, especially a nice piece of meat. Most cooks, even practiced ones, try to move the food too soon and break the sear before the surface of the protein has perfectly caramelized. Wait . . . for . . . it.

Active: Whether you're working on stiffening peaks in a whipped cream or emulsifying that hollandaise, whisk with authority. Let that mixture know you mean business, and serve no meringue until it stands up and salutes you back.

In cooking, easy is a state of mind. It may seem easy for anybody to open a boxed, pre-fabricated mac-and-cheese product and mechanically follow the instructions. They'll end up with something that resembles macaroni and cheese in a fairly short period of time. But you're not just anybody.

You'll start your macaroni water boiling, just as they will. But whilst it is heating, you'll take a little flour and butter, whisk it in a saucepot for two minutes, pour in a cup of milk, and add shredded cheese to make a Mornay sauce, which *they* likely don't even know about. As it thickens and shimmers in the pot, you'll cook your pasta, just like they will. In the time it takes them to add their manufactured powder to their macaroni, you'll be combining your macaroni with your cheese sauce in a baking dish and popping it under the broiler. During the few minutes it takes to finish baking your homemade, soon-to-be-legendary family classic, it's true that they'll already be gloomily ingesting their soulless, cheese product–based compound. But you, by persevering for perhaps five extra minutes, will instead be breaking into your cheesy, golden brown crust, inhaling the succulent aroma, and spooning and serving the warm, gooey perfection you created onto your plate and the plates of your family, their eyes glistening with gratitude and appreciation. Does that make you better than them? You'll have to decide. I'm not a philosopher; I'm a cook.

Everybody likes things to be easy once in a while, but I'd like to suggest that it's okay to feel stressed before, after, or whilst you are cooking. Anything worth doing (and cooking is worth doing, I assure you) is worth suffering at least a little stress over. Now, in the area of stress in the kitchen, I have been accused of being more a carrier than a sufferer ("Are you scared? You should be."), but I don't believe in tension for its own sake. I do believe that stress, when properly managed, can mean that you're alert and paying attention, not necessarily that you're having a nervous breakdown. Stoves are hot, ovens are hot, knives are sharp, and you have to stay on your toes and learn to know what you're doing if you are going to be happy in the kitchen. Cooking well and making little extra demands on yourself along the way—like paying a few extra dollars for organic meats and poultry, driving a few extra blocks for fresher fish, taking a few extra minutes and making a sauce for an entrée, dropping some fresh herbs on the plate just before service, and trying a new recipe every week or every month—can and will pay big dividends over even a short period of time. I prefer a take-charge attitude over takeout any day of the week.

There are few things I like better than the moment you've gotten something done, you stand back and look at it, and it's good. I am personally addicted to moments like these. Maybe it has something to do with my military background, but I believe in the rewards system, in the cause and effect of honest effort and pleasurable result. Creating pleasure with food is one of the pillars of my culinary philosophy.

Part of the pleasure and fun of cookbooks for me is being able to re-create the dishes I see in the pictures, either as prescribed by the author or with my own special touches added. Nothing has been more frustrating to me, especially in my early cooking years, than trying my hand at a recipe and having my finished product miserably fail to sparkle, shine, stand up, arch, swirl, or otherwise defy the laws of physics and gravity in the manner depicted on the page. There are tricks of the trade used in food photography, like the use of sticks and pins, oils and compounds, sprays, artificial supports, stand-ins, food colorings, and the like, that make it virtually impossible for the home cook to achieve the artistry the food stylist creates on picture day. I've learned over the years to spot these tricks, and they drive me crazy. The pictures in this book are honest. I cooked the food, I plated the food, and we took a picture. Some of my favorite platings may take a little more effort than just plopping the food on the plate, but I think you can do them all. I think you can be as good a cook as you want to be.

Believe me, some days you'll be better than others. Some days you'll be tired at the end of the day and hardly want to make anything at all. On those days, do not underestimate the power of a dish of pasta, some good olive oil, a little garlic, some grated cheese, and a fresh tomato. Other days you'll want to pull out all the stops. On those days, your starters will thrill, your flavors will have harmonious layers, your sauces will be silky, your meats robust, your fish light and flaky, your sides snappy, and your desserts rich, sweet, and satisfying. You'll be striking sparks on the taste buds of your friends and family. Whether you're cooking something simple and aiming for that warm inner glow or shooting for fireworks with your food, take that extra moment to enjoy looking at and appreciating what you've achieved. That feeling can keep you going meal after meal.

No dinner is impossible! You can keep your food simple and still make it great. You can allow yourself to use dried pasta instead of fresh, skinless boneless chicken breasts, and fresh frozen vegetables and still get great, flavorful results if you use fresh herbs to finish your dishes instead of dried, freshly ground spices instead of pre-ground, a squeeze of real lemon juice here, a splash of good wine there, or a well-timed dollop of butter where you may not have thought to use one before. Create, try new combinations and ideas, learn to use your imagination when you cook, and you'll never be lonely; the world might just beat a path to your door. To all those who want to cook: Cook to your heart's delight! And to all those who love to eat: Don't forget to say thank you, clear your own place when you've finished, help with the washing up—and all hail the cook!

1. MISE EN PLACE: IN THE BEGINNING . . .

Many chefs, myself included, like to say that there are no hard-and-fast rules in cooking. If pressed on the strict, absolute truth of this notion, though, I would have to quote the Irish philosopher who, when asked a direct question about the truth of virtually any statement, replied, "Well, it is and it isn't. . . ." As with most truisms, clichés, and platitudes, there are shades of rightness and wrongness that need to be taken into account.

The truest final test for any cook comes shortly after the plate leaves your hands and hits the table. Anyone who raises fork or spoon to their lips, any diner, old or young, gourmand or trencherman, is the ultimate arbiter of what they think tastes good. I can work my culinary fingers to the bone, creating dish after dish with the most luxurious ingredients, meticulously prepared and cunningly presented, but if you taste them and decide you don't like them, I'm through.

You may not like my food (which thankfully doesn't happen to me too often), but you're going to have a tough time telling me that it wasn't correctly prepared because I practice a craft. If I were a master carpenter and I made you a table, you might not like my choice of wood, the design, the size, or the shape, but it will damn well be, unmistakably, a table. Cooking does have many facets of artistry to it, allowing for sudden flights of inspiration and, on rare occasions, the appearance of poetry on a plate, but it is also a *profession* that has at its foundation generations of accepted practices, methods, and standards. You can master these one by one and become a good, even a great cook. Start with your understanding of *mise en place.*

Mise en place has to do primarily with the way you set yourself up to cook. When I played football (or soccer) as a younger man, I was reasonably fast and had a certain amount of athletic skill, but as I learned more about the game I found out how important it was to be able to set yourself up, that what you did *without* the ball was at least as important as what you did *with* the ball, if not more so. To rise to the highest levels you have to be able to see the whole field and what every player is doing or going to be doing. In cooking, especially in a professional kitchen, you have to do things in a certain order, control your pots and pans, and control the heat of your stoves and ovens, because every decision you make has a direct influence on the next, and on three or four decisions down the line.

If you want to mix some cloves of roasted garlic in with your mashed potatoes, you've got to get a head of garlic in the oven early, well before you finish your potatoes. At breakfast, you put the bacon on before you start frying the eggs. The bacon takes longer to cook. When you're breading a piece of veal, best to dip it in flour, then beaten eggs, then breadcrumbs to achieve a proper coating. When thickening soups, sauces, or stews, you need to add cold to hot or hot to cold, then raise all up to a boil for the desired effect.

The names of many of my dishes tell you nearly everything you need to know about the *mise en place* required right at the outset. When I write Endive with Granny Smith Apples, Smoked Bacon, and Creamy Cheddar Dressing (page 58), Garlic and Herb Pesto–Crusted Lamb Chops (page 153), Pan-Seared Salmon and Lemon Confit over Sage Ratatouille (page 182), or Pecan Bourbon Pralines (page 263), I'm giving you quite a lot of information about the ingredients, the methods, the timeline, and the flavor profile for the finished dish. Endive, apples, bacon, and dressing indicate a salad. My recipe might differ from yours, but if I left you to your own devices, you could likely make a version of this salad based on my description and probably do a pretty good job of it. Salmon, lemon confit, and sage ratatouille: You would undoubtedly start the ratatouille first, make the confit whilst the ratatouille is cooking, sear the salmon toward the end because it will cook the quickest, plate, and serve. Garlic and Herb Pesto–Crusted Lamb Chops: Make a simple pesto in a food processor or with a mortar and pestle, spread the mixture over the lamb chops, and pop them in the oven. If you want baked or roasted potatoes with your lamb chops, better get them in at least a half hour beforehand. Pecan Bourbon Pralines are easy to make, but you have to know that a praline is a type of nut candy. You need at least some technical knowledge to interpret all of these descriptions. You have to know what endive is, what a sear is, what ratatouille is, what comprises pesto . . . but with just a basic stockpile of information at your fingertips and just a little accumulated cooking skill, you can find your way.

As in comedy and demolition, an essential concept in cooking is timing. If you over-whip your hollandaise, you'll soon have a bowlful of goop as thick as butter. If you carve your meat before it has had a chance to rest, you'll sacrifice all of its natural juices. Overcook your roast, meat loaf, or soufflé, and you may find yourself on the phone with a takeout menu in your hand. Good cooking is about controlling the situation in which you place yourself, whether you're a restaurant chef, a home cook, a dad stationed in front of a barbecue grill, or a little kid roasting marshmallows over an open fire.

In cooking, the manner in which you begin your task may well determine the success of the outcome. "Well begun is nearly done" is never more true than in the kitchen. As ye begin, so shall ye finish.

Robert's Rules for Impossible Dinners

GET ORGANIZED: *Remember the rules for* mise en place: *a place for everything and everything in its place before you begin. Any task becomes less daunting when you break it into its component parts and go one step at a time.*

Think about the simplest example of *mise en place*: a bowl of cereal. Equipment: 1 spoon, 1 bowl; Ingredients: box of cereal; 1 cup milk. Place the bowl on the table, pour the cereal into a bowl, pour milk gently over the cereal. Eat with spoon.

Now think of this year's Thanksgiving dinner. Stop. I can already feel you seizing up in panic through the very pages of this book. The complexity level of these two examples varies, but your approach must be essentially the same. The bowl must go down on the table first, or the cereal will be scattered all over the place. The cereal must go into the bowl. Logical. But why does virtually everybody on the planet instinctively pour the cereal first, *then* the milk? Because by doing so, you can adjust the recipe as you go according to your likes and dislikes. If you just poured in an entire cup of milk first, you'd have to keep pouring cereal until you achieved the correct proportions. By pouring in the dry ingredient first, a lot or a little, followed by the wet ingredient, *you* retain control over the process. Just about everyone knows this without thinking about it, and nearly everyone knows how to make a good bowl of cereal.

The same concept of control applies when planning any meal, and more often than not, the process and the results are immediately subject to your personal judgment and inclinations. For some folks, the *mise en place* for a hamburger is grabbing the keys, driving to a drive-through, throwing some cash through the window, and driving away with a warm paper bag in hand. For others, the process starts with forming and cooking the patty, then placing it on a roll and finishing with prepackaged condiments. For a select few, the process may start considerably earlier. If you want to create your own freshly baked bun, you must allow time for making dough, proofing, and baking. If you'd like to create your own condiments, say, freshly made ketchup, you would have to cook down some tomatoes, then properly season and puree them, which is going to take some time. If you want to make your own pickles, you might have to start days, maybe weeks in advance to get them just the way you like them. In any case, you have to decide what you would like to make and how you would like to make it, and then apply your common sense and experience, which, like any well-exercised muscle, will grow and become stronger the more you use it.

Look at every meal, large or small, as a mechanical process. Make sure you understand each step in its proper order, and the method will fall into place for you like a line of dominoes.

CREATE A TIMELINE: *The items with the longest cooking times must be addressed first. Write down your menu, your to-do list, prep whatever possible as far in advance as you can, stay calm, and remember: You're the cook, and dinner's ready when you say it is.*

A lot of the advice I'll offer in this book is based on principles of common sense. I encourage you to use those things you already know to your advantage. You probably know that if you don't get the turkey in first thing Thanksgiving morning, you run the risk of eating at midnight. If you leave a steak under the broiler for half an hour, you're creating charcoal, not dinner. If you go shopping and forget to buy eggs for your soufflé, you can't make it; you're sunk. You cannot cook with ingredients you do not have. If you see six ounces of butter in an ingredients list for pan-searing a protein and dressing it with a reduction sauce, check ahead in the method and see what all that butter is being used for. If you're meant to reserve some until the end to finish your sauce, pay attention—don't just dump it all into the pan at the beginning. We'll remind you, too, as we go along, just to help you build good habits.

I'm suggesting not only that you take advantage of your common sense in the kitchen, but that you do so with an attitude of *command.* Be the boss. With even a little practice, the food will do what you want it to do. Don't let it push you around.

For a lot of the recipes in this book, we've created a timeline for you to follow. This will help you learn how to organize your work in the kitchen. Perform tasks in a logical manner, always keeping the end results in mind. Start the tasks that will take the longest first: Roasting a head of garlic can take nearly an hour (though we may offer you an alternative method or two); boiling potatoes takes about half an hour; mashing or whipping potatoes and finishing them with butter and cream, salt and pepper, and the roasted cloves of garlic is done only in the last few minutes. Thinking ahead and making time for that one extra step—roasting the garlic, for instance—can take your mashed potatoes from ordinary to over the moon with virtually no extra effort on your part.

There is an excellent example of this in *Kramer vs. Kramer*, the film starring Dustin Hoffman and Meryl Streep. Meryl walks out on Dustin and their marriage at the beginning of the film, leaving him to care for their young son on his own for the first time. The fun starts when father and son try to make breakfast before school on their first morning together. French toast is on the menu, and every element is put together *bass ackwards*, as a titanic power struggle erupts between small child and hapless adult. The eggs, shells mostly included, are smashed, manhandled, and dumped in a pan with bread just long enough to barely say hello to one another before they are incinerated with extreme prejudice. The scene closes to the blare of a fire alarm, and no one gets fed.

Later, near the end of the film, boy and man have come to a warm mutual understanding, and their new levels of respect and affection are reflected in their behavior whilst cooking. French toast is on again, but this time, after months of practice, their choreography is a wonder to behold. Nary a word is spoken as the eggs are cracked into a bowl, whisked to perfection, and introduced politely to the bread. All is slipped into a perfectly heated pan, flipped, and finished on two plates with just a whisper of maple syrup. In the kitchen, they have become Astaire and Rogers, Balanchine and Baryshnikov, Batman and Robin. They own their kitchen. In the end, it is a beautiful tale of familial love, but it's always my inner chef that cries for joy during this scene.

You sear the steak, *you* baste the roast, *you* whisk the sauce and mount it with butter to a silky smoothness. *You* decide what's on the menu, when and how it is cooked. *You* are in charge.

GO WITH WHAT YOU KNOW: *Under the gun is not the time to be experimenting with foie gras or trying your first soufflé. If you're a confident roaster, go with a roast. Make what you know and make it as well as you know how, and they'll love you for it.*

There are a lot of things I like about this piece of advice, and it covers more ground than it may look like at first glance.

First, I like it because it's practical. You can only do what you can do in any given situation. That doesn't mean you should put limits on yourself, but it does mean you should be realistic. Cooking is largely governed by scientific principles: chemistry, physics, biology, maybe with a little bit of anatomy and botany thrown in on the side. A certain amount of heat applied to certain combinations of molecules gets you certain, highly predictable results. Food generally doesn't burn itself; you burn it. When it's delicious, it's because you did something (usually a number of things) the right way.

Through practice and experience, you become a confident cook. Some cooks are more instinctive than others, but anyone can become a better cook by focusing their attention on the craft of cooking. Most of us started learning in the home kitchens of our youth. Chefs my age and older can generally point to the influence of mothers and fathers who cooked family meals in a time before the hyperscheduling of children and the demands of round-the-clock working schedules. A lot of the food from our childhood was basic, filling, and, if we were lucky, tasted really good. Favorite dishes from those early days of food consciousness form the base of the pyramid, the foundation from which most of us judge what we like and dislike throughout the rest of our lives. Later, experimentation and education take hold, and a repertoire is built.

There are always things you are good at and things you are better at. As hard as I work to diversify, I generally like to have a protein as a basis for my entrées, usually done in a straightforward manner, either seared, fried, braised, roasted, poached, or baked. I'll happily put any number of twists on a theme, but my variations are most often based on the basic tenets of my craft. Although I've had the chance to experiment, especially on *Dinner: Impossible,* with *sous vide* techniques, with the use of compounds that mess with the basic chemistry of certain types of food, even with the use of liquid nitrogen to flash freeze and alter the essential nature of ingredients, I know myself and what I like, and for the most part, that approach is not for me. Brilliant chefs like Ferran Adrià, Wiley Dufresne, and Homaro Cantu might tend to disagree.

We all cook from the inside out, informing our food with our creative imagination as well as our acquired cooking knowledge. My personal advice to you is to learn to braise, sear, fry, roast, or bake one thing exceptionally well, letting your own taste be your guide, then build from there.

KEEP IT SIMPLE: *When cooking for a crowd, especially on short notice, use the freshest ingredients you have on hand or can shop for quickly, and keep it simple, but as good as you can make it. You don't have to make fifty individual canapés; maybe just split a loaf of great bread, lay on some fresh mozzarella and basil, drizzle with good olive oil, cut it down, and you're in. You have the option of cooking family style in big bowls and platters and letting everybody serve themselves. Your food doesn't need to be complicated, it just has to taste great!*

Inevitably, when you press a great chef about his favorite dish, about what he or she likes to eat best, the answer is inevitably something laughably simple. Jacques Pépin will be incredibly satisfied with fresh asparagus with a poached egg and a little brown butter. Jean-Georges Vongerichten loves toast and collects toasters. Give Roberto Donna a plate of pasta with nice olive oil, fresh tomato, and basil and leave him alone . . . he's eating.

There's almost nothing I would rather eat than a great steak with French fries. Make a nice peppercorn sauce to go with it and you can put a fork in me, I'm done. We shot an episode of *Dinner: Impossible* at a Renaissance fair, cooking only with medieval tools and implements. My friend and *sous* chef for the day, David Britton, made bread boules in an outdoor clay oven from freshly made dough. When I grabbed a steaming loaf, slathered on some hand-churned butter, and ripped it to shreds, I could practically feel my eyes rolling back in my head from pleasure.

Feed any chef worth his salt a nice, thick, properly seasoned and well-cooked pork chop or a fresh, vine-ripened tomato with a little kosher salt or a few drops of aged balsamic vinegar on it, or a great slice of pie with a scoop of ice cream, and you'll have a happy chef on your hands.

When you're up against it, especially when cooking for a lot of people, racks of ribs on the grill, a big fish fry-up, a big pot of stew, gumbo, or jambalaya, a pile of boiled shrimp in the shell sprinkled with Old Bay, a big pot of fresh corn, or one or two freshly built big salads will happily satisfy a hungry crowd.

SIGN 'EM UP! *If there's another couple of good cooks handy, or if you've got kids at home, get them on the team and put them to work. It's a great way to build family memories—the more the merrier, and the faster things get done!*

This piece of advice stands at the crossroads where getting things done meets "Let's have some fun!" Getting everyone involved in the cooking process makes sense, makes time fly by, and makes for good times. In a classical French brigade system or in the military, one proceeds through the most basic skills to the most complex, from *commis* to grill chef, from potato peeler to garde-manger, from buck private to full bird colonel, from *sous* chef to *chef de cuisine*. Likewise, in a family kitchen, you may start with shelling peas, shucking corn, ripping bread for stuffing, or rolling meatballs. Soon you'll graduate to assembling the big pot of sauce (or red gravy, for the purists among you) on your own, maybe even dressing the chicken for roasting and popping it in the oven. You'll get your own knife and start adding to the family cooking canon with recipes of your own invention. Along the way you'll hear stirring and scandalous stories of family gossip, thrilling tales of family overachievement, and, if you're very lucky, all of your mother's, grandmothers', aunts', and uncles' methods for making everything just the way everyone likes it.

I've trained myself to walk off a plane, train, or boat or out of a car and move straight into just about any cooking situation and do my thing, on my own if need be. But I'm not crazy. I look for every available pair of hands I can find. As anybody who has seen *Dinner: Impossible* will tell you, I'll never turn away a willing cook in my kitchen, whether your name is "George!" or you're a professional chef, dishwasher, or innocent bystander. If you have opposable thumbs, I will find a job for you to do.

Your Personal Cooking Arsenal

As in most professions, there are certain essentials you will come to rely on in your personal pursuit of culinary excellence. Here are a few of my favorites:

Stone-ground mustard
Rice wine vinegar
Demi-glace
A blender
A mandoline
Titanium knives

In general, I feel that I can excel with whatever ingredients I might have at hand with these tools because they play to my strengths as a chef. I like using sauces and dressings as a counterpoint to the flavors of the best-quality ingredients in my recipes. Rice wine vinegar is an incredibly versatile acid that I employ to add brightness and tang to preparations. Stone-ground mustard is a great emulsifying agent for both sauces and dressings, and it adds texture as well as a rich and satisfying flavor element. Demi-glace is a very reduced, concentrated brown sauce, a mother sauce that delivers the intense power of classical French technique to savory dishes. A blender allows me the freedom to pull together nearly any kind of sauce, as well as to make purees for flavorful soups and sides. A mandoline is like a mini-version of the meat slicer that your deli counterman uses. It creates beautifully uniform thin slices of vegetables of various shapes and sizes that I love to work into designs and accents in the architecture of my platings—and it's also true that slicing vegetables in different sizes helps me create different and surprising textures and flavor profiles. Any chef can only go as far as a good sharp knife will take him. Generally, I like to have a chef's knife with a good sharp tip and a smaller paring knife on hand at all times.

There's a reason that the word *prepare* applies so often to food. Preparation makes everything possible in the kitchen. It's never too soon to start thinking about the next meal. Wake up and start thinking about dinner. Marinate a London broil or pork loin the night before you need it with rice wine vinegar, maybe ketchup, salt and pepper, soy sauce, dried herbs, lemon juice, even ginger ale—anything you think will tenderize and lend some flavor—then pop it in the oven when you get home, knock together some simple side dishes or a salad, and you'll feel an amazing sense of mastery. Drudgery has no place in the kitchen. Your kitchen is a place of unlimited potential, a place you can fill with amazing smells, textures, colors, and tastes, with sharing and fun and surprises whenever you choose.

From a good cast-iron skillet to an immersion blender (one of the handiest kitchen tools *ever* invented!), you'll develop your own tool kit of preferred equipment and methods based on what works for you. Here is a quick overview of some things every cook wants and needs.

Salt and Pepper

If you're going to cook, you're going to use salt and pepper. One is a mineral, one is a spice, and they're at the top or bottom of nearly every savory recipe you'll ever make. Do not overlook their level of quality just because they are commonplace. Make sure you use the best available of both. For most cooking, you'll be hard pressed to do better than kosher salt. It's natural and flavorful, and dissolves beautifully and evenly; it's also inexpensive. Sea salt is another great alternative, and can be either relatively inexpensive or a bit pricey, especially *fleur de sel*, which is gathered from specific regions in the Mediterranean and the Camargue. Alaea is Hawaiian sea salt mixed with volcanic baked red clay. *Fleur de sel* is grayish in color, alaea is reddish pink, and both have distinctive flavors that are perhaps not for everyday use, though I would recommend buying some of each if you get the chance and playing with them. Sea salt is a perfect source of iodine, a necessary nutrient, in your diet.

Sprinkle salt from about half an arm's length above the food you are cooking. It provides for more even distribution and makes you look cool.

Ground black peppercorns are most commonly used at table and in cooking. You'll want to grind them freshly almost exclusively in a pepper grinder with a metal burr, not a plastic one. Green peppercorns are handy in sauces because they're softer. White pepper gives you a slightly different flavor and no black specks if you don't want them. Pepper adds a distinctive, spicy flavor, and you can generally use as much or as little as you like within reason.

Overplaying your hand with the pepper may lead to catastrophic bouts of sneezing among your guests.

Generally, don't use salt and pepper shakers when you are cooking. Keep your kosher salt in a bowl that you can cover and uncover and grab it as you need it with clean fingers. Generally, grind your pepper unless you need one of your hands for something else, like holding the cavity of a turkey open whilst you are peppering the inside before roasting—then it's okay to shake or sprinkle from a shaker.

Cooking Oils

There are primarily three kinds of oils I like to use in cooking, and they pretty much cover the spectrum of what I like to use oils for. You can research all the various oils on the market and decide which ones you would like to experiment with, but they will mostly play these three basic roles.

Grapeseed oil has a high smoke point and a neutral flavor and is the oil I prefer to use for searing in a pan and for any high heat applications. Its qualities hold up really well under heat, and it's not showy—it doesn't add flavor of its own when it might not be welcome.

Canola oil is a good frying oil or salad oil. Its flavor is mild to neutral, it holds up well under heat, and it's versatile. I like to use it for deep-frying and sautéing, and in many applications where oil is used in room temperature or blending situations, such as in dressing and emulsifications.

Olive oil is healthy and amazingly flavorful, and I don't cook with it. I've had this argument with many of the greatest chefs all over the world, but I don't think olive oil can take the heat. I love it on greens, as a finish on pasta dishes, as an accent to soups and vegetables, and in dressings. When you use it, try to use extra virgin; opting for quality pays big dividends in the arena of flavor.

You might want to consider other infused or flavors of oils, like hazelnut or walnut, sesame seed or white truffle oil, but in the main, buy and keep these three oils in supply and you'll be in good shape whenever you're cooking out of this book and in most home cooking situations.

Fresh and Dried Herbs

Fresh herbs are irreplaceable in my opinion in great cooking. To quote the Temptations, fresh herbs are like sunshine on a cloudy day, and you can rely on them to work their magic on even the dreariest ingredients. I especially love parsley and thyme because of their ubiquity and because they go with so many savory preparations. Definitely keep parsley in your refrigerator at all times, preferably the flat-leaf Italian version over the curly leaf variety, which is okay for decorative purposes but has a less appealing flavor and texture. You cannot have too much thyme on your hands, and if you have direct sun shining on your property, you may be able to grow it for yourself in copious amounts.

You'll learn classic pairing of herbs as you progress as a cook: Sage goes with stuffing at Thanksgiving, fennel in sausages, allspice with pumpkin, basil with tomato, mint or rosemary with lamb. Over time you'll make discoveries on your own as you encounter different combinations. Let inspiration strike. Generally speaking, dried herbs need time to develop their flavors. As a rule of thumb, use dried herbs at the beginning of your sauce, sauté, or braise and fresh herbs at the end to finish.

Spices

Whole volumes have been and will be written about spices, their types and kinds, and their uses in cuisines from Asia to Europe and the Americas and back again. I have one big fat, drop-dead tip for you: *Grind your own*. Buy an inexpensive electric coffee grinder and buy whole spices—cardamom, allspice, cinnamon sticks, juniper berries, and so on—and grind them to a powder as you need them. Drop-dead tip number two? Toast whole spices lightly before you use them, to draw out their natural essences. Your flavors will improve immediately, and you'll look like a culinary genius to your friends and family.

The Allium Family

The members of this family, kissing cousins of the lily family, may be a cook's best friend. It includes onions of every kind: garlic, garlic chives, shallots, scallions, elephant garlic, leeks, and the like. It helps to think of them as vegetables and herbs at the same time because they can serve in both capacities. They are foundational, in that they form the bottom layer of flavor in so many savory preparations, certainly in Western cuisine. Try cooking without them once or twice in a favorite recipe and you'll be amazed at how bland it suddenly is and realize how much work the members of the allium family perform. They're even good for you, with their very powerful antioxidant qualities. If they didn't exist in nature (and in such fabulous abundance), we'd have to invent them. You can experiment by swapping different members of the family for one another: Use leeks when white onions are called for, red onions for shallots, or garlic chives for scallions. Or try the recipe on page 226, which uses many members of the allium family to great effect!

Wine, Beer, and Spirits

Celebrate the civilization of mankind and try to keep a supply of good wine in your house. *Good* does not have to mean expensive. There has been an explosion of great affordable wines in the last few years, and the trend looks likely to continue. Pairing wine with food should aim at bringing out the best in both. Remember that you and your guests have the final say in what works at your table. Wine, especially when used in sauces, provides a wonderful, versatile tool for any cook, mainly because their flavors concentrate so beautifully. I've also heard that wine makes for a nice libation for sipping whilst you're working in the kitchen. Beer can be used in much the same way as wine in cooking, to fortify soups and sauces, and there are literally hundreds of styles and brewers you can choose from. Spirits such as bourbon, Cognac, brandy, rum, and liqueurs like Grand Marnier, crème de menthe, Frangelico, and a multitude of others add a marvelous kick of concentrated flavor to be delivered at your discretion. You can burn off the alcohol during cooking, as when Cognac is used to fortify French onion soup, or you can leave it intact to provide a charge to the palate, as when you whisk a liqueur into a whipped cream. It's always a neat trick to serve an appropriately sized glass of whatever you've been cooking with next to the dish you've created at table.

Flours and Thickeners

The skillful use of liquids defines much of your proficiency as a chef. Thinning a liquid preparation is usually a simple matter of adding *more*, and in many, many cases, a little extra water will do the trick. But properly thickening sauces, soups and stews, pan juices, and so on requires a bit more skill, and there are a number of methods available to the good cook.

A *roux* is a mixture of flour and a fat, usually oil or butter. The flour is combined with the fat, usually by whisking, and the resultant roux is combined with liquid to make it as thick as the cook chooses. A quick and simple blond roux, a combination of white flour and butter, can be used to thicken a mother sauce such as a béchamel, which is a combination of a roux, salt and pepper, milk or cream, and maybe a sprinkle of paprika. A dark roux, a combination of white flour and vegetable oil cooked to caramel or even chocolate color, forms the basis of, for instance, a Cajun gumbo. Once a roux is heated, you must add a cool or room temperature liquid to it, then bring the mixture to a boil for the full thickening effect. A reverse roux, or beurre manié, can be made by mixing cold butter with flour with your fingers to form crumbs, which you can then add to a hot liquid to achieve the same effect. Most rouxs are made with white or wheat flour, although rice flour and some other flours may be used in different applications, especially when making a bisque. Rice flour thickens more lightly and delicately. Another way to thicken a hot liquid is the use of a slurry. Mix a tablespoon or so of flour with ½ cup of water or other liquid, mix briskly, then pour into the hot liquid and cook until you have achieved the desired consistency. Baked bread can classically act as a thickener for soups, especially in French and Italian family- or farmhouse-style cooking. Cream and butter are used for thickening soups and especially sauces (*monter au beurre*, or adding butter to a warm sauce just before service, is a favorite technique of mine). Yogurt is added as a thickener to sauces in some Indian and Middle Eastern dishes.

Feel free to adopt any of these methods to any dish of yours where you think it makes sense. Talented thievery is the hallmark of most good cooking.

Acids

I will avoid going into a lecture on the acidity, alkalinity, and pH content of various food-stuffs and simply say that in the daily working life of the home cook, the two most important sources of acidity are citrus and vinegars. To my mind, acids add tang, sharpness, and brightness on the palate.

Citrus generically includes lemons and limes, oranges and grapefruits. If you watch me cook over a period of time, you'll likely see me squeezing a lot of limes. I like to finish lots of fish and shellfish dishes, sauces, and vinaigrettes with fresh lime juice because I think it adds a spark and balance just before service. I like to microwave limes to get every last bit of natural oils out of them, including those in the skin. Along those lines, lemon, lime, and orange zest or very finely shaved peel can do some of the work that citrus juice does on top of fish, steamed vegetables, stir-fries, and loads of other applications, on a lighter, sweeter note and with a bit more texture.

Vinegar adds sharpness as well as a pleasant sour note of balance to many preparations. I prefer rice wine vinegar for its versatility. When you want to make a bit more of a statement with vinegar, there are a lot to choose from: red and white wine vinegars, apple cider, Champagne, sherry, and balsamic, to name a few. Aged balsamic is the big dog and delivers a wallop of flavor just sprinkled on greens or reduced by heat as part of a sauce. Aged balsamic vinegars can be very pricey, but even moderate to lower-priced versions are a worthy addition to your pantry. Also stock apple cider and red and white wine vinegars and you'll be in good shape.

Sugars

Guess what? Sugar is sweet and so are you! Sugars are for sweetening, whether they're Demerara, pure cane, light and dark brown, confectioners' or powdered sugar. Honey works;

so do maple syrup and molasses. Stock them all in your pantry. They're available at varying levels of price and quality, based on where they fall in the range from generic to artisanal. Honey in particular comes in many interesting varietals. Sometimes a good way to counter excessive spiciness, a sour taste, or too much saltiness is to balance the mix with honey or sugar in stages. The less processed the sweetener is, the better. High-fructose corn syrup comes from the devil, and I feel much the same way about it as I do about MSG. *Blecch.*

Natural sugars occur in both fruits and vegetables and in proteins, and are expressed by the taste of sweetness on your palate. A great way to draw out and enhance the sweetness of meats, fish, fruits, and veggies is to caramelize their surfaces with heat in a sauté pan, by roasting, or by grilling.

Knives

Samurai have their *kitana* blades, sheriffs have their six-shooters, great golfers have their drivers, Harry Potter has his magic wand, and Babe Ruth had a big baseball bat. It doesn't help to have the talent if you haven't got the tools. There are a million different knives for a million different uses. I believe that for nearly any cooking task, you need a chef's knife between six and eight inches long that fits your hand, has a pleasant, well-balanced heft, and is sharp, very sharp. Most accidents with knives occur because they slip when they should be cutting because of a dull blade. Keep your knives sharp—there are lots of gadgets and methods you can use, and you can call Alton Brown to explain them all to you, but pick one and use it every time you start to cook. When you're moving from butchering meats to filleting fish to julienning vegetables whilst cooking in the middle of a football field in Mississippi for more than a thousand people in less than eight hours, you want a reliable tool in your hand that doesn't weigh you down.

Pots and Pans

By any measure, I love doing *Dinner: Impossible.* But I have one nagging pet peeve with our production team: Too often I'm landed in some field, camp kitchen, desert landscape, nook, cranny, or cave with a stick, club, spoon, or flame but *no pots*! You cannot seriously cook anything for even one person without pots or pans! Sticking a stick in a weenie and poking it in a campfire gets old really fast. For your kitchen, make sure you have frying pans—eight-inch, twelve-inch, and bigger. Your twelve-inch pan should have a lid or splatter screen. (Sometimes these lids have to be sought out or purchased separately, but the effort is worth it.) You need big sauté pans, both a shallow one and one that is five inches deep, which will probably turn out to be the most useful pot you will ever buy. The big one must have a lid! You need at least one saucier or saucepan. A Dutch oven is a beautiful, deep pot that does double duty, both on top of the stove and in the oven. You need a big stockpot, six quarts or so, the better in which to boil. A cast-iron skillet costs about twenty bucks, and will last well into the next century. Your great-grandchildren will be able to cook in it if you take even remotely good care of it. You'll want to have a couple of good nonstick pans especially for crepes and omelets. Finally, you would do well to buy a great, high-quality roasting pan with an insert rack. Over and above these recommendations, if you see a pan and you get a sudden vision of it filled with food of your creation, buy it and cook in it.

Implements

You need implements with which to cook because you cannot safely touch burning-hot food. You can buy or likely already own a full complement of whisks, spatulas, spoons, ladles, and so on. Your inventory will grow or shrink as you grow older and especially every time you change homes. You probably have a good idea of what you need and use on that front on a daily basis, so I won't go into infinite detail. But here are some tools I think are particularly handy to have around the kitchen.

I've previously mentioned my high regard for the blender, which I find invaluable in both a professional and a home environment. Along those lines, I would also highly recommend that you acquire and learn how to use a good food processor with a dough blade, slicer, and shredder as well as the basic spinning blade. You can use it to chop onions or make dough, coleslaw, pesto, hummus, forcemeats (such as sausages), or purees, all within seconds. It's an all-purpose versatile addition to your arsenal and can do the work of many hands.

A burr mixer or immersion blender is a fantastic tool that consists of blender blades at the end of a rod. It allows you to agitate and puree food in the pot in which you have cooked it and is irreplaceable for making soups and purees with beautiful, uniform textures.

Colanders and strainers in various sizes will have innumerable uses. A good collection of nonreactive, stainless steel bowls are perfect for mixing anything; if nested, they take up very little room, they're lightweight, and you'll have them forever. Plastic bowls are worthless in my opinion: They stain, they melt, and they're unattractive.

Great cutting boards in different sizes are a must, and although I espouse plastic in a professional kitchen because of the wide range of possible cross-contamination issues, at home I love wooden cutting boards. They feel substantial, the nicer ones look like art objects, and in a home environment you can keep them scrupulously clean. But more important than having a big fancy cutting board is to have more than one cutting board. A good vegetable peeler makes quick work of cleaning and prepping vegetables and can function like a mini-mandoline, allowing you to create neat strips and shapes. I love meat mallets, the bigger the better. You can make inexpensive cuts of meat deliciously tender by pounding them into submission, and it is very satisfying and stress-releasing work. Also on the crushing and grinding side of things, get a substantial mortar and pestle set (another candidate as a family heirloom). It's the world's first food processor, and the act of grinding and pulverizing fruits, vegetables, herbs, and spices releases oils and flavors you'll never have access to with any other method. By the way, invest in a salad spinner. They come in all sizes and prices, but you can get a really good one with a pump-style lid for $20 to $30 (such as the one by OXO); kids can't wait to use it. I think it's worth $20 to have your child begin eating salads!

Prep bowls are a must because prepping is more important than most people realize. It may take as long or longer than the actual cooking, depending on what you're doing. In a professional kitchen a cadre of workers is available to devote all their time to this most important step. My team and I have gone to great lengths in this book's recipes to organize the steps in a realistic fashion for someone with the sole responsibility of pulling together a particular dish. Why am I saying this? Because while it may be tempting for you to skip some of the prep up front, thinking that it can be done in between while other elements of the dish are cooking, this often results in parts of the dish becoming overcooked or even burned because of the distraction of late prepping. More important, since you're likely to be preparing other dishes for your meal, you'll need that in-between time to organize the rest of your cooking. You'll see that some of the ingredients are followed by prep instructions such as "medium diced" or "drained," while others are prepped within the recipe itself. This is done to help you get the dish on the table with maximum organization and minimum stress. So, get yourself some vessels that can serve as prep bowls—anything from small stainless steel bowls to cereal bowls to the plastic containers you get when you order soup from Chinese takeout. Then take the ten or fifteen minutes to prep your ingredients as instructed in the list. Set the prepped ingredients in their bowls in your work area. Organize your work space. Now you have your *mise en place*.

Last, invest in big serving bowls and platters. They make great platforms for presentation for family-style dining, and they allow everybody to serve themselves. You have enough to do; make it easy on yourself every once in a while.

The Freezer

The freezer is an incredible weapon for the strategic cook. I'd like to make the case for preparing foods like sauces, soups, and stocks ahead of time, for breaking down ingredients for easy preparation as you bring them in from the grocery store, and for saving and freezing items you might otherwise have thrown away.

Some good vegetable and fish stocks are easy to find on store shelves. Store any extra stock for future use in your freezer in one-cup increments in freezer containers or heavy-duty freezer bags.

Soups, stews, chili, marinara sauce, and purees of every description can be put away in individual serving sizes in freezer containers to provide you with instant access to items freshly prepared by your own hand in your recipes when you simply do not have the time to make them *à la minute* (on the spot!).

When you come home with chicken parts, thighs, legs, or breasts, let them sit in a bowl of salt water for a few minutes to clean and purify them, then separate them into individual bags for the freezer as well. Divide packets of ground beef into flattened quarter-pound increments (for quick thawing) and store them in separate small freezer bags, as well as pork chops, beef cubes, fish steaks, and the like. This will allow you the freedom to choose only what you need for any dish when you are grabbing for ingredients later on, which helps with portion control and minimizes waste.

Whenever you separate shrimp or lobster from their shells, throw the remains in a bag and toss them into the back of your freezer. They can form the basis of flavorful stocks and sauces once you've collected enough of them. The same goes for end bits of broccoli, parsnips, carrots, cabbage leaves, and so on, which can be collected for vegetable stocks. Nothing replaces something you have created in your own home kitchen. You'll have the satisfaction of having made it yourself, and the peace of mind of knowing exactly what you put into it. For a discussion of stock-making, see page 42.

Fortune Favors the Prepared

Have paper and pen or pencil handy when you're cooking. You'll get ideas, you'll run out of things you'll need to inventory for your next shopping list, and you'll need to write down timings and reminders.

One last note about organization: One of the biggest challenges for many a cook is timing all the elements of a meal to arrive at their finished state at the same time, especially when multiple components are involved. You don't have to be a magician or a quantum mathematician to accomplish this. You have sources of refrigeration and heat at your command; use them. You have foils and plastic wrap to hold in heat and to protect finished foods from contamination. When I cook for a large event in a big hotel, the food needs to come out in waves. I have big walk-in refrigerators and hot boxes on wheels that can keep things cool or hot until I decide to serve them. You have the same range of options on a smaller scale in your kitchen.

Whenever you can make items ahead of time (such as salads and desserts) and hold them in a cool environment, do so. If you have finished cooking your protein of choice and want to take a few extra minutes to make a sauce, finish it or hold it in the oven covered with foil whilst you work on your sauce on the stovetop. You can hold potatoes, roasted vegetables, bread, and rolls in a warm oven for quite a long time.

Take advantage of carry-over cooking. Just because you've taken a piece of meat off the heat on the range does not mean it has stopped cooking, unless you've shocked it in cold water. If you have last-minute details to attend to, slightly undercook your meat and fish and let them carry-over cook in a warm oven or off to the side. With just a little practice and experience, you will become an excellent judge of when your dishes are ready using this method.

Think—not only when you are in the kitchen, but before and after. Learn from your mistakes as well as from your successes. And bear in mind in cooking, as in life, good fortune favors the prepared.

To get the ball rolling, I've selected some of my favorite recipes that demonstrate different aspects of *mise en place*. Keep the principles we've just discussed in mind as you work your way through the balance of this chapter, and add your own personal notes of style and organization.

Retro Caesar Salad
(with Pasteurized Eggs)

SERVES 4

If you've ever had a Caesar salad prepared tableside for you at a fine restaurant, you know it's a special experience. To see someone making this freshly just for you in a huge, deep wooden bowl nestled in its own stand is something fine indeed, particularly if that person has cultivated the elusive ability to make you feel it is his or her honor to do so. The practice faded away over safety concerns about raw eggs, but has made somewhat of a comeback with the advent of pasteurized eggs. The classical method is a beautiful example of correct *mise en place*. The garlic, anchovy, salt, and pepper are made into a paste; egg and lemon juice are blended in; olive oil is whisked in by hand to emulsify; Parmesan is added to the romaine; and it is tossed and served. It should ideally be performed with the requisite flourish to make the guest feel uniquely privileged at the moment it is served.

A blender-made version is presented here using the selfsame ingredients. (By the way, if you want to train yourself to do the tableside preparation, don't bring the blender to the table. The high-speed motor can put a damper on the moment, to say the least. Instead do a few practice runs to make sure you get the handmade technique down.) However, I *highly* recommend this easy blender version. The results are delicious and elegant.

INGREDIENTS FOR THE SALAD DRESSING

1 lemon

5 garlic cloves, peeled and quartered

1 pasteurized egg (These are identified in stores as "pasteurized" and although not cooked, have been sufficiently heated for food safety.)

1 teaspoon Worcestershire sauce

1 cup extra virgin olive oil

2 cups finely grated Parmigiano-Reggiano cheese

Freshly ground black pepper to taste

Salt to taste (Be careful, as the cheese lends saltiness.)

INGREDIENTS FOR THE CROUTONS

½ baguette loaf, cut into cubes

¼ cup olive oil

1 teaspoon garlic powder

Salt and freshly ground black pepper to taste

INGREDIENTS FOR THE SALAD

1 large head of romaine lettuce, soaked in salt water to remove grit and dried in a salad spinner

4 boneless anchovies (optional), sliced into ½-inch pieces

Method

To make the salad dressing, microwave the lemon in a small bowl to release the essential oils and set aside briefly until it has cooled off just enough to handle. One at a time through the feed tube of a running blender, add the garlic cloves, egg, and Worcestershire sauce. Whilst the blender is still running, squeeze the lemon juice from the microwaved lemon through the feed opening with the sliced side against your palm to contain the seeds. Add the olive oil in a thin stream and you will see the mixture begin to come together as it emulsifies. Turn off the blender and stir in the Parmigiano-Reggiano a little at a time. Season the dressing to taste with ground black pepper and salt only if needed.

To make the croutons, preheat the oven to 350°F. In a mixing bowl, toss the bread cubes with the olive oil, sprinkle with the garlic powder, salt, and pepper, and toss again to coat thoroughly. Place the bread cubes on a baking sheet and toast until golden, about 5 minutes. Set aside to cool.

Remove the large spines from the lettuce leaves and tear the tender portions of the leaves into bite-size pieces. Just before service, in a mixing bowl, toss the lettuce with only enough dressing to coat.

Presentation

Transfer to serving dishes and top with anchovies (if using) and sprinkle with the croutons.

Veal Milanese with Warm Fingerling Potato Salad

SERVES 6

An extremely useful technique, especially for serving family meals, is learning how to properly flour, egg wash, and bread thin slices of meat. Learn this *mise en place* once, and use it a million times over a lifetime in the kitchen. Be sure to refer to the photo in the insert for a presentation of this dish.

INGREDIENTS FOR THE POTATO SALAD

1½ pounds fingerling or baby Yukon Gold potatoes, scrubbed and cut into bite-size pieces

1 tablespoon stone-ground mustard

1 teaspoon salt

⅛ cup malt vinegar

½ cup olive oil

4 tablespoons sliced scallions, white and tender green parts only (about 6 scallions)

2 tablespoons chopped fresh flat-leaf parsley leaves (about 6 sprigs)

¼ cup lemon juice (the juice of 1 lemon)

4 strips cooked bacon, chopped

INGREDIENTS FOR THE VEAL

3 tablespoons minced fresh flat-leaf parsley (from 8 or 9 sprigs) (can be done in a food processor)

3 tablespoons minced fresh basil (from about 8 sprigs) (can be done in a food processor)

2 teaspoons garlic powder

1 teaspoon salt

¼ teaspoon freshly ground black pepper

½ cup freshly grated Parmesan cheese

3 cups Italian-flavored breadcrumbs

1½ to 2 pounds thinly sliced veal (scaloppine), pounded thin with a meat mallet

½ cup milk, or as needed to moisten the veal

1 cup all-purpose flour

2 to 4 eggs, beaten, or as needed for the egg wash

½ cup grapeseed oil

4 tablespoons butter

2 lemons, cut into slices, for garnish

Method for the warm potato salad

Boil the potatoes until fork-tender and drain.

In a bowl, mix together the mustard, salt, vinegar, oil, scallions, parsley, and lemon juice. Lightly fold in the potatoes and bacon pieces, being careful not to break up the potatoes.

Method for the veal

Add the parsley, basil, garlic powder, salt, pepper, and Parmesan cheese to the breadcrumbs and set up a breading station as follows:

1. Moisten the veal slices in the milk.
2. Dredge them in the flour, shaking off any excess.
3. Dip them in the beaten eggs.
4. Coat them with the breadcrumb mixture, pressing the crumbs into the veal.

Heat the oil over medium-high heat in a large sauté pan and melt the butter in the oil. Add the veal and cook until golden brown on both sides, allowing each side of the veal to cook undisturbed for the first 2 minutes or so, to avoid having the breading crust come off. Remove to a platter and let rest.

Presentation

Place the warm potato salad on a platter. Arrange the veal around the salad. Garnish with the lemon slices.

Champagne Peach and Mint Soup

SERVES 4

This is undoubtedly a problem you've had, probably not on a daily basis, but maybe around the holidays: "What am I going to do with this bottle of Champagne that's been lying around my house?" Sure, anybody can pop the cork and drink it, but let me suggest instead that you use it as part of your *mise en place* for the next few recipes. And if you must, buy a second bottle (or a third and fourth) to imbibe with your guests.

This soup makes an elegant meal with the Salad of Tender Greens with Mascarpone-Chive Dumplings and Candied Walnuts with Champagne Vinaigrette on page 30. Just use ½ cup Champagne from this bottle in that recipe and substitute ½ cup seltzer water in this one.

INGREDIENTS

1 bottle dry Champagne

6 large fresh peaches, peeled and sliced

⅛ teaspoon salt, plus some as needed

4 large fresh mint sprigs, left intact but well washed and dried in a salad spinner or with paper toweling

White pepper to taste

2 tablespoons crème fraîche

⅛ cup fresh mint leaves, cut in chiffonade

Method

Combine the Champagne, peaches, salt, mint sprigs, and white pepper in a large saucepan or deep pot. Cook for 20 minutes over medium heat to infuse the flavors. Remove from the heat and remove the mint sprigs. Taste and adjust the salt and white pepper if needed. Blend with an immersion blender and chill. Serve garnished with a dollop of crème fraîche swirled over the surface of the soup and the mint strips.

Champagne Brie Fondue

SERVES 4

There is a second element of *mise en place* you may wish to consider for this dish. As with any fondue, you don't have to limit yourself to bread cubes. Grape tomatoes, steamed pearl onions, cauliflorets, even cubes of cooked beef or chicken can be dipped into this cheesy mixture. Raid your pantry for ideas, prepare them in bite-size chunks, and dip away! P.S. Take a look at the beautiful photo of this fondue in the insert.

INGREDIENTS

2 tablespoons cornstarch

2 tablespoons kirsch

1 garlic clove, halved

1 cup dry Champagne

1 teaspoon freshly squeezed lemon juice

16 ounces (about 2 small wheels) Brie cheese, chilled, rind removed, and cut into small pieces

⅛ teaspoon white pepper

1 baguette loaf, cut into cubes, with each cube having some crust

Method

Create a slurry by whisking together the cornstarch and kirsch in a small bowl, and set it aside briefly.

Rub the inside of a saucepan with the garlic clove. In a medium saucepan over medium heat, bring the Champagne and lemon juice to a gentle boil. Immediately reduce the heat to low and stir in the Brie. Blend the cornstarch/kirsch slurry into the cheese mixture and stir for a couple of minutes, until the mixture is smooth and thick. Transfer to a fondue pot over a flame and season with white pepper. Serve with bread cubes on fondue forks.

Salad of Tender Greens with Mascarpone-Chive Dumplings and Candied Walnuts with Champagne Vinaigrette

SERVES 4

This salad is so delectable you'll find yourself daydreaming about it. With tender greens, sweet dried cranberry, mascarpone cheese, candied walnuts, and Champagne vinaigrette—what more could you ask for? This is a good lesson in creating balance with the ingredients you've assembled. Because it has so many levels of flavor and contains protein, it is amazingly satisfying.

INGREDIENTS FOR THE CANDIED WALNUTS

1 cup sugar

2 tablespoons light corn syrup

⅓ cup water

½ teaspoon salt

2 cups walnut halves

1 teaspoon vanilla extract

1 teaspoon ground cinnamon

INGREDIENTS FOR THE CHAMPAGNE VINAIGRETTE

¼ cup Champagne vinegar

2 tablespoons chopped chives

½ cup Champagne (which leaves you the rest to drink or to use in Champagne Peach and Mint Soup, page 28)

1 teaspoon vanilla extract

¼ teaspoon salt, or to taste

⅛ teaspoon freshly ground black pepper, or to taste

1 cup grapeseed oil

INGREDIENTS FOR THE DUMPLINGS AND SALAD

½ cup goat cheese

¼ cup mascarpone cheese

¼ cup chopped chives

4 cups loosely packed greens, such as red leaf and green leaf lettuce, radicchio, and romaine (stiff spines removed, soaked to remove grit, and dried in a salad spinner)

1 cup grape or cherry tomatoes, cut in half

½ cup dried cranberries

SPECIAL EQUIPMENT

Candy thermometer

Method for the candied walnuts

Mix the sugar, corn syrup, water, and salt in a heavy saucepan. Stir over low heat until the sugar dissolves. Heat until a candy thermometer reaches the hard crack stage, about 310°F. Remove from the heat and stir in the walnuts, vanilla, and cinnamon. Turn out on waxed paper and pull the walnuts apart while cooling, taking care to avoid getting burned.

Method for the vinaigrette

Prepare the vinaigrette just before use. Through the feed opening of a running blender, add one at a time the Champagne vinegar, chives, Champagne, vanilla extract, salt, and pepper. Leaving the blender running, add the oil in a slow stream. Adjust the seasoning to taste with salt and pepper as needed.

Method for the dumplings and salad

In a medium bowl, mix the goat cheese, mascarpone, and chives. Roll into small ½-inch- to ¾-inch-diameter balls (the dumplings) and set aside on a plate.

Toss the greens, tomatoes, cranberries, and candied walnuts in a large salad bowl with just enough of the vinaigrette to coat.

Presentation

Transfer the salad to serving dishes, top with the dumplings, and serve the remaining vinaigrette on the side.

Duck Confit with Three-Bean Cassoulet

SERVES 6

A confit (pronounced "cone-FEE") is meat, usually duck or goose, cooked in its own fat. The process originated as a way of preserving meat in the days before refrigeration. A cassoulet (pronounced "cass-oo-LAY") is a stew of beans cooked with said confit or other meat. It's all very French, very delicious, and very worth cooking at home, because you can do it the long way or the short way, depending on whether you want to cook for pleasure and challenge or just feel like getting directly to dinner. Here are three ways to prepare the duck and two ways to prepare the beans for the cassoulet; you just need to choose which works best for you. The recipe may seem complicated, but if you read all the directions ahead of time, you'll see it's not difficult at all. The use of three types of beans provides a beautiful visual presentation (as seen in the photo insert).

Duck option #1: INGREDIENTS FOR PREPARING YOUR OWN CONFIT OF DUCK

If you *really* want to feel like a cook, to get that deep-seated feeling you really know what you're doing and really know how to feed people, choose this option. Start early in the day or do it the day before, because of the long, slow cooking time.

1 whole duck, butchered into 8 pieces—2 legs, 2 breasts, 2 wings, and 2 thighs (rubbed with about 1 tablespoon each of salt and sugar, as for curing, and refrigerated overnight), with the extra skin and trimmings reserved

Approximately 2 cups grapeseed oil or melted lard

½ teaspoon kosher salt

½ teaspoon coarsely ground black pepper

½ teaspoon finely chopped garlic (about 1 clove)

Duck option #2: PRECOOKED CONFIT OF DUCK

Purchase a precooked confit of duck, such as those sold by D'Artagnan, and follow the directions on the package (www.dartagnan.com).

Duck option #3: INGREDIENTS FOR SEARED BREAST OF DUCK

This faster option isn't a confit, but seared sliced duck breast to be served on top of the cassoulet.

1 tablespoon grapeseed oil

2 duck breasts

Salt and freshly ground pepper

SPECIAL EQUIPMENT

Candy thermometer

Method for duck option #1

Rinse to remove the salt and sugar from the duck pieces, extra skin, and trimmings and pat dry with paper towels. In a large sauté pan over medium-high heat, heat 1 tablespoon of the grape-seed oil and add the extra skin and trimmings. It will take about 15 minutes to render the duck and obtain the fat—the pieces will look brown, and you'll see that they've given up their fat.

Meanwhile, mix the salt, pepper, and garlic and coat the 8 pieces of duck with the seasonings, rubbing them into the surface of the duck. Set aside.

Strain the rendered fat into a heatproof glass measuring container (such as a 2-cup Pyrex measuring pitcher). Supplement the rendered fat to the 2-cup mark with the grapeseed oil or lard. Discard the rendered skin and trimmings.

On the stovetop over medium heat, heat the rendered fat with the supplemental oil or lard in a deep roasting pan (if you'll be using the oven) or in a large Dutch oven (if you'll be cooking on the range) to 200°F as read on a candy thermometer. (Note: You'll be poaching the duck, not frying it, so it's important to avoid getting the oil too hot.) Add the duck to the warm oil. If you're using the oven, put the duck in at 200°F for 6 to 8 hours. If you're using the stovetop, cook the duck at a simmer between 3 and 4 hours. In either case, the duck must be cooked until it falls away from the bone. Remove all the duck meat from the bones, shred the meat, and reserve until needed.

Method for duck option #2

Shred the precooked duck and reserve until needed.

Method for duck option #3

Preheat the oven to 375°F. Add the oil to a heavy ovenproof skillet over high heat. Season the duck breasts with salt and pepper and place in the pan skin-side down. Sear for 3 to 4 minutes, or until golden brown. Turn over and cook 1 minute. Transfer the duck to the oven and roast 6 to 8 minutes, or until the desired doneness. Let the duck rest for about 5 minutes before cutting it into ½-inch slices.

Cassoulet option #1: INGREDIENTS FOR REHYDRATING DRIED BEANS

1 pound dried red kidney beans, rinsed and picked over to remove any stones or impurities

½ pound dried navy beans, rinsed and picked over to remove any stones or impurities

½ pound dried black beans, rinsed and picked over to remove any stones or impurities

Cassoulet option #2: INGREDIENTS FOR CANNED BEANS

One 16-ounce can dark red kidney beans, drained

One 16-ounce can light red kidney beans, drained

One 16-ounce can white kidney beans, drained

One 16-ounce can black beans, drained

OTHER INGREDIENTS FOR THE THREE-BEAN CASSOULET

4 ounces chopped raw bacon (about 4 strips, or about 3 strips if thick sliced)

2 shallot cloves, finely chopped

3 carrots, peeled and minced

3 celery ribs, well scrubbed and finely chopped

4 or 5 garlic cloves, minced

Salt and freshly ground black pepper to taste

½ cup dry red wine

1½ cups demi-glace or 1½ teaspoons beef base, stirred into 1½ cups water

2 tablespoons tomato paste

Leaves from 2 fresh rosemary sprigs, finely chopped

2 tablespoons minced fresh chives

1 tablespoon chopped fresh parsley, plus 6 small sprigs for garnish

1 tablespoon unsalted butter

½ cup goat cheese (about 3 ounces)

Method for the cassoulet

For cassoulet option #1 you will be rehydrating the dried beans. To do so, bring 9 cups water to a boil in a large pot and add the dried beans. Return to a boil and cook for 15 minutes, skimming off any foam or impurities that rise to the top. Remove from the heat, cover, and let stand for 1 hour. Drain the beans through a colander.

When your rehydrated or canned beans are ready, proceed with the rest of the recipe. In a large oven-safe saucepan, cook the bacon until browned and place on paper toweling. Drain most of the grease out of the pan. Crumble the bacon back into the pan and add the shallots, carrots, celery, garlic, and salt and pepper. Cook for about 8 minutes over medium heat, stirring occasionally, until the shallots are softened.

Preheat the oven to 375°F. Deglaze the pan with the red wine and cook over medium-high heat until the liquid is reduced by half. Stir in the demi-glace and tomato paste, lower the heat, and simmer for a few minutes to integrate the flavors. Stir in the drained beans, rosemary, and chives and season with salt and pepper to taste. If you're using confit of duck in the cassoulet (duck option #1 or #2), gently fold the shredded duck into the beans.

Cover, place the pot on the middle rack of the oven, and roast for about 20 minutes to allow the flavors to combine. Remember to use an oven mitt when you pull the cassoulet out of the oven. Many home cooks are not accustomed to putting a pan normally used on the stovetop into an oven and grab the hot handle without thinking.

Gently stir the chopped parsley and butter into the cassoulet. Correct the seasoning with salt and pepper as needed.

Presentation

The cassoulet can be served family style or in individual servings. Transfer the beans to a serving dish (making sure that each guest gets some duck if you are plating individually) and dot the surface of the cassoulet with small dollops of goat cheese. If you have cooked a duck breast as in option #3, place several slices of duck on top of the beans. Garnish with the parsley sprigs.

Peanut Butter and Jelly Donut Sandwiches

MAKES 16 DONUT TRIANGLES TO SERVE 8

I came up with this on an episode of *Dinner: Impossible,* and the kids went crazy for it. So did the adults! Hey—who doesn't like PB&J, and who doesn't like donuts? I think this is a neat lesson on how to take the world's second-easiest *mise en place* (after the bowl of cereal) to another level. You just make a PB&J, dip it in batter, and deep-fry it. It's sinful to eat, but I'm quite sure God will forgive you. After all, peanuts contain protein, a building block of nutrition, as I'm sure George Washington Carver would agree. Could be good for you—right? (I'm rationalizing as fast as I can.)

INGREDIENTS FOR THE SANDWICHES

8 slices white bread (or your choice of cinnamon swirl, raisin, apple, and so on)

¼ to ½ cup peanut butter

4 to 6 teaspoons grape jelly (or your choice of jelly, jam, or preserves)

SPECIAL EQUIPMENT

A deep fryer

INGREDIENTS FOR THE BATTER

3 to 4 quarts canola oil (as needed for deep-frying)

1½ cups all-purpose flour

¾ cup cornstarch

4½ teaspoons baking powder

1½ cups seltzer water (carbonation makes a lighter batter)

1 teaspoon ground cinnamon

2 tablespoons sugar

Method

Lay out the slices of bread and spread approximately 1 tablespoon peanut butter on each of 4 slices and approximately 1 teaspoon jelly on each of the other 4 slices. Pair them together to make peanut butter and jelly sandwiches, cut off the crusts, and cut into quarters diagonally.

Heat the canola oil in a deep fryer to 325°F, or as directed in the manufacturer's instructions for similar items. In a medium bowl, mix together the flour, cornstarch, and baking powder and add the seltzer water in a stream whilst you are whisking constantly. Dip the sandwiches into the batter or ladle the batter over them.

Deep-fry the sandwiches until golden brown, about 2 minutes. Don't overcrowd. Since the batter has a tendency to meld the item being fried to the bottom of the fryer basket, it would serve you to place the empty basket in the fryer first, and then add the battered donut sandwiches to the hot oil with tongs to sear off the batter before releasing them into the basket. Use mitts to protect your hands from spatters, and also take care to keep your face at a safe distance.

Drain the sandwiches on paper toweling. Mix the cinnamon and sugar in a bowl and sift onto the fried sandwiches whilst they are still hot. Serve warm or at room temperature.

2. FLAVOR IS THE KEY

Flavor is the most important element in cooking, just as rhythm is in dance and pitch is in music. The perception of it can be just as subjective. Yet without it, you just aren't cooking. The slightest and most profound variations and gradations can be achieved and perceived by those who really know what they are doing in the food world, but even the smallest child knows when the flavor of a dish is working or not. It is analogous to that old judicial chestnut about pornography: "I may not be able to define it, but I know it when I see it." Everyone knows great flavor when they taste it.

Great flavor can make your day. The absence of flavor can put you out of business, as many a restaurateur could tell you. As cooks, we must pay constant attention to it, even obsess over it, because it penetrates and provides the underpinnings of everything we put on the plate. Flavor involves but is not limited to the consideration of temperatures, textures, finishes, combinations and pairings, garnishes, the skill of the practitioner, the refinement of the diner, the quality of the ingredients, and the sophistication or simplicity of the methods of preparation employed.

Flavor is largely about choices, about what we as cooks have decided to do with an ingredient once we get our hands on it. The flavor of any item starts with its inherent qualities: its sweetness or bitterness, its tanginess or saltiness, its leanness or fattiness, its pungent or acidic or earthy flavor profile. Its flavor is then contingent on its condition: its ripeness or staleness, whether it was raised organically or genetically manipulated, freshly picked or freshly frozen, shipped around the corner or across the globe, packaged whole or sliced, diced, or pureed, raised indifferently or with great care and attention.

It's at that point the cook takes over and decides how to *develop* its flavor.

One of the first things you can consider is altering the basic shape of the ingredient, which usually involves your trusty sharp knife. One half of a tomato on a plate is very different from a thin slice or a wedge, a fine dice or a puree. A light shaving of black truffle is going to deliver more flavor impact than three or four chopped white button mushrooms. A slice of Ahi tuna under the blade of a master sushi chef will deliver a different flavor experience served up as sashimi than Hawaiian poke, which features the same ingredient in small cubes, or the same product finely diced as tuna tartare. A head of iceberg lettuce served in large wedges will eat differently than one chiffonaded into delicate strips. Mouthfeel and texture are important considerations here. If an item is crispy, do you want to deliver a big crunch in the mouth or just a slight accent to another, softer item? In either case, size matters. If an item is soft and luxurious, like filet mignon, do you want to show off its buttery mouthfeel by leaving it essentially alone on the plate, by accentuating it with a silky, buttery sauce, or by contrasting it with a salty, toothsome potato hash or crispy deep-fried strands of red onion?

There are other ways to alter the basic nature of an ingredient. By breaking down tough fibers, pounding meat with a mallet certainly does the trick. Curing with spices, salt, or smoke is a method that stretches back to the earliest days of food preparation. Marinades of different kinds, such as those used in ceviche or to tenderize tough cuts of meat, seep deeply into the flesh of meat, fish, and vegetables and change their essential makeup.

One of the most prominent ways to develop flavor is the application of heat. Let's have fun with verbs! Bake, broil, braise, steam, simmer, sear, fry, roast, poach, and toast all indicate one thing: You've decided to turn up the heat on the food you're working with. Your skill and judgment as reflected in your use of heat whilst cooking will be one of the hallmarks of how you will be remembered as a cook.

- Baking is the use of ambient heat to evenly cook and penetrate whatever it is you are making; e.g., bake a cake.

- Broiling uses intense heat, usually from above; broil to achieve a browned, crispy surface and very light cooking on the interior.

- Braising indicates the use of hot, flavorful liquid to slow cook an ingredient; braise tough cuts of meat or bland items into which you wish to infuse the flavor of your cooking liquid.

- Steaming is a great way to use wet ambient heat to warm and sharpen delicate flavors whilst keeping them fresh and vibrant; that's why we steam fresh vegetables.

- A simmer occurs just below the point where water begins to boil actively; a full boil occurs when you heat water to a temperature at or above 212°F and is very bubbly. Immersing a food item in simmering or boiling water cooks very fully and allows for a lot of control on your part. Pull something out of a pot of hot water and shock it in ice water and you stop the cooking process dead in its tracks, ideally at exactly the point you have chosen. You can cook a potato in boiling water until it literally falls apart or delicately poach an egg in simmering water so that the membrane on the yolk just barely holds together.

- Searing indicates cooking on a very hot surface, usually until caramelization occurs on the surface of your food. Caramelization describes heating and intensifying the natural sugars in a foodstuff, achieving a crispy brown, slightly sweet effect on its outer surface. It is an outstanding way to develop flavor. Caramelization just sounds really good, and it is.

- Frying means cooking something in very hot fat, like butter, oil, or natural animal fat. Fry chicken. Fry lots of things. It is so good.

- Roasting is another method that uses ambient heat. It describes a method used for meats, vegetables, and fruits rather than baked goods such as cakes, pies, and cookies, though both use ambient heat, usually in an oven (the term also applies to cooking on a spit over an open fire, as I learned in Colonial Williamsburg and other premodern locales). Roasting achieves caramelization on the outside and deep penetrating heat and flavor on the inside. Roast beef, onions, and potatoes together and take the rest of the day off; your job will practically be done for you.

- Poaching is a method of cooking just below a simmer by immersion in liquid, which doesn't always have to be water. Learn how to perfectly poach an egg and figure out new ways to slip it into your favorite savory dishes. Or toast a piece of bread, butter it, put a poached egg on top, and enjoy your breakfast.

Carefully consider this next word: *balance*. This may be the next most important concept in cooking after flavor. In many ways, cooking is a high-wire act. Tip the scales too far in any one direction, especially when baking; use too much or too little salt, too much acid, too much or too little yeast or baking powder; apply too much heat or too little; and you can ruin literally hours of work in a few seconds. Balance applies not only to whatever you have cooking right in front of you at any given moment but to everything else you are serving as well. Everything you put on the plate must work together, as well as everything you put on the table—and in my business, everything you do in the restaurant or on an episode of the TV show, and in a grander sense, everything I've ever cooked in my entire career. Paula Deen's sense of balance is quite different from Paul Bocuse's or Thomas Keller's, but it's there nonetheless. It's easy to spot, and it's as important to her cuisine as it is to theirs. Try serving turkey and gravy on Thanksgiving Day on the same plate as a hamburger, a jelly donut, a whole raw onion, a scoop of ice cream, and a wad of cotton candy and you'll see what I mean.

Pairings of food should aim at a sense of harmony on the plate and on the palate. Certain things just go together. But that doesn't mean you have to get stuck in a rut. Potatoes go really well with green onions, but I have paired both with butternut squash and cranberries in a rissole potato cake with a savory chocolate sauce, and it worked really well. Know what flavors the foods you are working with have to offer, then decide how you are going to put those flavors to their best uses for what you have in mind. Do you want to concentrate them, dilute them, mask some of them for use as an undertone, make one or more of them the stars of your dish or supporting players, use them as accents, or just leave them alone? For this book I've worked on putting together pairings that I feel work well together. Some are classic, and some may be a little bit surprising. If you've ever found yourself wondering what pineapples and artichokes might taste like together with pasta, and you think you're crazy, try it. I did, and the recipe is on page 232.

There are secret weapons in the quest to create great flavor. I refer to foundational preparations and mixtures of ingredients that create a rock solid bottom layer for a dish.

- Mirepoix is a mix of diced or chopped ingredients that forms one of the bedrocks of Western savory cooking. It consists of onion, celery, and carrot.

- In Creole and Cajun cooking, the trinity, a variation on this theme, is made up of onion, celery, and green bell pepper.

- In Asian cooking, garlic and ginger cooked quickly in hot oil is a vital combination.

- Bouquet garni is a classical combination of fresh herbs that is used to flavor soups and stocks and usually contains bay leaf, parsley, and thyme. Other aromatics such as cloves and marjoram may be included.

- Herbes de Provence form another essential flavoring bouquet, consisting of thyme, rosemary, basil, savory, marjoram, fennel, and lavender. They may be unbundled according to your specific needs, but provide a marvelous culinary vocabulary for accenting and enriching your flavors.

- Garam masala is an Indian spice mixture that typically includes cardamom pods, cloves, cumin seeds, peppercorns, cinnamon sticks, coriander, and nutmeg.

- Chinese five-spice powder is a combination of cloves, cinnamon, fennel seeds, Szechuan peppers, and star anise.

It doesn't really matter what part of the globe you hail from. These combinations are designed to excite and stimulate the human palate. We live in a wonderful age where many of these tastes and flavors are available on a wide basis. We are all united in our search for better and more delicious flavor combinations.

MAKE ONCE, USE TWENTY TIMES

Stocks, Soups, Spice Blends, and Purees

Certain spice mixtures like those I've just described and certain sauces, stocks, and purees are items that you can prepare ahead of time, maybe on Sunday when you have time on your hands to fool around in the kitchen. You can then stash them and use them to add a turbo boost of flavor to your weekday meals.

Garam masala, Chinese five-spice powder, Old Bay seasoning, chili powder, and curry powder can all be enlivened by buying fresh spices, whole berries and seeds, cardamom pods, and mace blades and combining them in a dedicated coffee grinder. Experiment with the mixes, let your inner mad scientist have free rein, and find combinations that work for you. Find a cheap spice rack and jars, fill them with your own personalized line of fresh ground spices, and enjoy the fruits of your (minimal) labors across an entire platform of dishes for weeks to come.

A well-made stock can make or break the flavor of a dish. There are certain types of stocks you don't want to make at home. Veal stock is one of the most common stocks we use in a professional kitchen. We have an endless supply of bones left over from fresh butchery, which we roast to bring out the fabulous flavor inherent in the marrow. We cook them in water, often for days at a time, with the endless supply of leftover end bits of freshly chopped vegetables and meat trimmings. We use more whole chickens than you could ever imagine, so we also make our own chicken stocks. Demi-glace, a rich stock that is reduced and concentrated over days, though simple in design, is too time consuming in execution for the home cook. At home, I grant you permission to buy ready-made demi-glace and prepared chicken, veal, and beef stocks (and there are some very good ones on the market).

But you can and should be able to make fresh and wonderfully flavorful fish and vegetable stocks easily. Once you get into the habit of seeing end bits of vegetables, parsley stems, outer cabbage leaves, tomato skins, leek roots, mushroom stems, and the like as *mise en place* for your stocks instead of as garbage, you're on your way to becoming a better cook. Fish heads and bones, shrimp and lobster shells, anything you might otherwise discard that is fresh and promises flavor should go into a freezer bag until you're ready to use it.

Start with oil or butter in a stockpot or any other big pot. First, prepare a bouquet garni, then start cooking with a flavor foundation, like a mirepoix. Heat until you've just begun to coax the flavor out of it, and add the desired collection of leftovers. Add a cup of chardonnay or chenin blanc, a squeeze of lemon juice, a bouquet garni, a touch of salt and pepper, and maybe a clove or two of garlic. For your fish stock, add the bones, heads, and shells, or for your vegetable stock, maybe throw in the odd chopped turnip or parsnip. Cover with cold water, bring to a boil, lower to a simmer, and walk away. Come back in about forty minutes for the fish stock, one hour for the veggie. Strain well and separate into convenient serving sizes in plastic bags or containers or even into ice cube trays for use in enlivening your flavors in many different kinds of recipes.

Certain soups and stews are amazingly easy to make in advance for use over several meals. There was a time when soup was served routinely as a first course for the evening meal, and it always makes for a nice lunch with a chunk of crusty bread. Tomato soup, chili, chicken soup, and bean and vegetable soups all fit the model: Make them once in a big pot, then dole them out in small bowls for lunch or dinner. It's just as easy as opening a can once you put in the initial effort, and the taste (as well as the impact on your reputation as a fantastic cook) is beyond comparison.

As long as you have your trusty immersion blender, you can make purees of both vegetables and fruits simply and affordably. You'll have difficulty finding an easier way to get the most out of everyday ingredients. You concentrate and enhance their flavors by simply boiling down and blending carrots, parsnips, celeriac, cauliflower, asparagus, broccoli, butternut squash, pumpkin—pretty much any starchy or fibrous vegetable—in either water or chicken stock, with maybe a little salt and pepper. You can achieve a smooth, silky, and delicious homemade product that falls somewhere between a sauce and a soup. Again, once made, portion out your purees into smaller portions for the week, and use them as elegant counterpoints, either as side dishes or sauces, to your main entrées.

You can make a big pot of marinara sauce easily enough as well. Start with onions and celery frying in oil, add salt and pepper, maybe some crushed red pepper, dried herbs such as oregano and basil, and a tablespoonful of tomato paste. Five minutes in, add chopped garlic. Pour in cans of crushed tomatoes and a cup of red wine, season again, bring to a simmer, reduce the heat, and add a handful of chopped fresh parsley. Once it's heated through, it's done (although if you want to let it simmer slowly for a couple of hours just to enjoy the aroma, I certainly won't stop you). Divide this into user-friendly portions and you have the basis for spaghetti alla puttanesca, eggplant Parmigiana, lasagne Bolognese, seafood fra diavolo, and any number of Italian classics at your fingertips. And you will have the deep inner satisfaction that comes from ladling out a sauce of your own creation rather than the cold, sterile feeling of unscrewing the lid of a jar.

Remember, at the end of the day you're in search of great flavor. And you want to feel like a cook, not a can opener!

Veal Saltimbocca

SERVES 6

In any contest of dishes with flavors that go well together, Veal Saltimbocca is a hands-down winner. The name literally means "jumps in your mouth." It's got savory, a little bit of sweet, some bitter, some salty, beautiful textures . . . this one's got it all.

INGREDIENTS

1 pound wilted spinach, soaked in salt water to remove grit and drained

½ cup grapeseed oil

2 to 3 pounds thinly sliced veal cutlets

1 cup potato flour or all-purpose flour to dust

10 tablespoons (1¼ sticks) unsalted butter (6 tablespoons to sauté and 4 tablespoons cut into cubes for the sauce)

2 garlic cloves, chopped

½ cup white wine

1 cup demi-glace or 1 teaspoon beef base stirred into 1 cup water

12 fresh sage leaves, chopped or whole

6 slices prosciutto, cut into enough pieces to top all the veal

6 ounces sliced Swiss cheese, cut into strips that mimic the size of the veal slices

Salt and freshly ground black pepper to taste

Buttered noodles or julienned steamed vegetables, as an accompaniment

Method

In a saucepan fitted with a steamer basket, steam the spinach, then set aside to drain well and cool.

In a large sauté pan, heat the oil over medium heat. Dust the veal cutlets with flour and shake off any excess. Sear the veal quickly, 1 or 2 minutes per side, just to brown the coating—but be careful not to overcook. Remove the cutlets to a baking sheet to stop the cooking and allow them to cool. To the same pan add 6 tablespoons of butter and the garlic, allowing the butter to melt and sizzle for a short while. Deglaze the pan with the white wine, then add the demi-glace and allow this sauce to reduce by half, stirring occasionally.

Set one of the oven racks at the topmost level and preheat the oven to 325°F. Top each of the veal cutlets with some spinach, sage leaves, a slice of prosciutto, and a slice of Swiss cheese. Place into the oven on the top rack only long enough to melt the cheese and warm the veal. Do not leave in too long; you don't want the veal to cook any further.

To finish the sauce, remove the pan from the heat and whisk in the cubed butter. Season with salt and pepper to taste.

Presentation

Spoon the sauce onto each serving plate and top with a veal cutlet. Serve with buttered noodles or steamed julienned vegetables.

(The finished dish is shown in the photo insert.)

Good Tidings Salad with Balsamic Thyme Vinaigrette

SERVES 4

This salad is born of the idea that large bunches of fresh herbs like parsley go to waste because the home cook often can't use them all before they go bad. The name of the dish came from the resemblance the combination of fresh cranberries and goat cheese bears to the garland used during the holidays, but I assure you, it can be enjoyed in July as easily as in December. Parsley is a natural herbal breath freshener and, as a dark green leafy vegetable, it qualifies as a source of vitamin A. It is so tasty in its own right and plays a major role in this salad.

INGREDIENTS FOR THE BALSAMIC THYME VINAIGRETTE

¼ cup balsamic vinegar

1 shallot clove, minced

2 tablespoons fresh thyme leaves (stripped from about 6 large sprigs)

2 teaspoons minced fresh rosemary leaves (stripped from about 1 or 2 large sprigs)

1 teaspoon whole grain Dijon mustard (such as Inglehoffer's)

2 teaspoons sugar

½ teaspoon ground black pepper

1 teaspoon ground allspice

½ cup extra virgin olive oil

INGREDIENTS FOR THE SALAD

2 cups fresh flat-leaf parsley leaves, packed (Before removing the stems, soak the parsley in salt water and agitate to remove any grit, then spin in a salad spinner and/or pat dry with paper towels. The parsley is easier to clean with the stems on, but make sure you have enough leaves for the salad once the stems are removed.)

4 cups tender lettuce, such as red leaf or green leaf (soaked in water and agitated to remove grit, dried in a salad spinner, spines of leaves removed, and leaves torn into bite-size pieces)

¾ cup fresh cranberries or ½ cup dried cranberries

3 ounces goat cheese (about ½ cup)

Method for the balsamic thyme vinaigrette

Through the feed opening of a running blender add one at a time the vinegar, shallot, thyme leaves, rosemary leaves, mustard, sugar, black pepper, and allspice. Scrape down the sides of the blender and blend again. Leaving the blender running, slowly pour the olive oil in a stream through the feed opening to emulsify. Season to taste with salt only if needed and pour into a small pitcher or cruet.

Method for the salad

Toss the parsley and lettuce together in a large bowl.

Presentation

Transfer the greens to salad plates and top with the cranberries. Crumble the goat cheese on top. Drizzle lightly with the thyme vinaigrette.

Sea Scallop Sandwiches in a Crisp Potato Crust with Citrus Jus

SERVES 6

Flavor is about texture, too. This recipe encapsulates tender scallops in a crispy, salty potato crust. The citrus adds a wonderful note of brightness.

INGREDIENTS FOR THE SCALLOP SANDWICHES

2 large baking potatoes

Salt and freshly ground black pepper

1 lemon

6 U-10–size dry-pack scallops
(U-10 refers to the size of the scallop: under 10, meaning there are fewer than 10 in a pound)

2 tablespoons grapeseed oil

2 tablespoons unsalted butter

INGREDIENTS FOR THE SAUCE

Juice of 3 lemons

1⅓ cups dry white wine

3 large thyme sprigs
(preferably lemon thyme)

1 shallot, chopped

1 tablespoon chopped fresh flat-leaf parsley leaves

1 cup chicken stock

1 teaspoon sugar

1 tablespoon honey

2 tablespoons unsalted butter, cut into chunks

¼ teaspoon white pepper

Salt to taste (only if needed)

4 fresh chives, chopped

TIMELINE

Ingredient prep:
Create potato strands................................. 10 minutes
Chop herbs and shallot .... 5 minutes
Subtotal ingredient prep .... 15 minutes

Sear scallops... 4 minutes
Finish scallops in oven (15 minutes)
Overlaps with:
Cook and reduce sauce (10 minutes)
Sweeten and strain
sauce (5 minutes)................................15 minutes
Let scallops rest
Overlaps with:
Finish sauce .... 5 minutes
Estimated active cooking time .... 24 minutes

Assembly ....5 minutes

Total estimated time..............................44 minutes

Method

Using a vegetable peeler, cut the potatoes into ribbons. Mix the potato ribbons with salt to taste and squeeze out some of their liquid by hand with paper toweling. Squeeze fresh lemon juice over the scallops, then sprinkle them on both sides with salt and pepper. Envelop each scallop with a thick layer of potatoes, pressing with your hands to make it adhere.

Preheat the oven to 375°F. Heat a 10-inch skillet with an oven-safe handle over medium-high heat for 2 to 3 minutes, then add the oil and butter. When the butter foam subsides, add the scallops. Cook until the potato crust is nicely browned, about 2 minutes, then turn once to brown the other side. Transfer to a baking sheet to finish the scallops in the oven. For U-10 scallops this will take about 10 to 15 minutes, but check them for doneness. They should be opaque on the inside, but don't overcook them—they'll continue to cook for another 15 to 20 minutes after they're out of the oven. (This is called carry-over cooking.) Remove the scallops to a platter.

Add the lemon juice, wine, thyme, shallot, parsley, and chicken stock to the same skillet and reduce by half over high heat, stirring with a wooden spoon. Add the sugar and honey and cook for 1 minute. Strain into a small bowl, then whisk in the chunks of butter. Taste and adjust the seasoning with white pepper and salt as necessary.

Presentation

To serve, make a small circle of the sauce on each serving plate, then place one of the potato-crusted scallops in the center. Sprinkle with chives.

Everybody Loves Scalloped Potatoes

SERVES 6

Kids of all ages love this dish. It's a flavor classic. I keep it visually simple, using only light-colored ingredients, because kids seem to prefer it without green things (like the green parts of scallions) or black stuff (like ground pepper). However, you can jazz up the color if you like. You can also top it with breadcrumbs and bake till golden brown—but I keep the basic recipe gluten-free.

INGREDIENTS

4 tablespoons (½ stick) butter

1 large white onion, diced

½ cup rice flour (or all-purpose flour if the dish doesn't have to be gluten-free)

¾ cup milk

White pepper to taste

Dash of salt

4 to 5 baking potatoes, peeled and thinly sliced

¾ cup shredded white Cheddar cheese

⅛ cup breadcrumbs for topping (omit for a gluten-free dish)

⅛ cup thinly sliced white parts of scallions, for garnish

Method

Preheat the oven to 350°F. Lightly grease an oven-to-table baking dish with some of the butter.

Melt the rest of the butter in a saucepan or small skillet and sauté the onion until it becomes translucent, about 2 to 4 minutes. Gradually blend in the flour to make a blond roux, then slowly add the milk and allow the mixture to thicken. Season with white pepper and a dash of salt and remove from the heat. (Be careful to avoid oversalting as there is salt in the cheese.)

Layer a third of the potato slices in the baking dish, followed by a third of the milk sauce and ¼ cup of the shredded white Cheddar. Repeat the sequence twice for a total of three layers. You may top with the breadcrumbs before baking, but omit them if making the dish gluten-free. Bake, covered, for about 45 minutes to 1 hour, removing the cover for the last 10 minutes. The dish is done when the potatoes are tender when pierced with a fork. Let rest a few minutes before serving. Garnish with the sliced scallions.

Note: You can speed up the cooking time by premicrowaving the potatoes for 10 to 15 minutes before baking, or even parboiling them.

Mesquite Beef Medallions with Tomato Demi-glace over Cheddar Grits

SERVES 6

For this recipe, I would like you to try your hand at a simple version of demi-glace with tomato to experience what the beautiful concentration of flavors can do. Be sure to read all the directions carefully first and follow the timeline, and you'll be a master of multitasking in the kitchen.

INGREDIENTS FOR THE CHEDDAR GRITS

2 cups grits

2 cups grated sharp Cheddar cheese

Milk (or water), or as needed to adjust the consistency of the grits

Salt and freshly ground black pepper to taste

INGREDIENTS FOR THE TOMATO DEMI-GLACE

1 tablespoon grapeseed oil

1 medium red onion, finely chopped

1 celery rib, finely chopped

1 garlic clove, lightly crushed with the side of a knife blade and minced

¼ cup dry red wine

1 cup low-sodium vegetable stock

2 tablespoons tomato paste

1 tablespoon minced fresh flat-leaf parsley leaves

1 large thyme sprig, leaves stripped from stem and minced

INGREDIENTS FOR THE MESQUITE BEEF MEDALLIONS

2 pounds thin-cut round tip steak, cut into about 2 dozen 2-inch medallions

Salt and freshly ground black pepper to taste

1 to 2 tablespoons McCormick Mesquite Seasoning (or as needed to season the breadcrumbs)

2 cups panko breadcrumbs

1 cup milk, or as needed to moisten the beef

1 cup all-purpose flour, or as needed to dredge the beef

2 to 4 eggs, beaten, or as needed to coat the beef

⅛ cup grapeseed oil, or as needed to sauté

2 tablespoons minced fresh flat-leaf parsley leaves

TIMELINE

Ingredient prep:
Chop vegetables and mince herbs .... 10 minutes
Measure ingredients .... 5 minutes
Subtotal estimated prep time .... 15 minutes

Cook grits (20 minutes)
   Overlaps with:
   Sauté vegetables for demi-glace (5 minutes)
   Deglaze pan of vegetables and allow
      alcohol to evaporate (5 minutes)
   Overlaps with:
   Tenderize beef (5 minutes)
   Add stock, tomato, and herbs to sauce
      and allow to reduce (10 minutes)
   Overlaps with:
   Bread beef (10 minutes)................. 20 minutes
Remove demi-glace from
   heat and strain... 2 minutes
Add Cheddar to grits, cover, and
   allow cheese to melt .... 3 minutes
Sauté beef medallions and let rest .... 10 minutes
Estimated active cooking time .... 35 minutes

Assembly ....5 minutes

Total estimated time ....50 minutes

Method for the Cheddar grits

Bring 5 cups of water to a boil, add the grits, reduce the heat to low, cover, and simmer for 20 minutes, undisturbed. (Meanwhile, begin the tomato demi-glace below.)

Stir the grated Cheddar into the grits, cover, and cook for 1 or 2 minutes to let the cheese melt. Remove from the heat and let sit for 5 minutes. Set aside in a warm place. (Meanwhile, sauté the beef medallions, below.)

If the grits are too thick when you're ready to serve, adjust the consistency with milk or water. Season to taste with salt and pepper.

Method for the tomato demi-glace

Heat the grapeseed oil in a medium saucepan over medium-high heat and sauté the red onion, celery, and garlic until the onion is translucent, about 5 minutes.

Deglaze the pan with the red wine, and allow most of the alcohol to evaporate, about 5 minutes. (Meanwhile, start to tenderize the meat, below.)

Add the vegetable stock, tomato paste, parsley, and thyme. Return to a gentle boil and let the liquid reduce by half. (Finish tenderizing and breading the meat, below.)

When the tomato demi-glace is at the desired consistency, strain and transfer to a small bowl. Set the bowl in a container of warm water to keep the sauce warm until needed. (Finish the cheese grits, below.)

Method for the beef medallions

Lay a long length of plastic wrap over a large cutting board and tuck the edges of the plastic wrap under it. (This will help keep down the mess.) Lay the slices of beef out on the wrap and season with salt and pepper. Cover the meat with a second layer of plastic wrap, tucking the edges under the cutting board. Pound the beef with a meat mallet down to a thickness of about ⅛ inch to tenderize the meat and integrate the seasonings into its surface. You may have to work in 2 or 3 batches, depending on the size of your cutting board. (Now, add the stock and other ingredients to the demi-glace, above.)

Mix the mesquite seasoning with the breadcrumbs, set up a breading station, and bread the beef medallions as follows:

1. Moisten the beef slices in the milk.
2. Dredge the slices in flour, allowing any excess to fall away.
3. Dip in the beaten egg.
4. Coat with the breadcrumb mixture, pressing the crumbs into the beef.

(Meanwhile, stir the Cheddar into the grits and, if the tomato demi-glace is done, place it in a bowl and set in a bowl of warm water.)

Heat the oil over medium-high heat in a large skillet. Sear the medallions, leaving them undisturbed until you see the edges turning golden brown, about 1 to 2 minutes per side, to avoid having the coating crust come off. Work in batches so as not to crowd the pan. Transfer to a platter, cover to keep warm, and let rest. (Strain the demi-glace now.)

Presentation

Spoon some Cheddar grits into the center of a serving dish. Top with about 4 mesquite medallions and spoon some tomato demi-glace over the meat. Sprinkle minced parsley on top.

Lamb Tenderloin over Rice with Sauce Robért

SERVES 4

I wish I could say that Sauce Robért was named for me, but it is a classical French mustard sauce that is paired here with lamb loin for an easy and satisfying dish. As an accompaniment consider Ginger Vichy Carrots (page 221).

The sauce uses beef base as an ingredient. Beef base is sold in a jar and is a pastelike form of beef bouillon.

INGREDIENTS FOR THE RICE

1 cup white rice

1 tablespoon unsalted butter

1 teaspoon salt

INGREDIENTS FOR THE SAUCE ROBÉRT

1 to 2 tablespoons grapeseed oil

2 shallot cloves, minced

6 ounces (about 2 cups) cremini mushrooms, cleaned, trimmed, and sliced

1 tablespoon cornstarch

1 cup merlot wine (such as Clos du Bois or Phelps 2004 or 2005)

1 tablespoon tomato paste

1 teaspoon stone-ground Dijon mustard (such as Inglehoffer brand)

½ teaspoon beef base

1 tablespoon minced fresh flat-leaf parsley leaves (from about 4 to 6 large sprigs)

Salt and freshly ground black pepper to taste

INGREDIENTS FOR THE LAMB TENDERLOIN

1 tablespoon grapeseed oil

Four ¼-pound lamb tenderloins

Salt and freshly ground black pepper to taste

1 tablespoon minced fresh flat-leaf parsley leaves (from about 4 to 6 large sprigs)

TIMELINE

Ingredient prep:
Mince shallots/herbs and clean and
    slice mushrooms .... 5 minutes

Boil rice (20 minutes)
    Overlaps with:
    Sauté shallots and mushrooms
        for sauce (5 minutes)
    Make slurry (1 minute) and
        reduce sauce (10 minutes)
        Overlaps with:
        Sear lamb loin (6 minutes)
        Finish lamb loin
        in oven (8 to 14 minutes) .... 20 minutes
Let rice rest (5 minutes)
    Overlaps with:
    Let lamb rest (5 minutes) .... 5 minutes

Slice lamb and assembly .... 8 minutes

Total estimated time .... 38 minutes

Method for the rice

Bring 2½ cups water to a boil in a 2 to 2½ quart saucepan. Add the rice, butter, and salt and return to a boil. Cover, reduce the heat to low, and cook undisturbed—without lifting the lid—for 20 minutes. (Meanwhile, begin the sauce, below.)

Remove from the heat and let stand, covered, for 5 minutes.

Method for the Sauce Robért

Heat the grapeseed oil over medium-high heat in a medium saucepan. Add the shallots and sauté until translucent, about 2 minutes. Add the mushrooms and cook until they soften and begin to give up their juices, about 3 minutes.

Create a slurry by gradually whisking the cornstarch into a small bowl with 1 tablespoon of the wine and set aside briefly.

Deglaze the pan with the rest of the wine. Stir in the cornstarch slurry, tomato paste, mustard, beef base, and parsley and let the sauce reduce and thicken, about 10 minutes. (Meanwhile, begin the lamb, below.)

Season the sauce with salt and pepper as desired and transfer to a small bowl. Keep warm until needed by covering it with foil and nesting the bowl in a slightly larger bowl of warm water.

Method for the lamb tenderloin

Preheat the oven to 375°F. Heat the grapeseed oil over medium-high heat in a large sauté pan. Season the tenderloins on both sides with salt and pepper and rub into the surface of the meat. Sear the lamb for about 2 to 4 minutes on each side and transfer to the oven to finish to an internal temperature of 125°F for medium rare, about 10 minutes. Allow the lamb to rest 5 minutes before slicing.

Presentation

Spoon some rice into the center of each serving dish. Slice each tenderloin and arrange overlapping slices on top of the rice. Spoon the sauce on top and sprinkle with parsley leaves.

Salad of Seasonal Greens and Fresh Herbs with Orange-Shallot Vinaigrette

SERVES 6

You've probably heard of mesclun (not to be confused with the illicit drug mescaline, reportedly popular in the 1960s). Rather than a specific kind of lettuce or green, mesclun is any mixture of young or tender, wild and/or cultivated greens that originated in the rural area of Provence in France many decades ago. The thing about mesclun is: It was not intended to be a *specific* mix of greens, but rather a mix of those that were fresh, in season, and characteristically delicate. Freshness and flavor are what counts the most. Because of today's modern shipping methods, the global market is able to supply very nearly any type of produce at very nearly any time of year. Despite this reality, I believe mesclun should still vary not only with the season, but also to give your palate some new experiences.

The idea is to experiment by balancing flavor and texture in a mix of greens that are naturally tender because they are harvested young. Some of the usual elements of mesclun are arugula, mâche, and chicory. Others you can try are sorrel (sour with beautiful red stems), young beet leaves (a rippled texture), baby spinach (slightly bitter), baby romaine (light green and crunchy), nasturtium leaves (peppery), and oak leaf lettuce (smooth delicate texture and slightly sweet). (By the way, avoid picking weeds from the lawn. You have to worry about toxins from your lawn care regimen.)

Serve your mesclun mix with a dressing that is fresh and deserving of the delicate flavors. One of my pet peeves is the veritable host of partially used bottles of salad dressing kept in refrigerators and brought directly to the table. It's difficult for me not to think, *Now how old is this bottle of dressing?* and *Is this one still three-quarters full because nobody really likes it and you don't want to waste it by throwing it away?* It's incredibly easy to make your own fresh dressing, and you can rid your refrigerator of nearly emptied bottles of dressing that stretch back into the last century. It helps to have a blender, but many dressings can be made by just whisking the ingredients together in a bowl. Making salad dressing is one of the greatest ways to get kids involved in cooking because there's usually no heat involved and minimal cutting and, as appliances go, the blender is one of the safest and least messy around, provided you use the feed opening (which all blenders have). A lot of kids refuse to eat salads, but most kids I know cannot resist eating something they've made themselves.

Try this one. It's loaded with vitamin C. The proportions can easily be halved if you want to sample the taste without worrying about waste. (If you make the vinaigrette just before use, it will remain emulsified—plus you can give the kids a science lesson about emulsification.)

INGREDIENTS FOR THE ORANGE-SHALLOT VINAIGRETTE

1 head of garlic

2 teaspoons grapeseed oil

2 tablespoons rice vinegar (or apple cider vinegar)

Zest of 1 large orange (use the rest of the orange for the salad below)

¼ cup orange juice

1 shallot, quartered

½ teaspoon freshly ground black pepper

1 teaspoon salt

1 tablespoon honey

¾ cup canola oil

INGREDIENTS FOR THE MESCLUN SALAD

6 cups mixed seasonal greens and fresh herbs (about 12 ounces to 1 pound), soaked in salt water to remove grit, thoroughly rinsed, and dried in a salad spinner

1 large orange, peeled, pith removed, and segmented into ½-inch pieces

TIMELINE

Roast garlic cloves (15 minutes)
Overlaps with:
   Grate orange zest and segment
     orange (5 minutes)
   Measure ingredients (5 minutes)
   Chop shallot (1 minute)
   Soak, rinse, and dry
     greens (4 minutes)..............................15 minutes
Make dressing .... 5 minutes

Assemble salad... 2 minutes

Total estimated time .... **22 minutes**

Method

To roast the garlic, preheat the oven to 475°F. Slice the root end off the garlic head and turn it upside down, wrapping it in heavy duty aluminum foil and molding the foil so that it allows the cut end to stand upright in the oven. Pour the grapeseed oil on the garlic so that it slips between the skin and the cloves and enclose the garlic with foil. Place it on a baking sheet to help it roast evenly without burning. Roast until sweet and very tender, about 15 to 20 minutes. Since you're roasting at such a high temperature, *monitor to make sure the garlic is not burning. Burned garlic will be bitter and ruin your recipe.* (The garlic can be roasted in advance—at a lower temperature, if you have the time—and stored in the refrigerator for about a week.) Set aside the roasted garlic until just cool enough to handle.

Through the feed opening of a running blender, add, one at a time, the vinegar, orange zest, orange juice, shallot, black pepper, salt, honey, and 4 roasted garlic cloves (save the rest of the cloves for another delicious use). Leaving the blender running, add the oil in a slow, thin stream until emulsified.

In a large salad bowl, fold the greens with enough of the dressing to coat and serve the rest of the dressing on the side in a small pitcher or cruet. (Or you can just let everyone dress their own salads.)

Endive with Granny Smith Apples, Smoked Bacon, and Creamy Cheddar Dressing

SERVES 6

This salad is about great pairings. The following Cheddar dressing uses buttermilk, a mildly acid form of cultured milk. If you're reluctant to purchase a container of buttermilk for fear that most of it will go to waste, consider using the rest to marinate chicken (see the recipe for Boneless Buttermilk-Marinated Fried Chicken on page 66).

This recipe is proportioned for use as an appetizer. However, it makes a great entrée salad, particularly for lunch, in which case I would double the amount of endive to two halves per person (rather than one half for each person).

Have fun making your own fresh salad dressing in a blender. It's a great activity to get the kids involved in cooking and a surefire way to get them to eat salad. (It's a rare kid who doesn't at least want to taste his or her own cooking, and in this case the apples and cheese go a very long way toward helping the child like the dish—and wanting to make it again and again.)

INGREDIENTS FOR THE CHEDDAR DRESSING

2 tablespoons apple cider vinegar

2 tablespoons apple juice

½ teaspoon freshly ground black pepper

⅔ cup buttermilk or plain yogurt

2 teaspoons sugar

3 cups grated yellow Cheddar cheese (about 12 ounces)

INGREDIENTS FOR THE SALAD

1 teaspoon grapeseed oil

1 pound smoked bacon (Allow about 2 thick slices or 3 regular slices per person. A pound of thick-sliced bacon has about 12 strips. A pound of regular-sliced bacon contains about 16 bacon strips.)

3 heads of Belgian endive, halved lengthwise

Salt to taste

Freshly ground black pepper to taste

About 2 teaspoons sugar

3 Granny Smith apples, unpeeled, quartered, cored, cut into ¼-inch-thick slices that are then halved crosswise, and tossed in a bowl with the juice of ½ lemon to prevent oxidation

6 cups mesclun greens (tender and/or baby greens such as chicory, frisée, arugula, mâche, see page 56), soaked and agitated in salt water to remove grit, carefully lifted out, dried in a salad spinner, and torn into bite-size pieces

Method for the Cheddar dressing

Through the feed opening of a running blender, add, one at a time, the vinegar, apple juice, pepper, buttermilk, and sugar. Leaving the blender running, add the Cheddar cheese, about 1 tablespoon at a time, through the feed opening to allow it to integrate smoothly and gradually into the dressing. Set aside until needed.

Method for the salad

Heat the grapeseed oil in a large skillet over medium-high heat and sauté the bacon until crispy, being careful not to burn it. Remove the cooked bacon to drain on paper towels. Pour most of the fat from the pan, leaving about 2 tablespoons. (Wipe off any fat that drips on the side of the pan.) Sprinkle the cut sides of the Belgian endive with salt, pepper, and sugar and add the endive to the pan cut-side down, leaving undisturbed for about 2 to 3 minutes to allow the caramelization process to begin and the flavors of the bacon to integrate into the sliced surface of the endive. Add the apples to the pan and cook for a few minutes to allow the apples to caramelize on the surface. As the apples just begin to soften, remove them to a utility platter. Because of the thickness of the endive, it is likely to take longer to cook than the apples, about 5 to 7 more minutes. Both the apples and the endive should be slightly tender but not mushy. When the endive is soft (when pierced with a fork), remove it to the utility platter.

In a large mixing bowl, toss together the greens and apples. Season with pepper. (Be careful with the salt, since both the cheese in the dressing and the bacon lend some saltiness. Your guests can always add salt, but it can't be taken away.)

Presentation

Place the greens mixture on a serving plate and top with an endive half. Crumble some bacon on top. Spoon the dressing over the greens, serving additional dressing on the side.

Asparagus "Benedict" with Hollandaise

SERVES 4

This is my variation on a French countryside classic. These flavors work so well together, you may find yourself counting down the minutes until the arrival of the freshest seasonal asparagus at your greengrocer's. It may even be a little bit better with white asparagus and pancetta. Please feel free to enjoy this dish both ways.

INGREDIENTS FOR THE EGGS

8 bacon strips

1 tablespoon olive oil

8 thin asparagus stalks, tough ends snapped or
    sliced off and green skin on the stalk peeled
    down to the white layer

Salt and freshly ground black pepper to taste

4 eggs

1 tablespoon vinegar

INGREDIENTS FOR THE HOLLANDAISE

2 egg yolks

1 tablespoon chilled white wine

Pinch of salt (1/16 of a teaspoon)

1 stick (1/2 cup) unsalted butter, melted

Juice of 1/2 lemon

SPECIAL EQUIPMENT

Double boiler

Candy thermometer

Method

Put a large pot of water over high heat in preparation for poaching the eggs.

Cook the bacon over medium-high heat in a sauté pan until crispy, drain on paper towels, and set aside. Wipe out the pan and heat the olive oil over medium heat. Add the asparagus and sauté gently until tender, about 6 to 8 minutes. Season the asparagus with salt and pepper and set aside on a plate.

When the pot of water for the eggs is gently boiling, add the vinegar (to help keep the whites from dispersing) and set up a separate bowl of water that has been heated to 150°F as measured with a candy thermometer (hot enough to cook microorganisms but not so hot that it will keep cooking the eggs).

Add the eggs, one at a time, gently to the boiling water so they don't cook into one mass. Poached eggs should be cooked until the whites are set and opaque but the centers are still soft.

In an ideal world the eggs will all float freely and independently without sinking to the bottom. However, in the real world if an egg sinks to the bottom, wait until it is nearly set before attempting to work it loose, or the yolk will surely break. Remove the eggs from the pot with a slotted wooden or plastic spoon and place them in the bowl of hot water. Let sit for about 5 minutes. Drain the eggs on a paper towel and pat them dry.

To make the hollandaise, set a double boiler over a pot of simmering water (just below boiling). Add the egg yolks, wine, and salt and whisk constantly for about 2 minutes. Add the melted butter in a slow, thin stream, whisking constantly until it is emulsified and the sauce begins to thicken. Whisk in the lemon juice and remove the double boiler from the heat. Cover the double boiler.

Presentation

Place 2 asparagus stalks on each serving plate. Lay 2 bacon strips across the asparagus. Top with a poached egg and spoon hollandaise sauce over the egg. (The finished dish is shown in the photo insert.)

Savory Shrimp and Celery Cream Tart with Lime Aioli

SERVES 4

Prebake your tart crusts ahead of time for this recipe to streamline the process. You can purchase premade pastry shells if you like, but I urge you to go the distance and make your own dough. Despite all the excellent products out there, there is nothing quite like a flaky homemade pastry. It's really very easy, especially with the food processor method used here. However, there's nothing wrong with using premade pastry or shells.

Also, if you don't have one by now, invest a few bucks for an immersion blender. You'll never regret the purchase. But remember—the blade has to be *immersed* in the liquid to use it (hence the name), or it will make a mess.

Refer to the timeline and arrange the elements of the recipe accordingly. You can break it into its component parts based on your schedule.

INGREDIENTS FOR THE TART PASTRY

1½ cups all-purpose flour

¼ teaspoon salt

½ stick (4 tablespoons) chilled unsalted butter

¼ cup chilled shortening

INGREDIENTS FOR THE LIME AIOLI

⅓ cup mayonnaise

½ lime (use the other half for the shrimp)

Freshly ground black pepper to taste

SPECIAL EQUIPMENT

Food processor equipped with a dough blade (if making your own pastry)

Four 4½- to 5½-inch flan pans (tart tins with removable bottoms)

Pastry cloth (if making your own pastry)

Rolling pin (if making your own pastry)

Parchment paper

Pastry weights or dried beans

Immersion blender

INGREDIENTS FOR THE SHRIMP FILLING

1 celeriac (celery root), peeled and cut into chunks

1 tablespoon grapeseed oil

1 medium white onion, diced medium

2 garlic cloves, lightly crushed with the side of a knife blade and minced

1 red bell pepper, diced medium

1 celery rib, diced small

1 tablespoon minced fresh thyme leaves, or ¼ teaspoon dried

1 tablespoon minced fresh parsley leaves, or ¼ teaspoon dried

¼ teaspoon crushed red pepper

¼ teaspoon poultry seasoning

½ cup white wine

1 pound 31-40-size shrimp, deveined, shells and tails removed (freeze them in a plastic bag for later use in making seafood stock, page 103)

2 teaspoons Old Bay seasoning

Salt and freshly ground black pepper to taste

½ lime (use the other half for the aioli)

2 tablespoons unsalted butter

½ cup heavy cream

1 tablespoon minced fresh flat-leaf parsley leaves

Method for the crust

Place a glass of ice water in your work area; you'll need 6 to 8 tablespoons. Sift the flour into the bowl of a food processor equipped with a dough blade. Add the salt, butter, and shortening and pulse just until the mixture resembles coarse meal. Add the water, 1 tablespoon at a time, through the feed tube, pulsing after each addition. Add just enough water to allow the dough to come together and form a cohesive whole. All flours are different, so this amount will vary each time. Transfer the dough to a mixing bowl and form it into a ball. Divide it into 4 portions, form each into a ball, and flatten them slightly. Wrap each dough disk in plastic and refrigerate for 30 minutes. Meanwhile, make the aioli.

Grease the 4 flan pans well. Use a pastry cloth dusted with just enough flour to keep the dough from sticking. A pastry cloth is usually rectangular and long enough so that you can place the dough on one half of the rectangle, fold the remaining half of the cloth over the dough, and roll out the crust between the two layers. Using a rolling pin, roll out 1 dough disk at a time in the pastry cloth into a circle 7 or 8 inches in diameter. Ease the dough into one of the flan pans and trim the top edge of the dough flush with the top edge of the pan. Repeat with the other dough disks. Cover them with plastic and refrigerate for 30 minutes. (Save any scraps of dough in case you have extra filling.)

Preheat the oven to 400°F.

Lay a circle of parchment paper on top of each chilled pastry shell and top with a layer of pastry weights or dried beans. Place the pans on a tray and blind bake (partially pre-bake without any filling) until you can see

---

TIMELINE

Prepare pastry dough in food processor
  (10 minutes)
Let rest (30 minutes)
  Overlaps with:
  Make aioli (2 minutes)
Grease pans, roll out pastry, ease .... 40 minutes
  into pans, cover, and let rest .... 30 minutes
**Subtotal for preparation and
  resting of pastry crust
  (if using purchased pastry crusts,
  adjust time accordingly)** .... **70 minutes**

Prep for ingredients:
  Remove shells from shrimp .... 10 minutes
  Cut celeriac, onion, garlic, pepper,
    celery, and herbs .... 10 minutes
  Measure ingredients .... 5 minutes
Subtotal for ingredient prep .... **25 minutes**

Parbake crusts (25 minutes + 5 minutes)
  Overlaps with:
  Boil celery root (10 minutes)
  Sauté vegetables and herbs (7 minutes)
  Deglaze pan with wine (5 minutes)
  Overlaps with:
  Mash celery root and puree (5 minutes)
  Cook shrimp (3 minutes) .... 30 minutes
Add lime juice, combine elements,
  and assemble .... 3 minutes
Active cooking time .... **33 minutes**

Bake filled tarts... 20 minutes
Resting time.. 10 minutes

**Total estimated time
if making your own
pastry** .... **2 hours and 38 minutes**

If using premade shells .....**1 hour and 28 minutes**

that the dough is beginning to turn golden, about 25 minutes. Remove the pastry weights or beans and parchment paper and prick the base of each shell with a fork. (This will provide some ventilation to the bottom of the crust so that it doesn't bubble up in the center.) Bake 5 minutes more in order to dry out the bottom of the crust, where the pastry weights were. Set the pans aside.

Method for the aioli

In a small bowl, thoroughly whisk together the mayonnaise, lime juice, and black pepper, and refrigerate until needed.

Method for the filling

In a medium pot of boiling water, cook the celeriac until tender, about 10 to 12 minutes.

Meanwhile, prepare the shrimp. In a large sauté pan over medium-high heat, heat the grapeseed oil. Add the onion, garlic, bell pepper, celery, thyme, parsley, crushed red pepper, and poultry seasoning and sauté until the onion begins to turn translucent and the bell pepper softens, about 5 to 7 minutes. Deglaze the pan with the white wine and let most of it sizzle off, about 3 minutes.

Stir the shrimp into the pan and season it with the Old Bay seasoning and salt and pepper to taste. Toss the shrimp until it is just pink, 1 or 2 minutes. Do not overcook it. Squeeze the juice from the ½ lime over the shrimp and remove the pan from heat. (If you squeeze the fresh lime with the sliced side against your palm, most of the seeds will remain in the rind.)

To make the celeriac puree, drain the celeriac well and place in a bowl that is deep enough to accommodate the use of an immersion blender. Add the butter and mash by hand. Add the cream and whip with an immersion blender until pureed. Season the puree to taste with salt and pepper.

Preheat the oven to 375°F. Reserve about 8 shrimp (2 per tart halved lengthwise) to adorn the tops of the tarts and cut the rest into ½-inch pieces. Stir the celeriac puree into the shrimp mixture a little at a time. Do not feel compelled to use all of the celeriac puree. It is used primarily to bind the mixture in the tart as a creamy base, so you don't want to use so much that it's runny or overflows the tart shells. Fill each tart with about ¼ to ⅓ cup of the shrimp mixture (do not overfill). (If you have extra filling and some dough scraps, you may wish to make 1 or 2 celeriac tarts for tomorrow's lunch, with or without shrimp.) Place the filled tarts on an aluminum-lined baking sheet (for easy cleanup) and bake for 20 minutes. Let rest for 10 minutes.

Presentation

Using oven mitts to protect your hands, remove the hot tarts from the flan pans by pressing the removable bottoms up to disengage the outer ring of the pan. While it is still sitting on the removable pan base, place the tart onto a serving plate, then slide the tart off the pan base using an offset spatula. Arrange 4 halves of the reserved shrimp in a "tails to center" circle on the surface of each tart, and spoon some aioli into the center of each "circle." Sprinkle with minced parsley and serve.

Boneless Buttermilk-Marinated Fried Chicken

SERVES 4

Achieving maximum flavor is sometimes just about knowing what works. Marinating chicken in buttermilk works. Once you try it and taste the results, you may never do it any other way again.

INGREDIENTS

4 boneless chicken breasts

4 boneless chicken thighs

Salt and pepper to taste

3 cups buttermilk

1 cup canola oil, or more as needed for frying

2 cups all-purpose flour, or more as needed for breading

3 to 5 eggs, beaten, as needed for the egg wash

3 cups cornmeal, or more as needed for breading

1 tablespoon paprika, or more as desired for the cornmeal

Method

Rinse the chicken breasts and thighs to remove any residue and pat dry with paper towels. Season with salt and pepper and place in a nonreactive bowl. Pour the buttermilk on top, cover, and marinate, preferably overnight, but at least 2 hours.

Heat the oil in a large sauté pan over medium-high heat. Set up your breading station as follows:

1. Place the flour in a bowl or plastic bag.
2. Pour the beaten eggs into a shallow bowl.
3. Place the cornmeal seasoned with the paprika, salt, and pepper in a bowl or plastic bag.

Remove the chicken one piece at a time from the buttermilk and dredge it in the flour. Press the chicken into the flour to help it adhere, but allow any excess flour to fall away. Dip the floured chicken in the egg wash and then coat with the cornmeal mixture.

Working in batches, fry the coated chicken pieces over medium heat on both sides until they are cooked through—the juices run clear and the interior is no longer pink, about 20 to 30 minutes per batch. Drain on paper towels and serve.

Asiago-Stuffed Chicken Cacciatore

SERVES 6

The beauty of this dish is that you make it better when you start to eat it. When you cut into the chicken, the cheese escapes and enriches the sauce with creamy goodness.

INGREDIENTS

Six 6-ounce chicken breasts, butterfly cut (see page 68)

Salt and freshly ground black pepper to taste

6 tablespoons sour cream

6 tablespoons grated Asiago cheese or other hard cheese of your choice

¼ cup oil-packed sun-dried tomatoes *or* if dehydrated, soaked in warm water to soften, cut into ¼-inch pieces

½ cup milk, or as needed for moistening chicken before dredging

½ to 1 cup all-purpose flour, as needed for dredging

2 tablespoons grapeseed oil

2 garlic cloves, lightly crushed with the side of a knife blade and minced

1 medium red onion, diced

½ cup red wine, such as Moulin-à-Vent cru 2005 or Beaujolais Villages Jadot 2006

2 teaspoons minced fresh rosemary leaves, or ½ teaspoon dried, pulverized in a mortar and pestle

2 fresh sage leaves, minced, or ¼ teaspoon dried

1 tablespoon minced fresh basil leaves, or ¼ teaspoon dried

1 bay leaf

1 green bell pepper, cut in julienne

1 cup sliced fresh mushrooms (about 3 ounces)

One 29- to 32-ounce can diced tomatoes

1 pound farfalle pasta

1 tablespoon minced fresh flat-leaf parsley

TIMELINE

Ingredient prep:
Butterfly chicken .... 6 minutes
Grate cheese .... 2 minutes
Chop vegetables .... 5 minutes
Mince herbs .... 2 minutes
Clean/slice mushrooms .... 5 minutes
Measure out ingredients .... 5 minutes
Subtotal ingredient prep .... 25 minutes

Pound chicken .... 2 minutes
Assemble stuffed breasts .... 12 minutes
Dredge chicken .... 5 minutes
Sear chicken .... 8 minutes
Sauté garlic and onions .... 3 minutes
Add wine and herbs and cook peppers
   and mushrooms until they soften .... 7 minutes
Add tomatoes and chicken and
   cook until done
   Overlaps with:
   Boil pasta (10 minutes) .... 25 minutes
Estimated active cooking time .... 62 minutes

Assembly .... 5 minutes

**Total estimated time,
start to finish .... 1 hour and 32 minutes**

Method

Cover a large cutting board with 1 or two long pieces of plastic wrap and tuck it under the board. Place the chicken in a single layer on the plastic and season with salt and pepper. Cover the chicken with plastic wrap and tuck it under the board as well. (This will help keep the mess down.) Pound the chicken with a meat mallet to integrate the seasonings into the surface and create a uniform thickness of about ¼ inch.

Spoon 1 tablespoon sour cream, 1 tablespoon cheese, and 1 teaspoon sun-dried tomatoes into the center of each chicken breast and spread evenly. Roll up the chicken, folding in the edges as you go, and secure with wooden skewers or toothpicks. Place in a pie plate or shallow bowl. Repeat with the remaining chicken breasts. (If you have extra time, place the stuffed chicken in the freezer for a few minutes at this stage to harden slightly. It will be a bit easier to handle if it's slightly frozen.) Pour the milk over the stuffed chicken to moisten.

Place the flour in a small bowl and season it with salt and pepper. Spread about a third of the flour onto a flat surface, such as a piece of wax paper. Carefully lift the chicken breasts and place them onto the floured surface. Place the balance of the seasoned flour into a sifter or strainer held over the chicken and dust the tops with flour. Do your best to allow any excess flour to fall away without damaging the chicken rolls.

Heat the grapeseed oil over medium-high heat in a large sauté pan that is deep enough to accommodate the stuffed chicken and the sauce when covered. When the oil begins to shimmer, add the chicken, seam-side down if possible. Leave the chicken undisturbed for 2 to 3 minutes to let the flour and seasoning integrate into the surface of the chicken and to prevent the crust from sticking to the pan. When you see that the edges are beginning to turn golden brown, carefully turn the chicken over and sear the other side. Remove the chicken to a utility platter.

To the same sauté pan over medium-high heat, add the garlic and onion. Sauté until the onion turns translucent, about 3 minutes, taking care not to burn them. Deglaze the pan with the wine and add the rosemary, sage, basil, and bay leaf. When most of the wine has evaporated, stir in the bell pepper

HOW TO BUTTERFLY POULTRY

The butterfly cut makes the poultry breast thinner and more uniform, the better to stuff and roll it, as in a roulade. Remove the skin from the breast (if necessary) and place the breast skin-side down on your work surface. With a sharp knife, start on one side and cut almost (but not quite) through the breast horizontally. Spread the breast open to make one single piece of meat with a thickness of ¼ to ⅜ inch.

and mushrooms and cook until they begin to soften, about 7 minutes. Add the tomatoes and season with salt and pepper. Mix well, then return the chicken to the pan. Reduce the heat to low, cover, and cook until the juices of the chicken run clear, 25 to 35 minutes.

Meanwhile, bring a large pot of salted water to a boil over high heat for the farfalle. Add the farfalle, cook until al dente, and drain.

Transfer the chicken to a plate and remove the toothpicks. Remove the bay leaf from the sauce and discard.

Presentation

Spoon some farfalle on each serving plate. Spoon on some sauce and top with a piece of stuffed chicken. Garnish with the parsley.

3. FOR STARTERS

Okay, I like a party. I like big banquets, soirees, birthday parties, inaugural bashes, yacht parties, after parties, premiere parties, cocktail parties, and backyard barbecues, and I even like a good surprise party, as long as I am not its primary target.

Call them appetizers, hors d'oeuvres, finger foods, *amuse-bouche,* or munchies, they are designed to do what food does best: Bring people together and satisfy. How many great conversations have been started by discussing delicious little bites of food? "What's in this?" "This is sooo good!" "Have you tried the ———?" "Can I get the recipe?" A good starter is an icebreaker, delivers a burst of flavor, is well balanced so that it satisfies in one or two bites, and can be easily held in one hand whilst holding a cocktail or making an emphatic point with the other.

They're meant to be quick and fun, and the best of them are surprising, too. An appetizer can be as simple as cheese on a cracker or as complex as an entire entrée in microcosm. One of my favorite tricks is to create something that looks simple on the surface—something akin to a paste, mousse, aioli, or cream—that has some complex elements in its composition related to its seasoning. This usually involves a simple main ingredient like cream cheese or a mayonnaise or white beans that I can extend out with salmon or crab or duck breast, whatever. I turn it into something I can spoon or put it into a piping bag and dollop onto a cracker or crostini or into a cucumber boat and garnish with fresh herbs or something spicy to kick it up a bit, to give it an extra dash of flavor. I like to make forcemeats, like pâtés, sausages, or meatballs, that incorporate a lot of layers or flavors, then land them on a platform or spear them with a skewer, which goes back to rule number one: You've got to be able to pick it up, hold it, pop it in your mouth, and get the full effect in a single bite.

You can challenge yourself with elaborate recipes when making hors d'oeuvres, and you should, because if you do a good job you'll not only give a pleasurable experience to your guests, but also most likely get praised to the skies. But there's an equal virtue in keeping it simple—as long as your flavors are great.

A good appetizer is a great tool to set the mood. In a restaurant setting, the *amuse-bouche* or *amuse-gueule* is a single bite served up prior to the main meal, literally to amuse the palate and set the tone for the meal, to give you an inkling in one bite what the chef has in store for you at that sitting. If you're throwing a grand affair, you may want to load up on the pâté, caviar, and crème fraîche and really make an elegant statement. But if it's just the family, a spouse, or some friends, Welsh rarebit, a cheese or chocolate fondue, or a loaf of fresh bread paired with some wonderful olives, pickles, and cheeses can easily make for a memorable affair.

Don't be afraid to put your personality into your dishes, especially when you're entertaining, whether formally or informally. If you honestly please yourself, it will proceed as night follows the day that others will be pleased with what you're offering them, too.

Artichoke Hearts Stuffed with Crab Salad

SERVES 8

There is a singular beauty in the unique appearance of the artichoke (as shown in the photo insert).

INGREDIENTS

8 fresh artichokes

Salt and freshly ground pepper to taste

¼ cup prepared mayonnaise

12 fresh chives, snipped into small pieces

2 teaspoons fresh chopped flat-leaf parsley plus 18 small (2-leaf) parsley sprigs

⅛ teaspoon Old Bay seasoning

Splash of Tabasco

1 shallot clove, diced small

Juice of 1 lemon

1 tablespoon whole grain mustard

8 ounces (½ pound) cooked fresh backfin or lump crabmeat, such as Graham and Rollins Old Point Comfort brand (avoid using canned), picked over for shells

Method

Slice the stems from the artichokes so that they have a flat base. Slice across the artichokes about halfway down, to trim off the prickly tops of the leaves. Arrange the artichokes upright in a large saucepan so that they support each other. Fill the pot with water to cover about three quarters of the way up the artichokes and season generously with salt and pepper. Boil the artichokes over medium-high heat, uncovered, about 15 minutes, or until tender. Remove the artichokes from the pan and set aside to cool.

In a large bowl, make a dressing by combining the mayonnaise, chives, chopped parsley, Old Bay seasoning, Tabasco, shallot, lemon juice, mustard, and salt and pepper to taste. Place the crabmeat in another bowl and add just enough dressing to coat. Toss the crabmeat very lightly—try not to break it up. Cover and set aside to chill in the refrigerator.

Each artichoke heart and the remaining tender leaves that surround it will serve as a vessel for the salad. When the artichokes are cool enough to handle, peel away most of the leathery outer leaves until you reach the layer that's clinging tightly around the artichoke heart (the disklike pad at the bottom that secures the leaves). Sitting on the top of the heart is a cone-shaped cluster of immature prickly leaves that are lighter in color. Use your fingers to pluck this cluster—the "choke"—from each artichoke heart. This will leave a cavity.

Spread the surrounding leaves apart and spoon some crab salad into each cavity. Top with a tiny parsley sprig.

Presentation

Serve on salad plates.

Pommes Frites with Chipotle Aioli

SERVES 8

I'm all for going back to making French fries with actual potatoes instead of buying the overprocessed potato products marketed as French fries in the frozen food section or fast-food restaurants. Remember the wire grid–type French fry cutter your mom had when you were a kid? Buy one. They're great. It may amaze you to realize that potatoes—real potatoes—actually contain fiber! In processed potatoes the fiber is pulverized down to practically nothing. Given the choice, which do you think is healthier to eat?

INGREDIENTS FOR THE POMMES FRITES

1 liter canola oil

8 large potatoes, peeled and sliced (just before use) lengthwise to medium (½-inch-thick) batonnet or large (¾-inch-thick) batonnet, but in either case a uniform thickness so that they cook at the same rate

INGREDIENTS FOR THE CHIPOTLE AIOLI

1 cup prepared mayonnaise

1 tablespoon McCormick Hot Mexican Style Chili Powder

Salt to taste

INGREDIENTS FOR THE TOPPING

1 to 2 teaspoons truffle oil

2 tablespoons freshly grated Parmesan cheese

Method

Heat the oil in a deep fryer to 375°F or in a deep sauté pan until it begins to shimmer. Fry the potatoes until golden brown, about 5 to 7 minutes, and drain them on paper toweling.

While the potatoes are frying, make the chipotle aioli by whisking the mayonnaise and chipotle chile powder together in a small bowl.

Season the fries with salt while they're still glistening. Drizzle them with truffle oil and sprinkle the Parmesan on top.

Serve the fries with the chipotle aioli as a dipping sauce. (See the gorgeous pommes frites in the photo insert.)

Seared Tuna with Hummus on Crostini

APPROXIMATELY 24 HORS D'OEUVRES

This combines the slightly salty richness of deftly seared tuna with the garlicky creaminess of hummus and the toothsome crunch of the crostini, all in one bite.

INGREDIENTS

One 16-ounce can chickpeas, drained

2 to 3 garlic cloves, lightly crushed with the side of a knife blade and quartered

2 tablespoons chopped fresh flat-leaf parsley

3 tablespoons sesame seeds

½ teaspoon crushed red pepper flakes

¼ cup extra virgin olive oil

1 tablespoon freshly squeezed lemon juice

¼ cup grapeseed oil

Two 6-ounce tuna steaks

½ teaspoon paprika

Salt and freshly ground black pepper to taste

1 French baguette or sesame seed loaf, cut into ½-inch slices

24 small (2-leaf) parsley sprigs

Method

To make the hummus, in a food processor, combine the chickpeas, garlic, chopped parsley, sesame seeds, and red pepper flakes and pulse until coarsely chopped and combined. Remove to a bowl and stir in the extra virgin olive oil and lemon juice.

Heat the grapeseed oil in a sauté pan over medium-high heat. On a plate, season the tuna with the paprika and salt and pepper to taste. When the oil begins to shimmer, add the tuna. Sear the tuna on both sides, leaving undisturbed for the first 2 minutes or so to let the seasonings integrate into the surface of the meat and to prevent tearing. When you see the edges beginning to turn golden, flip the tuna to sear the other side in the same way. After both sides have been seared for about 2 to 3 minutes, remove the tuna to a utility platter and cover to let carry-over cooking finish the job (see page 23 for a discussion of carry-over cooking).

While the tuna is resting, make the crostini by arranging the bread slices on a baking sheet and toast in a 325°F oven until lightly browned. Slice the tuna across the grain.

Assemble the hors d'oeuvres by spooning a bit of hummus on each piece of toast and topping with a piece of tuna. Add another small bit of hummus (about ⅛ teaspoon) and a small sprig of parsley.

Welsh Rarebit

SERVES 8

By now, everybody has their own opinion on whether it's Welsh rabbit or Welsh rarebit, and whether it's meant to be a savory treat or a poor man's supper. Suffice it to say, it's as close to my heart as it gets for a warm, satisfying snack with the kids.

INGREDIENTS

1 egg

4 ounces (1 stick) unsalted butter, softened

½ cup grated Parmesan cheese

2 cups heavy cream

3 tablespoons dry English mustard (such as Colman's)

4 dashes (about ½ teaspoon) Worcestershire sauce

¼ teaspoon cayenne pepper, or more if you like it hot

8 ounces English sharp Cheddar cheese, grated

Salt and freshly ground black pepper to taste

1 loaf French bread, cut into ½-inch-thick slices

2 tablespoons chopped chives

Method

Preheat the oven to 325°F.

In a large bowl, using an electric beater, beat the egg for a few seconds. Add the butter, Parmesan cheese, cream, dry mustard, Worcestershire sauce, cayenne pepper, and Cheddar (the mixture will be thick). Season the mixture with salt and pepper to taste, taking care not to oversalt, since the cheese is already salty. Lay the slices of bread on a baking sheet and spoon some of the cheese mixture over the entire surface of each slice. Sprinkle with the chopped chives and bake until golden brown, about 5 minutes.

Presentation

Serve as a casual appetizer with your favorite beer, wine, soft drink, or a nice cup of tea. Refer to the photo insert to see this treat.

Lobster Brie Quesadilla

SERVES 4

If you were to think that the simple tortilla would be elevated to a whole different level with the addition of creamy Brie and fresh lobster, you'd be right.

INGREDIENTS

8 large flour tortillas

1 tablespoon grapeseed oil

1 medium white onion, very thinly sliced

½ orange bell pepper, seeded and thinly sliced

Salt to taste

White pepper to taste

Smidgen or dash of cayenne pepper (between ⅟₃₂ and ⅟₁₆ teaspoon)

1 tablespoon chopped fresh cilantro leaves

2 pounds steamed lobster tail and/or lobster claw, sliced into ¼-inch-thick pieces

4 ounces chilled Brie cheese, sliced ⅛ to ¼ inch thick

2 tablespoons scallions, white and tender green parts only, sliced on the bias

Method

Preheat the oven to 350°F. Lay 4 large flour tortillas on a baking sheet.

Heat the oil in a skillet over medium-high heat. Add the onion, bell pepper, salt, white pepper, cayenne, and cilantro and sauté until the onion becomes translucent, about 5 minutes. Toss in the lobster and stir to integrate the flavors. Spoon a thin layer of the lobster mixture over the tortillas and top with the Brie and scallions. Place a tortilla on top of each quesadilla and heat until the Brie melts, about 5 minutes.

Use a pizza cutter to cut each tortilla into 4 wedges and serve.

Cheese Fritters with Sauce Tomate

SERVES 12 (4 FRITTERS EACH)

You may have heard of pâte à choux (cream puff paste). Choux translates literally to "cabbage," and it's so named because the dough balls resemble small cabbages when they're cooked. Here we add cheese to cream puff paste to make a savory treat.

INGREDIENTS FOR THE DIPPING SAUCE

1 tablespoon grapeseed oil

1 medium onion, minced

2 garlic cloves, minced

One 29- to 32-ounce can crushed tomatoes

1 teaspoon dried oregano

1 teaspoon dried thyme

1 teaspoon dried parsley

Pinch (1/16 teaspoon) of dried rosemary, pulverized with a mortar and pestle

Salt and freshly ground black pepper to taste

INGREDIENTS FOR THE COATING

1 cup grated Parmesan cheese

Freshly ground black pepper

INGREDIENTS FOR THE FRITTERS

3 to 4 quarts canola oil (approximately, as needed for deep frying)

8 tablespoons unsalted butter (1 stick), cut into chunks

1 teaspoon salt

1/4 teaspoon freshly ground black pepper

1 cup all-purpose flour

5 eggs

1 cup grated Swiss cheese

1/4 cup grated Parmesan cheese

SPECIAL EQUIPMENT

Deep fryer

Method for the sauce tomate

Heat the grapeseed oil over medium-high heat in a medium saucepan and sauté the onion and garlic until the onion turns translucent, about 5 minutes. Stir in the tomatoes, oregano, thyme, parsley, rosemary, and salt and pepper. Bring to a gentle boil, reduce the heat to low, cover, and simmer about 20 minutes while you prepare the fritters.

Method for the coating

Spread 1/4 cup at a time of the Parmesan cheese on a sheet of waxed paper and grind black pepper on top. Replenish the cheese/pepper mixture as needed for each batch of fritters.

Method for the fritters

Heat the oil in the deep fryer to 325°F, or as directed in the manufacturer's instructions for similar foods. Place the basket in the deep fryer.

Bring 1 cup water to a gentle boil in a medium saucepan and add the butter, salt, and pepper. Remove from the heat and add the flour, mixing well with a wooden spoon. Return the pot to the stovetop and stir constantly until the mixture forms a cohesive mass. Remove again from the heat and beat in the eggs, one at a time, with a wooden spoon until the mixture is well blended. Gradually add the cheeses, blending well after each addition.

Set out a utility platter and cover it with paper towels. Add the dough to a pastry bag fitted with a 1-inch tip and quickly squeeze six to eight ¾-inch-diameter dough balls into the deep fryer basket, protecting your face, hands, and body from spatters. Fry the fritters until golden brown, about 2 minutes, drain them on paper towels, and immediately roll them in the cheese and pepper mixture. Repeat the process until all the dough has been fried. Note that the formation of the fritters into the perfect shape is a skill that may take some practice. Your goal is to squeeze roughly the same amount of dough for each fritter in a given batch so they will be done at the same time. (Funnily, kids seem to prefer the bloopers that are shaped more like Cheetos to the cabbage shape.)

Presentation

Spoon the dipping sauce into a number of small bowls, such as 2-ounce ramekins. (It's nice for each guest to have his or her own mini dipping bowl.) Serve the fritters with cocktail forks or cocktail toothpicks.

Island-Style Bay Scallops Ceviche

SERVES 6

Those of you who are familiar with my cooking know I always strive to do things with style. I guarantee that if you improve the presentation of your dishes, they'll seem to taste even better, as you delight all the senses. Fortunately, this can be done affordably. Small, incremental upgrades make a huge difference. For example, you'll recognize the martini glass as one of my themes in presentation. (Maybe it's the James Bond influence, which most grown men have experienced to a certain extent.) Martini glasses can be obtained remarkably inexpensively in many places, even at the corner liquor store.

A ceviche is made by cooking with acid instead of heat. Here the scallops are cooked chemically by marinating them in lime juice and vinegar for several hours.

INGREDIENTS

1¼ pounds bay scallops, rinsed to remove residue and drained

Juice (about 2 tablespoons) and grated zest of 1 lime

2 tablespoons rice vinegar

Splash of Tabasco sauce

1 tablespoon ground coriander seed

1 teaspoon ground turmeric

½ teaspoon ground mace

1 mango, peeled and diced small

½ cup chopped fresh cilantro (from about a 2-ounce bunch)

2 medium radishes, very thinly sliced with a mandoline

1 red pepper (such as long hot or cayenne), diced small

½ teaspoon salt

¼ teaspoon freshly ground black pepper

5 tablespoons extra virgin olive oil

1 pint-size container alfalfa sprouts (about 2 or 3 ounces)

Method

Coat the scallops with lime juice and vinegar in a nonreactive bowl. Add the lime zest, Tabasco sauce, coriander seed, turmeric, mace, mango, cilantro, radishes, red pepper, salt, and pepper and stir to combine well. Fold in the olive oil, cover, and marinate in the refrigerator for 4 to 6 hours. The scallops must be opaque inside and out.

Presentation

Spoon into martini glasses and top with alfalfa sprouts.

Walnut Wontons with Goat Cheese over Apples

SERVES 6 (2 WONTONS EACH)

The pasta takes about 30 minutes of active preparation time plus 30 minutes resting time. It can easily be made in advance and stored for a day or so in the refrigerator, as long as it is wrapped in plastic to keep it from drying out. When you remove it from the refrigerator, knead it with your hands to warm it up.

The old-time way is to use a rolling pin, but if you like making pasta—there *is* something meditative about it—treat yourself to a pasta machine or ask for one for your birthday, and get one with an electric motor so you won't have to crank.

Alternatively, you can use purchased pasta dough or premade wonton skins.

INGREDIENTS FOR THE PASTA DOUGH

1 cup all-purpose flour

2 to 3 eggs (1 egg for the dough, plus 1 to 2 eggs as needed for the egg wash)

½ teaspoon olive oil

¼ to ½ cup milk, as needed to moisten the wonton dough

INGREDIENTS FOR THE WALNUT/RAISIN/ GOAT CHEESE FILLING AND APPLE BASE

4 tablespoons butter (½ stick)

1 Granny Smith apple, unpeeled, cored, thinly sliced, and tossed with lemon juice

1 cup walnut meats

½ cup golden raisins

4 teaspoons canola oil

¼ cup goat cheese (1 to 2 ounces)

12 wonton skins

¼ cup confectioners' sugar

1 tablespoon minced fresh mint leaves

TIMELINE

Ingredient prep:
Cut fruit and herbs .... 5 minutes
Measure out ingredients .... 5 minutes
Subtotal ingredient prep .... 10 minutes

Mixing and kneading time for dough... 30 minutes
Resting time for dough .... 30 minutes
Subtotal dough time .... 60 minutes

Roll out pasta .... 15 minutes
Cut wonton squares .... 2 minutes

Cook apples (14 minutes)
   Overlaps with:
    Make walnut paste (2 minutes)
    Fill wontons (5 minutes)
    Seal wontons (5 minutes)
    Boil wontons (2 minutes) .... 14 minutes
Plate wontons, dust with confectioners'
   sugar, and top with mint .... 2 minutes

Total estimated time if
making your own dough ....1 hour and 23 minutes

Total estimated time if
using purchased pasta dough .... 43 minutes

Total estimated time if
using wonton skins .... 26 minutes

Method for the pasta dough

(If you're using premade pasta dough, skip the next paragraph and proceed to roll out the dough and cut out the wontons. If you've bought wonton skins, skip directly to the method for the filling and apples. But you'll still need an egg for the egg wash to seal the wontons.)

Mound the flour in the center of a clean, room temperature work surface, such as a large wooden cutting board. Create a crater in the center of the mound, crack 1 egg into it, and add the olive oil. Pour enough of the egg mixture into the crater to fill it. With a fork, gently begin to whisk the egg within the confines of the crater while integrating the flour from the sides. Fully mix the flour, egg, and olive oil until they become a dough. (Remember that making pasta is not an exact science. Depending on the flour, you may need more moisture to make the dough come together, in which case use a little milk. Conversely, if the dough is too wet, add a little more flour—but just enough to make it the right consistency. This is an acquired skill, so be patient with yourself.)

Start kneading the dough with your palms, allowing the warmth of your hands to impart elasticity to the dough. Knead for a count of about 400 strokes, or until you've created a cohesive mass. Wrap the dough in plastic and allow it to rest for about 30 minutes.

Work with a third of the pasta dough at a time, keeping the balance wrapped in plastic to prevent it from drying out. Use a pasta machine to gradually roll each section of the pasta down, successively reducing the setting on the machine until it is at a thickness of 1/16 inch.

Cut into approximately twelve 3-inch squares of pasta.

Method for the walnut/raisin/goat cheese filling and apples

Bring a shallow pan of water to a boil over medium heat for the wontons.

In a large skillet, melt 2 tablespoons of the butter over low heat. Arrange the apple slices in a single layer and gently cook on one side, about 5 to 7 minutes.

Through the feed opening of a running food processor add, one at a time, the walnuts, raisins, and canola oil to form a smooth paste.

Spoon an even amount of the walnut paste, about 1 teaspoon, into the center of 1 wonton square and top with ½ teaspoon goat cheese. Fold the filled square into a triangle, sealing the edges with egg wash and carefully pressing the wonton closed with your fingers or the tines of a fork.

Repeat to create the rest of the wontons. (If you're adventurous, you can experiment with various wonton folding techniques, which seem to roughly mimic the way napkins are folded in restaurants.)

Meanwhile, add the remaining 2 tablespoons of butter to the pan with the apples and flip them to cook on the other side until tender, about 5 to 7 minutes.

Gently simmer the stuffed wontons in batches for 2 or 3 minutes. When you see that the wonton dough is hydrated and slightly translucent, use a slotted wooden spoon to transfer them to a plate to drain.

Presentation

Place some of the apples on each serving dish and top with 2 wontons. Use a sifter or strainer to dust confectioners' sugar on top, then garnish with mint leaves.

Swedish Meatballs in a Bag

SERVES 6 PEOPLE (6 TO 8 MEATBALLS EACH)

The fine texture and fluffiness of Swedish meatballs has kept them a timeless classic. The miracle of the food processor allows you to keep the meat smooth and the composition light, all in one step—a result once achieved only by grinding the meat successively, pushing it through a sieve, and beating it.

INGREDIENTS

1 cup fresh breadcrumbs

1 tablespoon Wondra flour (a flour that will dissolve readily)

2 tablespoons butter, cubed

1 cup beef stock

¼ cup dry sherry

1 bay leaf

1½ pounds ground beef

1 onion, halved, then each half quartered

1 egg

½ teaspoon salt

¼ teaspoon freshly ground black pepper

¼ teaspoon ground nutmeg

¼ teaspoon allspice

¼ cup heavy cream

2 tablespoons grapeseed oil

2 tablespoons minced fresh flat-leaf parsley leaves

Method

Hydrate the breadcrumbs in the bowl of a food processor by pouring ½ to ¾ cup water over them.

Preheat the oven to 350°F. Have on hand a large oven bag, or make an oven pouch out of a 3-foot length of heavy-duty foil by bringing the two ends to the center and folding the sides to seal, leaving an opening at the center through which to place the sauce and meatballs. Shake the flour in the pouch to coat the inside, and place in a roasting pan. Add the butter, stock, sherry, and bay leaf to the pouch.

Add the ground beef, onion, egg, salt, pepper, nutmeg, and allspice to the hydrated breadcrumbs in the food processor. Process until the mixture is chopped, then—with the processor still running—add the cream gradually through the feed opening and mix until fluffy. Form the meat mixture into small meatballs. Heat the oil over medium-high heat in a large skillet. Sear the meatballs briefly on all sides in the skillet and remove them to paper toweling to drain. Place them in the sauce in the oven pouch. Seal the oven pouch, pierce the bag with about 6 ventilation holes, and bake for 35 minutes, or until the meatballs are firm and cooked through. Remove the bay leaf from the sauce before serving.

Presentation

Place the meatballs in a chafing dish and sprinkle with parsley. Provide small plates and either toothpicks or tiny forks for your guests.

4. WHAT IS LIFE WITHOUT SOUPS, SAUCES, AND STEWS?

Soups, sauces, and stews express the very essence of cooking in that they meld, concentrate, and bring together flavors in a very fundamental way. Whether they're comprised of one or two simple ingredients (Fresh Pea Soup, page 89) or many ingredients combined into a harmonious whole (Unbeatable Bouillabaisse, page 102); whether it's a time-tested classic that has made the journey from the farmhouse to the finest cooking schools (Veal Blanquette, page 104) or a mother sauce that provides a platform for both unlimited comfort and experimentation (Béchamel Sauce, page 116), these preparations are among the most deeply satisfying in our craft.

Their common element is liquid. The method is basically cooking down, breaking down or concentrating your ingredients to their most essential flavors, and through that process imparting and incorporating those flavors into a liquid. Each sip of the broth of a good soup or stew is invigorating because it's infused with all its best component ingredients working together. You need only the smallest teaspoonful of a well-executed sauce to know that it's great.

Every soup, sauce, and stew starts with a foundation on which you build your flavors. In stews especially, it's often a mirepoix (onions, carrots, and celery) or in the case of a good gumbo, the trinity (onions, celery, and green bell pepper). There's always, with very rare exceptions, a member of the allium family involved, most often onion, but also shallots, leeks, and garlic. If you're going to make up a soup out of your head or based on ingredients you happen to have handy, start there.

Dried herbs can be used at the beginning if there's going to be a long, slow cooking process, as is the case with soups and stews, because they will have the time to release their

Champagne Brie Fondue (page 29)

Pommes Frites with Chipotle Aioli (page 74)

Duck Confit with Three-Bean Cassoulet (page 32)

Asparagus "Benedict" with Hollandaise (page 60)

Veal Saltimbocca (page 44)

Artichoke Hearts Stuffed with Crab Salad (page 72)

Veal Milanese with Warm Fingerling Potato Salad (page 26)

Cauliflower Soup with Maine Lobster and Herb-Lemon Oil (page 88)

Veal Chops with Honey-Roasted Figs, Caramelized Onion–Potato Puree, and Port Wine Sauce (page 127)

Roasted Parsnip and Vanilla Chocolate Soup (page 96)

Roasted Cornish Game Hen with Sweet Potato Gnocchi (page 144)

Shrimp and Melon Gazpacho (page 98)

Mahimahi with Orange Beurre Blanc Sauce (page 114)

Ragout of Brussels Sprouts, Roasted Shallots, Navy Beans, and Tiny Carrots (page 223)

Chicken Marsala with Garlic-Scented Red Bliss Potato Salad (page 134)

Welsh Rarebit (page 76)

innate flavors. But finish your sauces with fresh herbs, especially pan sauces that are going to be served right after preparation to showcase their bright, vibrant freshness.

Soups should be invigorating. They are best if freshly made, and trust me, it's not hard to do. If you can chop and boil water, there's a good chance you can make a delicious pot of soup. And the bigger the pot, the more fresh soup you'll have on hand. Cook up a big pot on Sunday, buy a couple of loaves of sourdough bread and some butter, and you've got lunch for a week.

Stews should be sustaining. A big part of the theory behind most stews is to take a primary element, such as beef, chicken, or pork, and make it feed more people by extending it with other more plentiful and less expensive items, such as potatoes, carrots, or mushrooms, whilst enriching a broth with its essence. There's always a sense of family or community implied when you're hunched over a steaming plate of stew.

Sauces should be perfect. Don't be scared. It's true that sauces live in rarefied air right near the top of our profession, and there are men and women who have spent their entire careers perfecting their saucier techniques. But when it comes down to what's on the table, a sauce is a delicious liquid that's put on or around your food to make it taste even better. Your mother's turkey gravy is perfect. Chocolate sauce on an ice cream sundae is perfect. Your grandmother's marinara sauce is perfect, and will probably be one of your favorite tastes until you're tottering on the edge of the grave. As long as it's made with care, goes with the dish, and brings pleasure to the palate, the sauces you will make are perfect.

You can make a sauce out of the simplest, most easily available ingredients, like onion and celery, wine and butter, fresh herbs, vinegars, and fruit juices. It's an area where you can unleash your imagination, as long as you take just a few minutes to understand some very basic techniques. Sauces were a big part of my training, and I'm frankly somewhat uncomfortable serving you a piece of meat or fish without a sauce. I encourage you to make sauces. When you sear something in a pan, the lovely brown bits at the bottom of the pan, called the *fond*, are the basis for a sauce; they are pure flavor. If you've got an open bottle of wine, you can reduce it in a saucepan with shallots and herbs whilst you're working on the rest of your dinner and get it done in time for service, no problem. You can learn to make a mother sauce, such as a béchamel or basic white sauce, in next to no time, and you'll be making essentially the same sauce that Escoffier himself made.

The warmth in a bowl of soup, the welcome in a plate of stew, the care and craftsmanship that goes into a great sauce are among the great pleasures in life. Pursue them with gusto.

Cauliflower Soup with Maine Lobster and Herb-Lemon Oil

SERVES 6

It seems so simple, but this is a powerful flavor combination. The cauliflower soup delivers the essence of the real taste of cauliflower; it's a beautifully balanced dish.

INGREDIENTS FOR THE SOUP

1 large head of cauliflower

1 tablespoon kosher salt

4 tablespoons (½ stick) unsalted butter, at room temperature

1¼ to 1½ pounds cooked lobster, meat separated from shell and cut into large bite-size pieces

INGREDIENTS FOR THE HERB-LEMON OIL

2 tablespoons finely sliced fresh chives

1 tablespoon finely chopped lemon zest

½ teaspoon freshly ground black pepper

6 tablespoons extra virgin olive oil

Method for the soup

Remove and discard the outer leaves of the cauliflower, cut out the core, and separate into florets. Put the cauliflower florets in a large saucepan with the salt and 6 cups of water and bring to a boil over high heat. Maintain a lively simmer and cook for 8 to 12 minutes, or until very tender. Drain through a sieve placed over a bowl to reserve the cooking liquid. Let cool for a few minutes, reserve 6 cauliflower florets for garnish, and then put the rest of the cauliflower and 2½ cups of the reserved cooking liquid back into the pot. Add the butter and puree until smooth, using an immersion blender. (If you need to use a conventional blender, work in small batches with a clean folded kitchen towel held securely over the vented feed opening to avoid a major blender explosion of hot liquid.) Add more of the cooking liquid if the soup is too thick, then strain again through a fine-mesh sieve. The soup should be silky and just coat the back of a spoon. Taste and season with salt if needed. Set aside and keep warm, or let cool and refrigerate, covered, for up to 4 hours and reheat before serving.

Method for the herb-lemon oil

Whisk the chives, lemon zest, pepper, and olive oil together in a small bowl until combined. Set aside for up to 4 hours.

Presentation

Ladle the soup into serving bowls. Mound the lobster pieces in the center. Place a cauliflower floret into the center of the lobster and drizzle the herb-lemon oil over the surface of the soup. (The finished dish is shown in the photo insert.)

Fresh Pea Soup

SERVES 2

When you can make something this good and this fresh in less than a half hour's time, and it will keep for a few days and you can take it to work or have it on hand for a snack, why open a can or a packet of something with compromised flavor or lesser nutritive value?

INGREDIENTS

1 pat butter (½ tablespoon or 1½ teaspoons)

2 or 3 shallots, finely chopped

3 cups fresh or frozen peas (from about 3 pounds fresh garden peas in pods or 1 pound thawed frozen peas), rinsed before use

1 tablespoon minced fresh mint leaves

Salt and white pepper to taste

3 to 4 tablespoons heavy cream

Croutons or crumbled crisp bacon, for garnish

Method

Melt the butter in a heavy saucepan. Add the shallots and cook until translucent, about 3 minutes, stirring occasionally.

Add 2 cups water, the peas, and the mint leaves and season with salt and a little pepper. Cover and simmer for about 12 minutes for young or frozen peas and up to 18 minutes for large or older peas, stirring occasionally.

When the peas are tender, ladle them into a food processor or blender with a little of the cooking liquid and process until smooth.

Strain the soup back into the saucepan, stir in the cream, and heat through without boiling. Add salt and pepper to taste if needed.

Presentation

Serve hot, garnished with croutons or bacon.

Lime-Cured Shrimp and Roasted Corn Chowder

SERVES 8

Here's the deal: If you prefer the warm weather over the cold as I do, you can prepare a summery pick-me-up for when you get home in the dark, short days of winter. Put the shrimp in the marinade in the morning before you leave for work. When you get home, invest 15 minutes of prep time, and in 30 more minutes you can make this hearty and spirit-warming chowder.

INGREDIENTS

1 pound 31–40–size shrimp, shelled and deveined

1 teaspoon Old Bay seasoning

3 limes (2 to squeeze for marinating, plus 1 for the soup)

2 cups fresh corn kernels (from about 4 ears) or thawed frozen corn kernels (I like the white/yellow combo)

¼ cup plus 1 teaspoon canola oil

1 cup chopped raw bacon (6 to 8 strips)

1 red onion, diced

½ cup finely diced celery (about 1 or 2 large ribs)

1 green bell pepper, diced

1 red bell pepper, diced

6 garlic cloves, lightly crushed with the side of a knife blade and minced

1 cup dry white wine

½ cup all-purpose flour

6 cups chicken stock

½ pound red bliss potatoes, diced

2 cups (1 pint) heavy cream

3 tablespoons freshly squeezed lime juice

2 tablespoons chopped fresh flat-leaf parsley

¼ to ½ teaspoon cayenne pepper (according to your preference—I like about ½ teaspoon)

Salt and freshly ground black pepper to taste

½ cup scallions, white and tender green parts only, cut on the diagonal (about 6 to 8 scallions)

Oyster crackers as an accompaniment

Method

Early in the day, place the shrimp in a bowl and season with the Old Bay. Squeeze the juice from 2 limes into the bowl (toss in the rinds as well), stir to coat, cover, and refrigerate for 4 to 6 hours.

Preheat the oven to 375°F. On a baking sheet, coat the corn kernels with ¼ cup canola oil (reserving the 1 teaspoon oil) and roast 5 to 10 minutes, or until the corn is lightly browned.

Heat the remaining 1 teaspoon canola oil in a heavy-bottomed pan over low heat, add the bacon, and cook until crisp. Remove the bacon to paper toweling and drain off most of the bacon fat, leaving just a coating in the pan. Return the bacon to the pan, add the onion and celery, and cook over medium heat until the onion is softened but not browned, about 5 minutes. Add the green and red bell peppers, garlic, and corn and cook 5 minutes. Deglaze the pan with the white wine. Whisk in the flour, then gradually add the chicken stock. Add the potatoes and, maintaining medium to medium-high heat, cook, covered, until the potatoes are soft, about 20 to 30 minutes, stirring occasionally to prevent them from sticking. (Please note: Vegetables in soups are more palatable if you cook them until they are softer than you would usually serve them.) Reduce the heat to medium-low, gradually stir in the cream, and cook 3 to 5 minutes or so to allow the flavors to mingle.

Microwave the remaining lime for approximately 1 minute in a small bowl to release the essential oils and set aside until just cool enough to handle. Squeeze the lime juice into the small bowl. Remove the shrimp from the marinade and discard the marinating liquid.

Stir the shrimp, lime juice, parsley, and cayenne pepper into the chowder and cook just until the shrimp are pink and just cooked through, only about 3 to 5 minutes. Taste the chowder and adjust the seasoning with salt and pepper.

Presentation

Spoon into soup bowls and top with the scallions. Serve with oyster crackers.

Roasted Elephant Garlic Soup with Warm "Salad" of Fennel and Cumin-Scented Eggplant Drizzled with Fennel Emulsion

SERVES 4

Don't be afraid of garlic soup. The aggressive taste of raw garlic is tamed to sweet, nutty goodness by the roasting and simmering cooking processes.

INGREDIENTS FOR THE SOUP

2 heads of elephant garlic

2 tablespoons olive oil

1 stick (½ cup) butter

¾ cup rice flour

4 cups (1 quart) chicken stock

2 teaspoons Old Bay seasoning

Salt and freshly ground black pepper to taste

¼ cup heavy cream

INGREDIENTS FOR THE WARM "SALAD" AND FENNEL EMULSION

1 small eggplant, peeled and sliced into ¼-inch-thick pieces and drizzled with lemon juice

3 tablespoons olive oil (2 tablespoons for the eggplant, 1 tablespoon for the fennel)

1 teaspoon ground cumin

1 tablespoon butter

2 shallot cloves, diced small

1 fennel bulb, thinly sliced, core parts removed, layers separated

1 cup sherry (such as Sandeman Don Fino or Osborne Manzanilla)

¼ teaspoon crushed red pepper

¼ teaspoon cayenne pepper

½ cup extra virgin olive oil

Salt and freshly ground black pepper

Fennel fronds, for garnish

Method for the soup

Preheat the oven to 375°F. Cut the root ends off the garlic heads and wrap each head of garlic upside down in a sheet of aluminum foil, molding the foil into a base that supports the garlic

---

TIMELINE

Ingredient prep:
Roast elephant garlic (1 hour)
  Overlaps with:
  Peel and slice eggplant, fennel, and shallots
    (10 minutes)
  Measure ingredients (5 minutes)
  Concurrently roast eggplant during
    last 25 minutes .... 60 minutes
Subtotal for ingredient prep .... 60 minutes

Make roux, assemble and
  cook soup (35 minutes)
  Overlaps with:
  Sauté shallots and fennel, slice eggplant,
    and assemble warm salad (10 minutes)
  Reduce sherry in remaining fennel and
    shallots (5 minutes)
  Prepare emulsion in blender
    (5 minutes) ....35 minutes
Blend soup with immersion blender .... 5 minutes
Estimated active cooking time ....40 minutes

Assemble soup bowls for
  presentation ....5 minutes

Total estimated time .... 1 hour and 45 minutes

---

upright and leaving an opening at the top. Pour 2 tablespoons of the oil over the garlic cloves so that it flows under the skin and coats the cloves. Seal the foil packages (still with the cut-side up) and place them on a baking sheet. Roast until tender for about 40 minutes. (After about 35 minutes, add the eggplant to roast, below.)

In a deep pot over medium heat, melt the butter. Whisk in the rice flour to make a roux to thicken the soup. Stir in the chicken stock and bring to a simmer, then squeeze the roasted garlic cloves directly from their skins into the pot. Add the Old Bay seasoning and salt and pepper and simmer until the flavors are well integrated, about 30 minutes. (Meanwhile, begin the warm salad and fennel emulsion, below.)

Remove the pot of soup from the heat and add the cream. Blend to a smooth puree with an immersion blender (you'll be using the regular blender for the emulsion in the method below). Season with salt and pepper to taste and keep warm.

Method for the warm "salad" and fennel emulsion

After the garlic has been roasting for 30 minutes, brush the eggplant lightly with 2 tablespoons of the olive oil and sprinkle with the cumin. Lay the eggplant on the baking sheet with the garlic and roast until tender for about 25 minutes. Set aside until cool enough to handle.

While the soup is cooking, melt the butter in the remaining 1 tablespoon of olive oil over medium-high heat and sauté the shallots and fennel until tender, about 5 minutes. Remove half the shallots and fennel to a medium utility bowl and keep the rest in the pan. Cut the eggplant into thin slices about 1 inch long, add to the bowl with the shallots and fennel, and toss together. Cover and keep in a warm place.

To prepare the emulsion, add the sherry to the pan containing the remaining shallots and fennel and reduce by half over medium-high heat, about 5 minutes. (Meanwhile, blend the garlic soup, above.)

Puree the sherry/shallot/fennel reduction in a blender until smooth. Leaving the blender running, add the crushed red pepper, cayenne pepper, and extra virgin olive oil in a slow, thin stream. Season to taste with salt and pepper and set aside briefly.

Presentation

Ladle the garlic soup into serving bowls. Spoon some of the fennel/eggplant mixture into the center and drizzle the emulsion onto the surface of the soup surrounding and over the fennel/eggplant mixture. Garnish with fennel fronds.

Black Bean and Mocha Chocolate Soup

SERVES 8 TO 10

This recipe, and its fellow that follows, were inspired by a trip to the real-life equivalent of Willy Wonka's Chocolate Factory. These tastes have a foundational relationship in authentic Mexican cooking and work together really well here, I think.

INGREDIENTS

1 head of garlic (only 4 cloves will be needed after roasting)

1 tablespoon grapeseed oil (2 teaspoons to roast the garlic, 1 teaspoon to cook the bacon)

3 to 6 bacon strips, cut into 1-inch strips

1 teaspoon dried oregano

3 shallot cloves, diced

1 celery rib, diced

1 medium poblano pepper, diced (protect your hands and face while handling)

¼ cup chopped fresh cilantro leaves (2 tablespoons for the soup, 2 tablespoons for garnish)

1 tablespoon tomato paste

Salt and freshly ground black pepper

1 cup chicken stock

Four 16-ounce cans black beans (including the liquid)

2 prepared chipotle peppers in adobo sauce, chopped (protect your hands and face while handling)

One 14 ½- to 16-ounce can diced tomatoes, drained

4 teaspoons brown sugar

2 tablespoons plus 1 teaspoon high-quality sweet ground chocolate (such as Ghirardelli)

1 cup brewed coffee

1 lime, halved

SPECIAL EQUIPMENT

Vinyl gloves to wear while cutting the hot peppers

TIMELINE

Prepare garlic cloves for roasting .... 5 minutes
Roast garlic cloves (40 minutes)
  Overlaps with:
  Chop/dice bacon, onion, celery, pepper, and cilantro (10 minutes)
  Measure ingredients, open containers (5 minutes)
  Cook and drain bacon (5 minutes)
  Sauté vegetables and add ingredients (10 minutes)
  Cooking time (10 minutes)
Net time .... 40 minutes

Squeeze garlic cloves and blend .... 5 minutes

Total time .... 50 minutes

Method

Preheat the oven to 350°F. Cut the root end off the garlic head and wrap it upside down in a sheet of aluminum foil, molding the foil into a base that supports the garlic upright and leaving an opening at the top. Pour 2 teaspoons of the oil over the garlic so that it flows under the skin and coats the cloves. Seal the foil package (still with the cut-side up) and place it on a baking sheet. Roast for about 40 minutes, or until tender.

Heat the remaining teaspoon of grapeseed oil in a large pot over medium-high heat. Add the bacon and oregano and cook until the bacon is crispy. Remove the bacon to paper toweling to drain and pour all but 1 tablespoon of the fat from the pot. Add the onion, celery, poblano, and 2 tablespoons of the cilantro (reserving the rest of the cilantro for garnish) and sauté until the onion turns translucent, about 5 to 7 minutes. Stir in the tomato paste and season with salt and pepper. Return the bacon to the pot and add the chicken stock, black beans and their liquid, chipotles, tomatoes, brown sugar, chocolate, and coffee. Squeeze the juice of a lime half into the soup, holding it against your palm to catch the seeds. Reduce the heat to medium and cook the soup for about 10 minutes to let all the flavors integrate. Squeeze 4 of the roasted garlic cloves from their skins into the soup. Refrigerate the rest of the cloves for another use. Using an immersion blender, blend the soup right in the pot until smooth.

Presentation

Ladle the soup into serving bowls. Use the other lime half to squeeze a bit of lime juice over the surface of the soup. Garnish with the remaining 2 tablespoons chopped cilantro.

Roasted Parsnip and Vanilla Chocolate Soup

SERVES 6 TO 8

This is another great example of how setting your imagination free to wander over ingredients that you may have on hand can lead to delicious results. Parsnips have a great earthy quality, and in a time before the widespread use of refined sugars they were prized for their sweetness. The fusion of vanilla, a hint of chocolate, and the full-flavored parsnip is amazingly smooth, and the lemon, rather than introducing a sour note, serves to shine a light on this harmonious combination.

INGREDIENTS

2 pounds parsnips (about 4 or 5 large), peeled and cut into 1-inch chunks

¼ cup canola oil (2 tablespoons to brush on parsnips, 2 tablespoons to brush on bread for croutons)

8 tablespoons (1 stick) unsalted butter

1 large white onion, chopped

2 quarts chicken stock

1 whole vanilla bean, preferably Tahitian (sold 1 or 2 to a jar in the spice section of the store) or 1 tablespoon vanilla extract (preferably pure extract, not artificial flavoring)

Salt and pepper

1 epi French bread loaf (the kind with slits cut along the sides before baking to look like "petals," which are easily broken into serving-size chunks at the table) or 1 baguette loaf

¼ cup dark cocoa powder

1 cup Hershey's Premier White Chips (vanilla white chocolate chips)

1 cup heavy cream

2 lemons, halved crosswise (1 for the soup, 1 for garnish)

2 tablespoons minced fresh dill

SPECIAL EQUIPMENT

Immersion blender

Method

Preheat the oven to 400°F. Brush the parsnips lightly with 2 tablespoons of oil and place on a baking sheet lined with heavy-duty aluminum foil for easy cleanup. Roast until the parsnips begin to soften (as tested with a knife blade) and until the tips begin to turn golden brown, about 40 minutes. Set the parsnips aside to carry-over cook (see page 23 for definition) for a few minutes while you start the other ingredients in the stockpot. (Leave the oven on to toast the croutons.)

Melt the butter in a large stockpot over medium-low heat and gently sauté the onion until translucent. (This takes about 10 minutes, but the more important thing is that it *looks* translucent.) Add the chicken stock. Slice open the vanilla bean lengthwise, scrape the seeds into the pot, and drop in the vanilla pod itself. Increase the heat to medium, add the roasted parsnips, and bring to a boil. Season with salt and pepper, cover, and cook until the parsnips are completely tender, about 20 minutes.

Meanwhile, prepare the croutons. Break the epi loaf into serving-size chunks or cut the baguette into ¾-inch-thick slices. Brush the bread with the remaining 2 tablespoons of oil and place on a foil-lined baking sheet (again, for easy cleanup). Sift the dark cocoa over the bread and toast briefly in the oven just until crispy, about 2 or 3 minutes. Remove and set aside.

Stir the white chocolate chips into the soup and cook 5 minutes, to allow them to melt and to integrate the flavors.

Remove the soup from the heat, discard the vanilla pod, and stir in the heavy cream. Using an immersion blender, blend until smooth. (Remember—when using an immersion blender, the blade end has to be *immersed* or it will make a big mess.) Squeeze 2 lemon halves into the pot and stir to combine. (Note: If you hold the sliced end of the fresh lemon against your palm while you squeeze in the juice, the seeds are likely to stay in the rind.)

Presentation

Ladle the soup into bowls and garnish with fresh dill. Serve with lemon wedges and dark cocoa–dusted croutons. (The finished dish is shown in the photo insert.)

Shrimp and Melon Gazpacho

SERVES 18 TO 24 AS HORS D'OEUVRES
OR 6 AS APPETIZERS IN SOUP BOWLS

You'll have trouble finding a more refreshing and satisfying dish on a hot summer's day.

INGREDIENTS

1 pint vegetable broth

1 to 1½ pounds 21–30–size deveined shrimp, with shells on (use smaller shrimp if you like, but these are easy to clean and still economical)

2 cucumbers, peeled, seeded, and cut brunoise (first cut julienne, then crosswise into small dice of ⅛ inch)

2 ripe tomatoes, halved, seeds scooped out, and cut brunoise

1 teaspoon fresh jalapeño, stem and seeds removed and cut brunoise (Protect your hands and eyes and avoid breathing in the fumes of any hot peppers.)

1 small red onion, cut brunoise

2 tomatillos, cut brunoise

½ cantaloupe, seeds removed, fruit cut from the rind and cut brunoise

½ honeydew melon, seeds removed, fruit cut from the rind and cut brunoise

Juice of 1 lemon

2 tablespoons chopped chives

Salt and freshly ground black pepper

SPECIAL EQUIPMENT
Vinyl gloves for cutting the jalapeño

Method

Bring the vegetable broth to a boil in a saucepan over medium heat. You'll be using it as a court bouillon—a poaching liquid for the shrimp. Poach the shrimp in their shells until just pink, about 2 or 3 minutes, and use a slotted spoon to remove them to a platter to cool. (Shrimp cooked in its shell retains more flavor.) Strain and reserve the court bouillon and let cool to add to the gazpacho later.

While the shrimp are cooling, in a large mixing bowl, fold together the cucumbers, tomatoes, jalapeño, onion, tomatillos, cantaloupe, honeydew, and lemon juice. Add 1 tablespoon of chives (reserving the rest of the chives for garnish), and the cooled court bouillon and stir to combine.

Peel the shrimp and dice them small, reserving 6 shrimp, halved lengthwise, for the garnish if you'll be serving the gazpacho in appetizer-size portions. Stir the diced shrimp into the fruit/vegetable mixture and season to taste with salt and pepper. Chill well.

Presentation

This gazpacho can be served as an hors d'oeuvre in porcelain Chinese spoons, or be creative and use your own choice of small serving vessels, such as sake cups, rice bowls, or even 2-ounce ramekins with demitasse spoons. It can also be served as an appetizer in soup bowls. If you're serving the gazpacho in soup bowls, arrange 2 reserved shrimp halves "tails to center" on the surface of each serving and sprinkle with the remaining 1 tablespoon of chopped chives as a garnish. (The finished dish is shown in the photo insert.)

Saffron Mussel Soup

SERVES 4 TO 6

This soup combines wonderful flavors, but the color provided by the saffron makes it really special.

INGREDIENTS

3 tablespoons unsalted butter

8 shallot cloves, finely chopped

1 bouquet garni (a small bunch of parsley, 8 fresh thyme sprigs, and a bay leaf in a cheesecloth bag)

1 teaspoon black peppercorns

1½ cups dry white wine

2 pounds (about 48) mussels, scrubbed and debearded, soaked for 30 minutes in ice water

Pinch of saffron strands

2 medium leeks, tough top leaves removed, soaked several times in salt water to remove the grit, trimmed, and finely chopped

1 fennel bulb, finely chopped

1 carrot, peeled and finely chopped

4 cups fish or chicken stock

Salt and freshly ground black pepper

2 tablespoons cornstarch, whisked in a small bowl of 3 tablespoons cold water to create a slurry

½ cup heavy cream

1 medium tomato, stem end cut out, blanched for 1 minute to peel off skins, seeds removed, and finely chopped

2 tablespoons Pernod (optional)

1 red bell pepper, stemmed, seeded, and diced small

About 3 dozen tiny mint leaves

Method

In a large heavy sauté pan, melt 1½ tablespoons of the butter over medium-high heat. Add half the shallots and cook for 1 to 2 minutes, until softened but not darkened. Add the bouquet garni, peppercorns, and white wine and bring to a boil. Add the mussels, cover tightly, and cook over high heat for 3 to 5 minutes, shaking the pan occasionally, until the mussels have opened. (Discard any mussels that do not open.)

With a slotted spoon, transfer the mussels to a bowl. Strain the cooking liquid through a cheesecloth-lined strainer into a bowl and reserve, keeping both the bowl and strainer handy to catch additional juices (see below).

Spoon 2 tablespoons of the warmed cooking liquid into a small bowl. Add the saffron threads and let sit for 10 minutes to let the saffron "bloom." (This will bring them to the height of their flavor.)

When the mussel shells are cool enough to handle, pull them open and remove the mussel meat to a utility dish (the heat from the soup will warm the mussels at the time of service). Pour any extra juices from the shells and from the bottom of the bowl through the cheesecloth-lined strainer into the bowl of reserved cooking liquid. Squeeze the cheesecloth into the bowl to capture every bit of liquid and discard the cheesecloth and solids.

Rinse and dry the sauté pan and melt the remaining 1½ tablespoons butter over medium heat. Add the remaining shallots and cook for 1 to 2 minutes, until softened. Add the reserved cooking liquid, leeks, fennel, carrot, and bowl of bloomed saffron liquid and bring to a boil, cooking until the vegetables are tender and the liquid is slightly reduced, about 5 minutes. Add the fish or chicken stock and bring to a boil. Season with salt and pepper to taste and cook for 5 minutes.

Stir the cornstarch slurry into the soup. Simmer for 2 to 3 minutes, until the soup is slightly thickened, and add the cream and chopped tomato. Puree in batches in a blender, or use an immersion blender if the pot is deep enough (be sure to immerse the blade to avoid a mess). Stir in the Pernod, if using, and cook for 1 or 2 minutes, until hot.

Presentation

Ladle the soup into bowls and spoon about 8 mussels into the center of each bowl. Top the mussels with a teaspoon of the diced red bell pepper and about 6 small mint leaves. Serve at once.

Unbeatable Bouillabaisse

SERVES 6 TO 8

This seafood stew is an example of something you can labor over for hours or make relatively quickly. It originated as a meal for Marseilles fishermen, who used the catch of the day, and should feature the freshest fish available to you. I like this quicker version; it seems to me that the fishermen led a busy life and probably had to eat and get back to work.

INGREDIENTS FOR THE BOUILLABAISSE

1 tablespoon grapeseed oil

1 large red onion, finely diced

1 cup diced fennel (including the bulb, fresh green part of the stalk, and fronds)

2 garlic cloves, lightly crushed with the side of a knife blade, peeled, and minced

1 teaspoon dried basil

2 bay leaves

4 cups seafood stock (such as Kitchen Basics brand)

¾ pound 21–25–size shrimp, peeled and deveined, with shells and tails reserved to cook in the stock

1 tablespoon tomato paste

Salt and freshly ground black pepper to taste

½ cup dry vermouth

3 or 4 dozen (about 2 pounds) mussels, debearded, well scrubbed, and soaked for 30 minutes in ice water

3 or 4 dozen littleneck clams, well scrubbed, and soaked for 30 minutes in ice water

2 pinches of saffron threads

1 teaspoon grated lemon zest

3 medium vine-ripened tomatoes, seeded and diced

2 tablespoons fresh thyme leaves (from about 4 large sprigs)

2 tablespoons Pernod (Sambuca or any anise-flavored liqueur can be substituted)

1½ pounds snapper, or other non-oily white fish such as cod or haddock

TIMELINE

Ingredient prep:
Scrub mussels and clams .... 30 minutes
Soak mussels and clams
   in ice water ....28 minutes
   Overlaps with:
   Chop onion, fennel, and garlic (10 minutes)
   Peel shells from shrimp and reserve
      shells for stock (10 minutes)
   Cut and remove skin from fish (5 minutes)
   Grate lemon zest (1 minute)
   Strip thyme leaves (2 minutes)
Subtotal for prep time .... 58 minutes

Sauté onion, fennel, garlic, and herbs
Overlaps with:
   Boiling shrimp shells in stock .... 5 minutes
   Deglaze pan with vermouth .... 2 minutes
   Add part of broth and cook
      mussels and clams .... 7 minutes
Spoon ¼ cup broth in small bowl
  and allow saffron to "bloom" in it (10 minutes)
   Overlaps with:
   Remove mussels and clams to platter
      and remove half from shells to return
      to broth
   Add rest of stock, lemon zest,
      thyme, and bowl of "bloomed"
      saffron to broth and cook .... 10 minutes
Add shrimp and cook .... 5 minutes
Subtotal for active cooking time .... 39 minutes

Total time .... 1 hour and 37 minutes

Method

Heat the oil in a 6-quart sauté pan or large pot over medium-high heat and sauté the onion, fennel, garlic, basil, and bay leaves until the onion turns translucent, about 5 minutes.

Meanwhile, bring 3 cups of the seafood stock and the shrimp shells and tails (*not* the shrimp themselves!) to a boil in a large saucepan over medium-high heat. Cook the shells and tails until they turn pink, about 8 minutes. Turn off the heat and set aside.

Return to the pan with the onion mixture and stir in the tomato paste and salt and pepper to taste. Deglaze the pan with the vermouth. (Meanwhile, get a large utility platter and a large bowl ready to use for the cooked mussels and clams.) When most of the alcohol has evaporated, add the remaining 1 cup of seafood stock and the mussels and clams. Tightly cover and cook for about 5 to 7 minutes, until they open. (Clams seem to take slightly longer to open than mussels, probably because of the difference in the thickness of the shells.) Using a slotted spoon, remove the mussels and clams to the utility platter. For each serving, set aside 3 mussels and 3 clams in the shell; place these in the utility bowl and cover to keep warm.

Spoon about ¼ cup of the broth into a small bowl and add the saffron. Let it stand for about 10 minutes to allow it to "bloom."

Meanwhile, scoop out the meat from the rest of the mussels and clams, place the meat in the broth, and discard the empty shells. Using a large strainer, strain the saucepan of shrimp shells and liquid into the saucepan with the bouillabaisse broth. Discard the shrimp shells.

Add the lemon zest, tomatoes, thyme, the saffron and liquid, and the Pernod to the bouillabaisse and cook 10 minutes to let the flavors integrate. Add the shrimp and snapper and cook 5 minutes more, or until just opaque. Discard the bay leaves.

Presentation

Place soup bowls on dinner plates and ladle in the bouillabaisse. Surround the bowl with 3 mussels in the shell and 3 clams in the shell, arranged alternately.

Veal Blanquette

SERVES 6

This is a beautiful stew to look at, all creamy and white. It's even better to eat.

INGREDIENTS

4 pounds boneless veal breast, cut into large dice

20 pearl onions

2 quarts beef stock

1 sachet d'epices (1 tablespoon parsley, 1 tablespoon peppercorns, 1 tablespoon thyme, and 1 bay leaf in a cheesecloth bag)

6 tablespoons (¾ stick) unsalted butter

½ cup all-purpose flour

6 ounces (about 2 cups) white button mushrooms, cleaned and sliced

2 tablespoons freshly squeezed lemon juice

½ teaspoon salt, plus more to taste if desired

¼ teaspoon freshly ground black pepper, plus more to taste if desired

2 egg yolks

1 cup heavy cream

1 tablespoon chopped fresh flat-leaf parsley

Method

In a large bowl, cover the veal with cold water to "blanch" it. Drain and rinse the veal.

Bring 2 cups of water to boil in a saucepan over medium-high heat and add the pearl onions briefly to scald them. Drain, slip the skins from the pearl onions, and set them aside.

In a large saucepan or Dutch oven, combine the veal with the stock and simmer, covered, over medium-low heat until the veal is tender, about 1½ hours. After the veal has been simmering about 30 minutes, add the sachet d'epices and keep the pot uncovered to allow the stock to reduce to intensify the flavor.

When the veal is tender, melt 4 tablespoons of the butter in a small saucepan and gradually whisk in the flour to make a white roux. (Do not allow the roux to brown.) Remove and discard the sachet. Whisk the roux into the veal and simmer until thickened, about 8 to 10 minutes.

Meanwhile, in a medium sauté pan, heat the remaining 2 tablespoons of butter and gently cook the pearl onions and mushrooms until they are tender and the mushrooms give up their juices, about 8 minutes. Stir in the lemon juice, salt, and pepper and set aside.

The heat under the blanquette (stew) must be such that the liquid is just simmering. In a separate small pot, whisk together the egg yolks and cream and temper it (known as a liaison) by gradually adding some warm stew and heat it gently over low heat. (Do not boil it or allow it to cook.) Stir the liaison into the blanquette, add the pearl onions and mushrooms, and adjust the salt and pepper if needed.

Presentation

Serve in earthenware bowls and sprinkle with chopped parsley.

Beef Carbonnade

SERVES 6

This is a warm, slow-cooking Flemish masterpiece that combines sweet and sour in a succulent beef stew. Take the time to caramelize the onions slowly. They provide a signature flavor in this dish, and the longer you take to cook them down (without burning them, of course), the better it will be. I use Guinness in this recipe, but you could use any good porter or Belgian dark ale. The very real danger with this dish is that more beer ends up in the cook than in the pot, but it's a risk worth taking.

INGREDIENTS

¼ cup grapeseed oil

3 red onions, sliced

½ cup all-purpose flour, or as needed for dredging

Salt and freshly ground black pepper to taste

3 pounds beef such as London broil or chuck roast, cut into 1½-inch cubes

One 12-ounce bottle beer, such as Guinness

1 quart beef stock

1 tablespoon honey

½ cup apple cider vinegar

1 tablespoon minced fresh thyme leaves (stripped from about 3 or 4 large sprigs)

3 turnips, peeled and cut into 1-inch pieces

½ pound brussels sprouts

3 apples, peeled and cut into 1-inch pieces

2 tablespoons minced fresh flat-leaf parsley leaves

1 loaf French bread or crusty Italian bread

Method

Heat 1 tablespoon of oil in a skillet over medium-low heat and add the onions. Let them cook down over low heat, stirring occasionally, until golden brown, about 40 minutes. Remove to a bowl.

Add the flour to a plate, season with salt and pepper, and dredge the beef cubes, allowing any excess flour to fall away.

Heat 1 more tablespoon of the oil in a Dutch oven over medium high-heat. In batches, brown the beef cubes on all sides, about 5 to 7 minutes, transferring the browned beef to a utility platter as you go and gradually using the remaining oil as needed. Deglaze the pan with the beer and return the beef cubes and caramelized onions to the pan. Stir in 2 cups of the beef stock, the honey, vinegar, and thyme. Cover, reduce the heat to medium-low, and simmer for 1 hour. Add the turnips and 1 more cup of beef stock (reserving the balance), cover, and cook for about 30 minutes, or until the meat is tender and easily pierced with a fork. Add the sprouts, apples, and remaining 1 cup stock to the pot. Cover and cook about 15 minutes, or until the beef is fork-tender and the turnips, sprouts, and apples are cooked through. Remove the cover and let the liquids reduce and thicken for about 15 minutes, until they reach the desired consistency.

Presentation

Spoon into bowls or crocks and sprinkle parsley on top. Serve with crusty bread and beer.

Salmon Fillets over Whipped Potatoes with White Wine Sauce

SERVES 6

This ultra-easy recipe illustrates the use of the *fond* (the delicious fish essence that remains in the pan after searing fish) as the basis for the construction of a simple sauce that will elevate your meal from no-frills to fancy with practically no additional effort.

INGREDIENTS

1½ pounds potatoes (about 2 to 4 medium to large potatoes), peeled, cut into 1-inch pieces, and placed in a 2-quart saucepan with enough water to cover

1 to 2 tablespoons grapeseed oil, as needed to sauté the fish and shallot

Four 6-ounce salmon fillets

Salt and freshly ground black pepper

1 shallot clove, minced

½ cup dry white wine

2 teaspoons minced fresh thyme leaves (stripped from about 2 or 3 branches)

2 cups low-sodium chicken stock

6 tablespoons (¾ stick) unsalted butter, cut into cubes (4 tablespoons for the potatoes, 2 for the sauce)

¾ to 1 cup milk, as needed to make the potatoes smooth

1 tablespoon minced fresh dill

Method

Boil the potatoes over high heat until tender, about 10 to 15 minutes.

Preheat the oven to 375°F.

In a large sauté pan, heat the grapeseed oil over medium-high heat. Season the salmon fillets with salt and pepper. When the oil begins to shimmer, add the salmon to the pan, flesh side down first, and sear *undisturbed* for 2 or 3 minutes to allow the seasoning to integrate into the surface of the fish and to allow the fish to caramelize, which will prevent tearing. Flip over the fillets and sear the other side in the same way. Transfer the salmon to a baking pan and finish in the oven until they are done, about 6 to 8 minutes. The time will depend on the thickness of the fish, but generally the fish is done when the surface springs back upon gentle pressing. *Do not overcook the fish.*

To the *fond* (the material that's still in the sauté pan), add the shallot (and 1 teaspoon grapeseed oil, if it's too dry). Sauté until the shallot turns translucent, stirring frequently to avoid burning, about 2 minutes. Deglaze the pan with the white wine and cook for a minute or so to let most of the alcohol evaporate. Add the thyme leaves and chicken stock and increase the heat to allow the sauce to reduce quickly by two thirds.

Remove the fish from the oven and let it rest for a few minutes.

Drain the potatoes, add 4 tablespoons of the butter, and mash by hand.

Strain the sauce into a bowl and nest the bowl of sauce in a larger bowl of warm water to keep it warm. Just before service whisk in the remaining 2 tablespoons cubed butter a little at a time to make it smooth and silky. Adjust the seasoning with salt and pepper.

Add the milk to the potatoes, season to taste with salt and pepper, and whip with an electric beater until smooth.

Presentation

Spoon some potatoes into the center of a serving dish, top with a salmon fillet, and spoon some sauce on top. Sprinkle with dill.

Pork Chops with Asian Diable Sauce, Parsnip Puree, and Potato Galettes

SERVES 4

This recipe features a sauce-making method that, once learned, you can repeat with different ingredients over and over again. Pork chops are easy to make and usually popular with family members. If you're tired of doing them the same old way, here's a change of pace that will help you use up the bottle of sake you have in the house from the last time you went for sushi.

INGREDIENTS FOR THE SAUCE

Step 1

1 celery rib, finely chopped

1 carrot, peeled and finely chopped

1 medium onion, finely chopped

1 tablespoon chopped fresh flat-leaf parsley leaves

1 bay leaf

1 cup beef stock

1 cup sake

Step 2

1 tablespoon unsalted butter

2 shallot cloves, minced

1 cup sake

⅛ teaspoon freshly ground black pepper

1/16 teaspoon cayenne pepper

Salt to taste if needed

INGREDIENTS FOR THE POTATO GALETTES

1 pound potatoes (3 or 4 medium to large potatoes)

Salt and freshly ground black pepper to taste

1 tablespoon grapeseed oil

INGREDIENTS FOR THE PARSNIP PUREE

2 parsnips, peeled and cut into 1-inch chunks

2 tablespoons unsalted butter, cut into chunks

½ cup milk

Salt and freshly ground black pepper to taste

INGREDIENTS FOR THE PORK CHOPS

1 tablespoon grapeseed oil

Four 6-ounce boneless pork chops, about ¾ inch thick

¼ teaspoon cayenne pepper (or as desired)

Salt and freshly ground black pepper to taste

TIMELINE

Ingredient prep:

Chop celery, carrot, onion, and
    shallots .... 5 minutes
Peel and cut parsnips.................................... 2 minutes
Subtotal for ingredient prep .... 7 minutes

Cook ingredients for
    step 1 of sauce (20 minutes)
    Overlaps with:
    Shred potatoes (2 minutes)
    Form potato patties (3 minutes)
    Fry potato galettes (8 minutes)
    Boil parsnips (10 minutes).....................23 minutes
Strain vegetables from step 1 of sauce
    and sauté shallot in step 2 of sauce..... 5 minutes
Begin reduction (10 minutes)
    Overlaps with:
    Sauté pork chops and
        put in oven (8 minutes)
    Puree parsnips (2 minutes).................. 10 minutes
Remove pork chops and let rest (2 minutes)
Overlaps with:
    Strain sauce (2 minutes)......................... 2 minutes
Slice meat.. 5 minutes
Assembly... 5 minutes
Active cooking time .... 50 minutes

Total estimated time, start to finish ... 57 minutes

Method for the sauce

In a medium saucepan, combine the ingredients for step 1, bring to a boil, and allow the liquid to reduce by two thirds, about 20 minutes. (Meanwhile, start the potato galettes using the method below.)

Strain the liquid into a bowl. Using a wooden spoon, press on the vegetables in the strainer to squeeze out most of the liquid. Discard the vegetable pulp.

For Step 2, in the same saucepan, melt the butter over medium heat and sauté the shallots until they begin to turn translucent, about 2 or 3 minutes. Add the sake to deglaze the pan. Stir in the strained liquid from step 1, the black pepper, and the cayenne pepper. Allow the liquid to reduce by half, about 10 to 15 minutes. Meanwhile, begin the pork chops using the method below.

After you've removed the pork chops from the oven, strain the sauce and adjust the seasonings with salt, only if needed. (Slice the pork now.)

Method for the potato galettes

Preheat the oven to 375°F.

Peel the potatoes and shred them, using the shredding blade of a food processor or a handheld grater. Place the potatoes in a bowl, season with salt and pepper, and toss to coat with your hands. Heat the grapeseed oil over medium-high heat in a large sauté pan with an oven-safe handle (in case they need to be finished in the oven). Form the potatoes into 4 hamburger-size patties, squeezing the excess moisture out, and place in the hot oil, leaving undisturbed for the first 2 or 3 minutes to allow the potatoes to begin to caramelize, making them less likely to fall apart when you flip them. When you see the edges beginning to turn golden brown, flip the galettes and cook the other side in the same way, leaving them undisturbed until they brown. Transfer the galettes to a baking pan and bake until crispy on the outside and tender on the inside, about 20 minutes. (Meanwhile, start on the parsnips.)

Keep the oven heated and reserve the sauté pan for use with the pork chops.

Method for the parsnips

Add the parsnips to a saucepan and cover with water. Boil until tender over high heat, 10 to 15 minutes. (Meanwhile, strain the step 1 sauce ingredients.)

Drain the parsnips, add the butter, and mash by hand. Add the milk and whip until smooth with an electric beater. Season with salt and pepper to taste. Cover and keep warm. (Remove the pork chops from the pan.)

Method for the pork chops

Using the sauté pan you used for the potato galettes, heat the grapeseed oil over medium-high heat. Season the pork chops with cayenne, salt, and pepper. Sear the pork chops, leaving undisturbed for the first 2 to 3 minutes to allow the seasonings to integrate into the surface of the meat and to allow the meat to caramelize a bit, which will prevent sticking. When you see the edges beginning to turn golden, flip the pork chops and sear on the other side in the same way. Cover the pan and let them carry over cook for 4 or 5 minutes. Pork chops are easily overcooked and in a few minutes they can inadvertently become as tough as leather. However, if you want to ensure that the meat is cooked through, it would be prudent to slice a section and take a peek. If the inside is still pink you can transfer the pork chops to the oven to finish cooking, about 4 or 5 minutes (the pork chops and galettes may share the oven). (Drain the parsnips now.)

Remove the pork chops from the pan (protecting your hand with a mitt if they've been in the oven) and let rest for a few minutes. (Meanwhile, strain the sauce.)

Cut the pork chops on the bias into ⅛- to ¼-inch-thick slices.

Presentation

Spoon some parsnip puree into the center of each serving dish. Top with a potato galette, and place the pork on top of the potato, fanning out the slices. Spoon the diable sauce on top.

Basic Beurre Blanc Sauce

MAKES 1 CUP

This is a great basic sauce for fish; just by adding lemongrass or lime juice or even paprika you can create an incredibly well-flavored sauce that will enhance your dish.

INGREDIENTS

3 shallot cloves, minced

1 cup dry white wine

¼ cup white wine or Champagne vinegar

½ cup unsalted butter, cut into ½-inch cubes

Salt and white pepper to taste

Method

In a small saucepan, simmer the shallots, wine, and vinegar until reduced by three fourths. Add the butter and incorporate by stirring continuously until it's fully emulsified. Season to taste with salt and white pepper.

Mahimahi with Orange Beurre Blanc Sauce

SERVES 8

Note that this application of beurre blanc sauce uses orange juice to stand in as the acid to replace the vinegar in the basic beurre blanc sauce recipe, and the fat in the cream means that less butter is required in this version. Replacements like this are common in cooking, especially in sauces and dressings.

INGREDIENTS FOR THE MARINADE AND FISH

2 limes

Eight 6-ounce mahimahi fillets

½ teaspoon salt

⅛ teaspoon freshly ground black pepper

½ cup tequila

2 tablespoons canola oil

2 tablespoons unsalted butter

INGREDIENTS FOR THE ORANGE BEURRE BLANC SAUCE

1 cup orange juice (not from concentrate)

½ cup dry white wine

1 cup heavy cream

1 tablespoon minced fresh parsley, plus 8 small sprigs for garnish

½ stick (4 tablespoons) unsalted butter, cut into cubes

Method for the marinade

Microwave the limes in a small bowl for a minute or so (depending on your microwave) to release the essential oils. Set them aside until just cool enough to handle. Season the fish with salt and pepper and place in a nonreactive container for marinating. Squeeze the lime juice over the fish and add the rinds to the bowl. Pour the tequila on top, cover, and marinate in refrigerator for at least 2 hours.

Method for the sauce

About 20 to 25 minutes before mealtime, prepare the orange beurre blanc sauce by combining the orange juice and wine in a saucepan and simmering over medium heat until the volume is reduced by half, about 10 to 15 minutes. (After the sauce has cooked about 10 minutes, start on the fish, below.)

Stir in the cream, bring to a gentle simmer, and allow to reduce and thicken over low heat. Stir in the parsley and set aside briefly in a warm place. Whisk the butter into the sauce just before serving.

Method for the fish

Heat the oil over medium heat in a large sauté pan and add the butter. Sear the fillets flesh-side first, leaving undisturbed for at least 2 to 3 minutes to allow the surface to begin to caramelize and prevent tearing of the fish. Flip over to sear, skin-side down, and cook for 5 to 8 minutes, or until the flesh springs back when gently prodded. Remove to a tray and let rest.

Presentation

Spoon the sauce over and around the fish and top with parsley sprigs. (The finished dish is shown in the photo insert.)

Béchamel Sauce

MAKES 1 CUP

Béchamel, commonly called white sauce, is one of the most versatile and irreplaceable sauces in your arsenal. Béchamel pairs beautifully with mushrooms, tomatoes, and pasta, especially fresh pasta. One of the mother sauces, a béchamel sauce is thickened with a roux, which is made by gradually adding flour to melted butter. A mother sauce—such as those set down by Escoffier, the father of classical French cooking—is a basic sauce that can also serve as a jumping-off point for other sauces, although chefs don't always agree about how many mother sauces there are. You can adjust the mother sauce by adding ingredients to the recipe or by creating a variation on a theme, such as switching the acid-lending ingredient. Sauces are so important in fine restaurants that many employ an expert chef in sauces, known as a saucier, to prepare a daily battery of sauces once or twice daily to accompany the offerings on the menu. You've probably used a sauce as a mother sauce whether you actively intended to or not. For example, a sauce tomate, as one of the sauces that purists sometimes define as a classical mother sauce and others deny, worked as a mother sauce for you if you served it over pasta and later used it for chicken Parmigiana and yet again for a pizza topping.

Clarified butter is whole butter (what we usually buy in the store) with the water and milk solids removed. You can buy clarified butter, but making it yourself is remarkably easy. Start with 25 percent more whole butter than you'll need or what the recipe calls for. (The water and milk solids you'll be removing account for about a quarter of the volume.) Simply melt the butter in a small saucepan, skim off and discard the foam that rises to the top, and carefully pour the clear center layer—the clarified butter—into a small bowl without disturbing the water or solids at the bottom of the pot.

INGREDIENTS

1 small onion, peeled

1 small bay leaf

3 whole cloves

1 cup hot milk

1 small piece of whole nutmeg or ¼ teaspoon ground nutmeg

4 ½ teaspoons unsalted clarified butter

4 ½ teaspoons all-purpose flour

Salt and white pepper to taste

Method

Make a cut into the onion about 1 inch deep, and slide the bay leaf into this slit. Stick the cloves into the onion and place it, along with the milk and nutmeg, into a heavy-gauge, noncorrosive saucepan over medium heat.

Begin a roux in a separate sauté pan. Cook the butter and flour for about 5 minutes, whisking continuously, without browning, until it emits a nutty aroma. Remove from the heat and set aside to cool for a minute or two.

Discard the onion. Pour a small amount of the hot milk into the roux, stirring until the milk is thoroughly blended in. Combine the roux mixture with the remaining milk and simmer for 15 minutes, stirring frequently. Season to taste with salt and white pepper, strain, and set aside until ready to use.

Note: Béchamel has a tendency to form a skin on top, in part because of its exposure to air. To prevent this, impale a piece of butter on a fork and dab it on top of the sauce. This will leave a thin coating of butter that will prevent a skin from forming.

Velouté Sauce

MAKES 1 CUP

One way of describing velouté is to say that it is a white sauce—like béchamel, thickened with a white roux—but chicken stock is used instead of milk. The recipe for Braised Drumsticks with Potato Gnocchi and White Onion Sauce (page 119) uses a gluten-free variation of velouté sauce.

INGREDIENTS

1 cup chicken stock

1 sachet d'epices (4 thyme sprigs, 1 bay leaf, 4 peppercorns, and 4 parsley sprigs in a cheesecloth bag)

1 small onion, minced

4 ½ teaspoons unsalted clarified butter

4 ½ teaspoons all-purpose flour

Salt and white pepper to taste

Method

Place the chicken stock, sachet d'epices, and onion into a heavy-gauge, noncorrosive saucepan over medium heat.

Begin a roux in a separate sauté pan. Cook the butter and flour for about 5 minutes, whisking continuously, without browning, until it emits a nutty aroma. Remove from the heat and set aside to cool for a minute or two.

When the stock mixture is hot, pour a small amount of it into the cooled-down roux, stirring until the stock is thoroughly blended in. Return the roux mixture to the remaining stock and simmer for 15 minutes, stirring frequently. Season to taste with salt and white pepper, strain, and set aside until ready to use.

Braised Drumsticks with Potato Gnocchi and White Onion Sauce

SERVES 6 (ABOUT 6 GNOCCHI PER PERSON)

Everybody seems to love this recipe because it is so reminiscent of chicken and dumplings, which, even if we didn't have it as kids, still has a Main Street, USA, feeling to it. It's remarkably economical to make, because you can get a 4- to 5-pound value pack of chicken drumsticks for very little investment.

I have used a gluten-free recipe for the gnocchi. "Why," you may ask. Well, frankly, why not? Since potatoes are naturally gluten-free, we're already halfway to producing a gluten-free recipe, and because wheat flour is not mandatory for making gnocchi, it seems nice to be inclusive of people who can't eat gluten. Rice flour helps to provide a lovely light texture as well. If you prefer not to use the gluten-free recipe or if you don't feel like buying rice flour or potato starch, feel free to replace those two ingredients and the cornstarch with all-purpose flour.

The gnocchi take just about an hour to make from start to finish, as does the braised chicken. We've set up the timeline to overlap the two processes. However, if you decide to make the gnocchi in advance, consider making a bigger batch and freezing it for future use. Be sure to freeze the gnocchi in a single layer and spaced far enough apart so that they don't become one giant blob in the freezing process!

INGREDIENTS FOR THE POTATO GNOCCHI

1 pound potatoes (about 2 or 3 medium potatoes), peeled and cut into 1-inch chunks, boiled until tender, drained well, and cooled to room temperature

½ cup white rice flour, plus some to flour the board

3 tablespoons potato starch

2 tablespoons cornstarch

1½ teaspoons butter

1 tablespoon grated Parmigiano-Reggiano cheese

1 egg, beaten

½ teaspoon salt

INGREDIENTS FOR THE BRAISED DRUMSTICKS AND WHITE ONION SAUCE

1 tablespoon grapeseed oil

Twelve 4- to 5-ounce chicken drumsticks (2 per person, as found in a 4- to 5-pound value pack)

1 teaspoon garlic powder

Salt and freshly ground black pepper to taste

1 large white onion, sliced

1 cup dry white wine

1 bay leaf

Smidgen of ground cloves (1/32 teaspoon)

Smidgen of ground nutmeg (1/32 teaspoon)

1 cup chicken stock

4 tablespoons butter, cubed

¼ cup white rice flour

1 tablespoon minced fresh flat-leaf parsley leaves

Method for the gnocchi

Mash the potatoes in a large bowl and add the rice flour, potato starch, cornstarch, butter, cheese, egg, and salt. Mix well and knead lightly. Divide the dough into 4 portions in a bowl, shaping each into a ball. Cover with a damp towel and let rest for about 20 minutes. (Meanwhile, start seasoning and searing the chicken, below.)

Bring a large, shallow pan of water to a boil. On a floured surface (such as a large wooden cutting board), roll each portion of dough into a long cylinder, about ¾ inch diameter. Cut each cylinder into nine 1-inch pieces and set aside to rest until the chicken is well along in the cooking process.

Add the gnocchi to the boiling water. They will puff up as they cook. As they set up (after about 2 to 4 minutes), remove them to a utility platter with a slotted or wooden spoon, cover, and keep warm.

Method for the braised drumsticks and white onion sauce

In a large sauté pan with a cover, heat the grapeseed oil over medium-high heat. Rinse the drumsticks and season with the garlic powder and salt and pepper. Brown the chicken on all sides to allow the seasonings to integrate into the skin of the drumsticks.

Place the onion slices on top of the drumsticks and deglaze the pan with the wine, pouring some over the onions. Add the bay leaf, cloves, and nutmeg to the liquid in the pan and allow the wine to reduce by two thirds, about 10 minutes. Add the chicken stock, reduce the heat to low, cover the pan, and braise the chicken until fork-tender, about 40 minutes. (When the chicken has been braising about 30 to 35 minutes, you can start to boil the gnocchi.)

TIMELINE

Ingredient prep:
Peel potatoes.. 2 minutes
Boil potatoes (10 minutes)
   Overlaps with:
   Slice onion (2 minutes)
   Measure out ingredients
     (5 minutes) .... 10 minutes
   Cooling time for potatoes .... 10 minutes
Subtotal .... **22 minutes**

Mash potatoes with dry and wet ingredients,
   knead, and let rest (22 minutes)
   Overlaps with:
   Season chicken (1 minute)
   Sear chicken (8 minutes)
   Add onions and deglaze with wine (1 minute)
   Allow wine to evaporate
     (10 minutes)..22 minutes

Add chicken stock to chicken and braise
   (40 minutes)
   Overlaps with:
   Start pot of boiling water (2 minutes)
   Make gnocchi (15 minutes)
   Boil gnocchi (2 minutes) .... 40 minutes
Blend sauce....................................... 5 minutes

Assembly ....**5 minutes**

Total estimated time .... 1 hour and 34 minutes

Remove the chicken to a utility platter, leaving the onion in the pan. Cover the chicken to keep warm.

Begin a white roux in a separate sauté pan. Melt the butter over medium heat and gradually add the flour, whisking continuously. Cook without browning until the roux emits a nutty aroma, about 3 to 5 minutes, and remove from the heat.

Strain the braising liquid and return it to the pot (if using an immersion blender) or transfer it to a conventional blender. Add the roux to the strained braising liquid and blend the sauce until smooth. Add salt and pepper only if needed.

Presentation

Spoon some sauce onto a serving plate. Place 6 gnocchi on the plate for each serving, with 2 drumsticks on the side. Garnish with the parsley.

Mornay Sauce

MAKES 1½ CUPS

A Mornay sauce is simply a béchamel sauce with cheese added. Making a sauce as a vehicle for the cheese will ensure that it is smoothly and evenly delivered to the elements of the dish. The kind of cheese will vary depending on what you are making, and I encourage you to change things up once in a while, to keep your palate on its toes, so to speak.

INGREDIENTS

⅓ cup grated Gruyère or other variety of Swiss cheese

3 tablespoons grated Parmesan cheese

4 tablespoons cold cubed butter

1 cup just-made or warmed béchamel (cream sauce) (from the recipe on page 116)

Method

Gradually blend the cheeses and butter into the warm cream sauce, allowing each addition to melt before adding the next.

Broccoli with Mornay Sauce

SERVES 4

There's a school of thought that says kids are more likely to eat vegetables (or almost anything except breakfast cereal) if it's covered in a nice cheesy sauce. My kind of school.

INGREDIENTS

1 pound fresh broccoli, broken into florets, with stems peeled and cut into chunks

1 small onion, minced

1 bay leaf

Smidgen ($\frac{1}{32}$ teaspoon) of ground cloves

2 cups milk (or as needed to achieve a smooth consistency in the sauce)

Smidgen ($\frac{1}{32}$ teaspoon) of ground nutmeg

3 tablespoons unsalted butter

3 tablespoons all-purpose flour

Salt and white pepper to taste

½ cup grated Cheddar cheese (or as needed for your desired cheesiness)

3 tablespoons Parmesan cheese

Method

Steam the broccoli until tender, rinse with cool water to stop the cooking, cover, and set aside briefly.

Place the onion, bay leaf, cloves, milk, and nutmeg into a heavy-gauge, noncorrosive saucepan over medium heat. Do not let the milk scald.

Begin a roux in a separate sauté pan. Cook the butter and flour for about 5 minutes, whisking continuously, without browning, until it emits a nutty aroma. Remove from the heat and set aside to cool for a minute or two.

Pour a small amount of the hot milk into the roux, stirring until the milk is thoroughly blended in. Combine the roux mixture with the remaining milk and simmer for 15 minutes, stirring frequently. The sauce should be thick enough to coat the back of a spoon. Season to taste with salt and white pepper, strain, and set aside until ready to use.

Blend the cheeses into the cream sauce until smooth and melted and fold the broccoli into the sauce.

5. THE IMPORTANCE OF BEING PROTEIN: MEATS AND POULTRY

Meat speaks to both our most primal instincts and our most sublime. There is something atavistic about the very notion of a hunk of meat on a spit turning over an open fire, its juices spattering into the flames, its intoxicating aromas permeating the air. Yet it also represents the backbone of human civilization. For thousands of years, man scrounged out a living from gathering shrubs, grubs, and greens. But once we acquired the tools and knowledge to bag and cook fresh meat, things really started to take off. Our brains grew bigger (well, most of ours anyway), our muscles grew strong enough to build towns and cities, great nations, armies and navies, cooking schools, restaurants, and book publishing companies, and well, here we are. We've come full circle.

In chef's circles, we often lump the whole category of meat, fish, and poultry together as protein. (I've devoted a separate chapter to fish.) The first question you'll often hear me ask on any given mission on *Dinner: Impossible* is, "What proteins do we have?" They generally provide the cornerstone for my overall design of an entrée. Part of it is based on my training, part on personal preference. Protein is satisfying and nourishing, and a little goes a long way. Its preparation can be as basic as barbecue or as refined as a truffled foie gras terrine. It easily fills the starring role in an entrée artfully and against any number of supporting players. You can cut, pound, or roll it; slice it thick or thin; keep the bone in or take it out; pair it with starches, greens, vegetables, or fruits—it always shines through.

I have a good working familiarity with the construction of pigs, cows, chickens, and their various brethren. In my time of apprenticeship, we seldom worked with anything less than the whole animal. Our bacon didn't inevitably come vacuum-packed in plastic wrap; we often butchered it from the whole hog. I learned invaluable lessons in breaking down venison, game birds, rabbits, and sides of beef, all of which have combined to give me a great respect for fresh product and a great foundation in roasting, frying, braising, and sautéing from the ground up. Unless you're a butcher or plan to take up butchering as a hobby, you don't necessarily have to memorize the entire canon of cuts of meat or familiarize yourself with every cookable part of every animal. Do not be overwhelmed—let experience and the marketplace be your guide. I could give you a tour of the types and qualities of muscle fiber in beef cattle, discuss the impact of exercise or a more sedentary lifestyle on the bovine in question, or discourse on the value of good marbling (the quantity and type of fat found throughout a cut of meat) or on grass feeding versus grain feeding, but a good guide is this: The more you pay, the less you have to cook.

A whole tenderloin of beef, depending on its weight and quality, could cost you more than a hundred dollars. It's a very fine-quality meat that does not need much cooking. Indeed, it's the main ingredient in beef tartare and carpaccio; in both cases, it is not cooked at all. It consists of soft muscle tissue, with a low gristle and fat content and, as a result, a very light flavor and a wonderful texture. Do not marinate it and do not overcook it. It will be tender, it will be buttery, and it will practically cut with a fork with just a little persuasion from you.

On the other hand, if you buy a big, well-marbled–looking slab of meat whose nickname is "Chuck," go ahead and cook the hell of it. Chuck can take it. Chuck is cheap. You'll likely want to braise it or stew it, the longer the better. Your great-grandmother wasn't out spending an arm and a leg buying her world-renowned brisket. Likely she knew the value of a dollar as well as the value of patience and long, slow cooking. In meat cookery, the name of the game is breaking down the tougher muscle fibers and allowing the inherent fat in a cut of meat free rein to express itself. In the case of ground beef (which is, in fact, pretty cheap), the breaking down has been done mechanically through a meat grinder. In a good burger, meatball, or meat loaf, the fat is still left in to do its good work.

What else is on the menu—pork, venison, veal, chicken, duck, goose, turkey, pheasant? All have their charms. Generally, the leaner it is, the quicker the cooking time and the lighter and less intense the flavor. A nice lean pork chop, the other white meat? Just sear it on both sides and give it a finish in the oven. Pork belly? Go out, buy a juicy novel, and rent *Gone With the Wind*. This is going to take a while, but the resulting flavor will be well worth the wait.

Poultry is very different from beef or pork. The fat content is lower and mainly contained just under the skin. Chickens may have been designed by the Creator for cooking. Their meat is varied and flavorful, with delectable dark and white meat contained in the same easy-to-pop-in-the-oven package. If you're cooking the whole bird, it has just the right amount of fat available for self-basting. Fried or roasted, it offers its succulent flavors up generously, with little effort. In a sauté pan, in a wok, or as part of a plated entrée, you can pair it with almost any other savory item and come up with a winning dish.

Practice makes perfect when it comes to understanding poultry. Duck will render more fat than pheasant, and you have to figure that into your game plan. You can cook a staggeringly tasty duck confit by cooking a duck in its own fat. That rendered fat will also be available to you to put extra flavor into your beans, potatoes, or other accompaniments. When working with pheasant, you might have to bard the bird—wrap it in caul fat or bacon—because it's so naturally lean. But the wild life it leads will offer you a different and exciting gamey flavor you won't find in more domesticated birds.

In any case, whether dealing with beef, lamb, pork, or chicken, if you have pan drippings, keep going! Making sauces and gravies from the golden brown remains and irreplaceable juices left over in the bottom of the pan or pot is one of the greatest joys in working with meat. The easiest method is to make a gravy by deglazing the pan with water, sprinkling in some Wondra (or rice flour, for a light, gluten-free version), stirring until integrated, and bringing up the heat to thicken. Season and serve.

Veal Chops with Honey-Roasted Figs, Caramelized Onion-Potato Puree, and Port Wine Sauce

SERVES 6

The sweet notes of the honey-roasted figs in this recipe take it over the top. Try to get them in season if you can, though dried will work, too, in a pinch.

INGREDIENTS FOR THE CARAMELIZED ONION-POTATO PUREE

8 tablespoons (1 stick) unsalted butter (1 tablespoon for the onion, the rest for the potatoes)

1 tablespoon grapeseed oil

1 large white onion, thinly sliced

6 large white potatoes (about 1 pound), peeled, cut into 1-inch pieces, and placed in a pot of enough water to cover

Salt and white pepper to taste

1 cup heavy cream

INGREDIENTS FOR THE WINE SAUCE

3 tablespoons grapeseed oil

2 garlic cloves, chopped

2 shallots or 1 white onion, finely diced

Trimmings from the veal (see below)

One-half 750 ml bottle tawny port wine

1 cup strong beef stock or demi-glace

1 tablespoon chopped fresh thyme

1 tablespoon chopped fresh rosemary

½ cup (1 stick) unsalted butter, cubed

INGREDIENTS FOR THE HONEY-ROASTED FIGS

6 fresh figs, tough stem ends cut off and halved lengthwise

½ cup honey (your choice)

INGREDIENTS FOR THE VEAL

⅛ cup grapeseed oil

Six 8-ounce ½-inch-thick veal chops, sirloin and tenderloin cut from the bone (save the trimmings for the port wine sauce and freeze the bones to make stock)

2 tablespoons minced fresh flat-leaf parsley leaves

Method for the onion-potato puree

Melt 1 tablespoon of butter in the oil in a large saucepan over medium heat. (Reserve the rest of the butter for the potatoes.) Add the onion and allow to caramelize. Keep an eye on it to make sure it doesn't burn.

Boil the potatoes until tender. (Meanwhile, begin the sauce, below.)

While the veal is finishing in the oven (as described below), drain the potatoes well and transfer them to the pot with the caramelized onions. Add the remaining 7 tablespoons butter and mash by hand. Season with salt and white pepper to taste. Whip the potato-onion mixture with a beater, gradually adding the cream. Cover and set aside until the veal is finished.

Method for the sauce

In a large saucepan, add the oil and sauté the garlic and shallots over gentle heat until translucent. (If you have any trimmings from the veal, add them at this time.) Deglaze the pan with the port, and add the beef stock or demi-glace, thyme, and rosemary. Allow this mixture to reduce at a rolling boil, uncovered, until the liquid evaporates by about two thirds, to intensify the flavor. (While the sauce is reducing, boil the potatoes and begin the figs, as directed below.) Remove the sauce from the heat and set aside to rest in a warm place. Just before plating, strain the sauce through a chinois (a conical strainer) or some cheesecloth in order to remove all the vegetables and herbs, and gradually whisk in the butter, allowing each addition to melt before adding the next to make the texture velvety smooth.

TIMELINE

Slice onion (1 minute) and immediately begin
  caramelizing in butter over very low heat
  (35 minutes)
Overlaps with:
Cut potatoes, shallots, herbs, and figs
  (8 minutes)
Sauté garlic and shallots for sauce (4 minutes)
Deglaze pan with wine, add stock and herbs,
  and let reduce (20 minutes)
Overlaps with:
Roast figs (20 minutes)
Overlaps with:
Boil potatoes until tender (10 minutes)
Overlaps with:
Glaze figs with honey during last 5 minutes
Season veal chops and heat pan (2 minutes)
Remove figs from oven,
remove sauce from heat and cover,
and drain potatoes (1 minute) .... 35 minutes

Add caramelized onion to potatoes
  and cover to keep warm .... 1 minute
Sear veal chops .... 8 minutes

Finish veal chops in oven (8 minutes)
  Overlaps with:
  Strain sauce and finish with butter (4 minutes)
  Whip potatoes and
    onions (4 minutes) .... 8 minutes

Assembly .... **5 minutes**

Total estimated time, start to finish ... **57 minutes**

Method for the honey-roasted figs

Preheat the oven to 375°F. While the sauce is reducing and the potatoes are boiling, place the figs cut-side up on a foil-lined roasting pan and roast for about 20 minutes. During the last 5 minutes of roasting, spoon the honey over the figs. Set the figs aside in a warm place until needed. (Keep the oven on.)

Method for the veal chop

In a heavy-bottomed oven-safe sauté pan, add the oil (it should just cover the bottom of the pan) and heat on medium-high. Season the veal on both sides with salt and pepper.

When the sauté pan is hot, cook the veal until golden brown, about 4 minutes per side. Leave the veal undisturbed for the first 2 minutes on each side to allow the seasoning to integrate into the surface of the meat. Using the same pan in which you seared them, place the veal in the oven and cook another 6 to 8 minutes, depending on the thickness. Remember—the times given in any recipe are relative because all ovens are different and only *you* know your oven.

Presentation

Spoon about ½ cup of the onion-potato puree into the center of each individual serving dish. Top with a veal chop and spoon some sauce on top. Garnish each plate with 1 teaspoon parsley and 2 fig halves. (The finished dish is shown in the photo insert.)

Veal Scaloppine and Lemon Confit over Warm Salade Niçoise with Potato Puree

SERVES 6

I'm sure you've encountered a number of words that have different meanings in the food and cooking world. For example, to keep it from burning, you reduce the heat under your saucepan when you add cream. You also reduce the sauce to intensify the flavor by allowing the liquids to evaporate. *Blanch* is another great one. You blanch the green beans by briefly cooking them in water. You also purchase cauliflower that is blanched white by farmers and the plant's own leaves by shielding it from the sun. *Confit* is another one of those words. As a term describing a way of preserving (and cooking) meat—usually poultry—in its own fat, it actually translates to "jam" in French, which is what is referred to in this recipe.

INGREDIENTS FOR THE LEMON CONFIT

½ cup sugar

⅛ teaspoon salt

1 tablespoon cornstarch, made into a slurry with ¼ cup water

1 shallot, peeled and thinly sliced

Zest and juice of 1 lemon

1 tablespoon honey

INGREDIENTS FOR THE SALAD DRESSING

3 tablespoons Champagne vinegar

2 teaspoons Dijon mustard

¼ teaspoon salt

Dash of pepper

6 tablespoons extra virgin olive oil

INGREDIENTS FOR THE SALADE NIÇOISE

1 pound haricots verts, trimmed, steamed until just tender but still bright green, and set aside to cool

½ cup niçoise olives, seeded

1 pint grape tomatoes, halved and seeded

¼ cup minced fresh parsley leaves (about 1 ounce)

2 tablespoons capers, drained

Salt and freshly ground black pepper to taste

6 hard-boiled eggs, peeled while still warm, set aside to cool, and cut lengthwise into 4 wedges

INGREDIENTS FOR THE POTATO PUREE

1½ pounds red bliss potatoes (about 6 large potatoes), peeled and cut into 1-inch chunks

6 tablespoons (¾ stick) unsalted butter, cut into pieces

Kosher salt to taste

White pepper to taste

½ cup heavy cream

1 cup all-purpose flour (use rice flour for a gluten-free meal)

Kosher salt and freshly ground black pepper to taste

1½ pounds veal scaloppine slices (12 to 18 slices), pounded thin between layers of plastic wrap

½ cup clarified butter (start with 10 tablespoons or 1¼ sticks of unsalted butter if you're clarifying your own; see the instructions on page 116)

Method for the lemon confit

In a medium saucepan, whisk together the sugar, salt, and cornstarch slurry until well mixed. Blend in the shallot and lemon juice and zest. Bring to a simmer for 1 minute over low heat, stir in the honey, and set aside to cool to room temperature.

Method for the dressing and salade niçoise

Prepare the salad dressing by adding the vinegar, mustard, salt, and pepper one at a time through the feed opening of a running blender. Then, leaving the blender running, add the olive oil in a slow, steady stream.

Into a mixing bowl, slice the green beans into ¾- to 1-inch lengths. Just for fun, stuff an olive into each of the halved grape tomatoes. Cut any extra olives into ¼-inch pieces and add the tomatoes and olives to the bowl. Add the parsley and capers, toss gently, and set aside until needed.

Method for the potato puree

Boil the potatoes over medium heat in a saucepan of water until tender and drain. Add the butter, salt, and white pepper. Mash the potatoes and butter by hand and use a beater to whip in the heavy cream (do not use a blender or food processor). Keep covered in a warm place.

Method for the veal

Season the flour with salt and pepper and dredge the veal slices in flour. Heat the clarified butter in a large sauté pan over medium-high heat and sauté the veal until golden, about 2 minutes per side. Remove to drain on paper toweling.

Presentation

Just before serving, season the salad with salt and pepper and toss with enough dressing to coat.

Spoon some of the potato puree into the middle of each individual serving dish. Top with 2 or 3 pieces of veal and arrange some salad around the plate, garnished with 4 wedges of the hard-boiled egg for each serving. Spoon a small amount of the confit on top of the veal.

Grilled Skirt Steak with Roast Corn Haricot Salad

SERVES 8

Skirt steak is the meat that "skirts" the rib and loin. It contains enough fat to stay pleasantly tender as long as it is sliced against the grain and not overcooked.

INGREDIENTS FOR THE SALAD

2 pounds trimmed haricots
   (very thin fresh green beans)

2 ears fresh corn

½ teaspoon grapeseed oil

Kosher salt and freshly ground black pepper

INGREDIENTS FOR THE STEAK

1 teaspoon grapeseed oil

Kosher salt and freshly ground black pepper to taste

3 pounds skirt steak

INGREDIENTS FOR THE SALAD DRESSING

5 tablespoons raspberry vinegar

1 teaspoon chopped fresh cilantro (about 2 sprigs)

2 teaspoons chopped fresh basil (2 or 3 sprigs)

2 teaspoons Dijon mustard

3 tablespoons extra virgin olive oil

Kosher salt and freshly ground black pepper
   to taste

Method for the salad

Preheat the grill to medium-high heat, about 275°F.

Bring 2 quarts salted water to a boil. Have a bowl of ice water handy. Blanch the haricots for 2 or 3 minutes, until tender yet crisp. Drain through a strainer, plunge into cold water to stop the cooking, and drain again.

Rub the corn with the oil and salt and pepper to taste. Place on the hot grill. Turn the corn until evenly golden brown, about 5 to 7 minutes. Wrap the corn in foil and move it to a rack on the grill away from direct heat while you make the dressing, about 5 to 10 minutes.

Remove the corn from the grill and set aside to cool while you grill the steak; then cut the corn kernels from the cob with a sharp knife.

Combine the green beans and corn and toss with enough dressing to coat, reserving some for the steak.

Method for the salad dressing

Through the feed opening of a running blender, add, one at a time, the raspberry vinegar, cilantro, basil, and Dijon mustard. With the blender still running, add the olive oil in a slow stream. Season with salt and pepper to taste.

Method for the skirt steak

Rub the grapeseed oil and salt and pepper to taste on the steak. Sear each side on the grill for 1 to 2 minutes, then finish until the preferred doneness is reached, either on the grill or in a preheated 450°F oven. Let rest 3 to 7 minutes.

Presentation

Place the bean and corn salad on a platter. Slice the steak on the bias and place on top of the salad.

Drizzle the remaining dressing onto the steak.

Chicken Marsala with Garlic-Scented Red Bliss Potato Salad

SERVES 6

Round, moist red bliss potatoes make a special accompaniment to mouthwatering marsala chicken. I like the salad best at room temperature.

INGREDIENTS FOR THE POTATO SALAD

1 whole head of garlic

1 tablespoon olive oil

2 large celery ribs, very thinly sliced

1 to 1½ pounds small red bliss potatoes, scrubbed, cut into ¼-inch disks, boiled until just tender, drained, and rinsed with cold water to stop the cooking process (Be careful not to overcook them or they will break apart in the salad.)

4 to 6 scallions, white and tender green parts, sliced

3 tablespoons chopped fresh chives (about 9 chives)

Salt and freshly ground black pepper to taste

INGREDIENTS FOR THE CHICKEN, MUSHROOMS, AND MARSALA SAUCE

½ cup all-purpose flour approximately

Salt and freshly ground black pepper to taste

Six 6-ounce chicken breasts, pounded with a meat mallet to tenderize

½ cup clarified butter (see the directions on page 116)

2 cups white mushrooms, cleaned, trimmed, and (if large) sliced

1 cup marsala wine

1 cup chicken stock

2 tablespoons unsalted butter, cut into chunks

INGREDIENTS FOR THE DRESSING

Juice of 1 lemon

Leaves from 2 or 3 thyme sprigs

1 teaspoon Dijon mustard

1 garlic clove, lightly crushed with the side of a knife blade and quartered

1 tablespoon honey

1 teaspoon salt

¼ teaspoon freshly ground black pepper

¾ cup olive oil

Method for the potato salad

Preheat the oven to 400°F. Slice the root end off the entire head of garlic and turn it upside down, wrapping it in aluminum foil so the cut end stands upright in the oven. Pour the oil on the garlic so it slips between the skin and the cloves and enclose it with the foil. Roast until tender and sweet, about 35 to 50 minutes. Squeeze the garlic cloves into a large bowl and mash them. Gently fold the celery, potatoes, scallions, and 2 tablespoons of the chives into the bowl with the garlic. Add enough dressing to coat. Do not feel compelled to use all the dressing. Taste and adjust the salt and pepper as needed.

Method for the salad dressing

Through the feed opening of a running blender, add, one at a time, the lemon juice, thyme, mustard, garlic, honey, salt, and pepper. Leaving the blender running, slowly add the olive oil in a thin stream.

Method for the chicken and marsala sauce

Season the flour with salt and pepper and dredge the chicken breasts in it, pressing the flour into the chicken and allowing any excess to fall away. Heat ¼ cup of the clarified butter over medium-high heat in a large skillet and add the chicken breasts and mushrooms. Leave the chicken undisturbed for 3 to 4 minutes to let the flour and seasonings integrate into the surface. Add the remaining clarified butter to the pan and push the mushrooms out of the way. Flip the chicken breasts over and cook the other side, leaving the chicken undisturbed for another 3 to 4 minutes. Add the marsala wine to the pan, pouring over the chicken and deglazing the pan, and let the wine reduce by half. Add the chicken stock and simmer until the chicken is cooked through, about 25 to 30 minutes, and the liquids are reduced by half again.

Remove the chicken and mushrooms to a utility platter and keep warm. Remove the pan from the heat and gradually whisk the chunks of butter into the sauce. Season to taste with salt and pepper.

Presentation

Arrange the chicken and potato salad on a serving plate. Spoon the marsala sauce and mushrooms over the chicken. Garnish the potato salad with the remaining tablespoon of chives. Serve any extra dressing or sauce on the side. (The finished dish is shown in the photo insert.)

TIMELINE

Roast garlic (35 to 50 minutes)
  Overlaps with:
Ingredient prep:
Cut potatoes (3 minutes)
Boil potatoes (10 minutes)
Chop celery, scallions, chives,
  thyme, and garlic (5 minutes)
Tenderize chicken (2 minutes)
**Subtotal estimated time for
  ingredient prep**.................................. **20 minutes**

Season chicken and heat oil........................ 2 minutes
Sear chicken and add mushrooms........... 4 minutes
Add and reduce marsala (10 minutes)
  and add and reduce
  chicken stock (10 minutes)
  Overlaps with:
Cook chicken (about 20 minutes)
  Overlaps with:
Combine elements of salad dressing
  in blender (5 minutes)
  Overlaps with:
Remove roasted garlic from oven
  and let cool
Fold together garlic potatoes
  and other elements of salad
  together and coat with
  dressing (3 minutes) .... 20 minutes
Subtotal cooking time .... **26 minutes**

Finish sauce and assembly......................**5 minutes**

Total estimated time, start to finish ... **51 minutes**

Citrus-Braised Chicken Breast with Sweet Roasted Garlic and Savory Artichoke Tart

SERVES 4

Roasted garlic cloves and lemon juice are made into a paste that becomes a top crust for the chicken. Yum! The vegetable tart paired here with the chicken can be also be prepared as an accompaniment for other dishes and can even be served as an appetizer or vegetarian luncheon entrée.

Assembling your own vol-au-vent pastry crusts with premade puff pastry is extremely easy. You can obtain prepared puff pastry, such as that made by Pepperidge Farm, in the frozen foods section of the grocery. Be sure it is thoroughly defrosted before unfolding and using it (so it doesn't crack), and follow the instructions below.

INGREDIENTS FOR THE CHICKEN

1 whole head of garlic

3 tablespoons grapeseed oil

Juice and zest of 2 lemons

⅛ cup fresh rosemary leaves

2 tablespoons lemon pepper

Four 6- to 8-ounce boneless chicken breasts, skin on if possible

Salt and freshly ground black pepper to taste

4 tablespoons unsalted butter (2 tablespoons cut into slices for the chicken, 2 tablespoons cut into cubes for the sauce)

1 cup dry white wine

1 cup orange juice

1 tablespoon cornstarch

2 tablespoons finely chopped parsley leaves

INGREDIENTS FOR THE VOL-AU-VENT PASTRY

2 sheets of puff pastry dough (often sold in 17- or 18-ounce packages containing two 9- or 10-inch-square sheets of puff pastry), thoroughly defrosted

1 to 2 eggs, beaten, for egg wash

INGREDIENTS FOR THE TART FILLING

2 parsnips, peeled and cut into 1-inch segments

One 8-ounce can artichoke hearts, drained (4 artichoke hearts)

1 tablespoon grapeseed oil

1 shallot, minced

2 garlic cloves, minced

1 teaspoon dried basil, or 1 tablespoon minced fresh

1 teaspoon dried marjoram, or 1 tablespoon minced fresh

2 tablespoons pine nuts

Salt and freshly ground black pepper to taste

1 tablespoon unsalted butter

2 tablespoons heavy cream

1 tablespoon minced fresh basil leaves, for garnish

Method for the chicken

First, roast the garlic cloves. Preheat the oven to 425°F. Slice the root end of the entire head of garlic and turn it upside down, wrapping it in aluminum foil and molding the foil so that it allows the cut end to stand upright in the oven. Pour 1 tablespoon of the grapeseed oil on the garlic so that it oozes between the skin and the garlic cloves and enclose the head of garlic with foil. Roast for about 30 to 35 minutes, checking occasionally to make sure the garlic isn't burning. (Meanwhile, prep the herbs and vegetables for the rest of the recipe and begin making vol-au-vent pastry, below.)

TIMELINE

Prep and roast time for garlic (35 minutes)
Overlaps with:
Chop herbs and slice vegetables (10 minutes)
Measure ingredients (5 minutes)
Assemble vol-au-vent pastry
(20 minutes) ....35 minutes

Active cooking time:
Make paste for chicken crust ....7 minutes
Sear chicken ....7 minutes
Deglaze pan ....3 minutes
Subtotal active cooking time ....17 minutes

Cook time for chicken (35 minutes)
Overlaps with:
Bake pastry shells (20 minutes)
Overlaps with:
Boil parsnips (10 minutes)
Sauté herbs and artichokes (5 minutes)
Mash parsnips (5 minutes)
Rest time for pastry shells (5 minutes)
Overlaps with:
Combine elements for
filling (5 minutes)................................35 minutes
Chicken resting time (5 minutes)
Overlaps with:
Make sauce (5 minutes)...........................5 minutes
Subtotal cooking time ....40 minutes

Assemble tarts and presentation ....5 minutes

Total estimated time ....1 hour and 37 minutes

Total estimated time
if using premade
pastry shells ....1 hour and 17 minutes

Remove the garlic from the oven and set aside to cool. Lower the heat to 400°F for the tarts.

(Please note that the oven temperature must be allowed to cool to 400°F before using it for the rest of the elements in this recipe.)

To make the paste that will be the chicken crust, add one at a time through the feed opening of a running blender the lemon juice and zest, rosemary, and lemon pepper. Transfer to a bowl and squeeze in the roasted garlic cloves. Mash into a paste.

Season the chicken breasts with salt and pepper. Press the lemon/garlic paste onto the surface of the curved side of the chicken breasts to form what will be a crust. In a large sauté pan, heat the remaining 2 tablespoons grapeseed oil over medium heat and add the 2 tablespoons of sliced butter (reserving the other 2 tablespoons for the sauce). When the oil/butter mixture is hot, add the chicken, crust-side down, and sear it, leaving it undisturbed for about 4 minutes to allow the seasonings to integrate into the surface of the chicken and prevent them from "crusting off." Flip the chicken breasts over and sauté the other side for about 3 minutes. Add the wine to the pan and cook for a few minutes to let the flavors integrate. Reduce the heat to low and add the orange juice. Cover and let simmer until fork-tender, about 25 to 35 minutes, spooning the sauce over the chicken intermittently. (While the chicken is cooking, begin the tart filling, below.)

Remove the chicken to a utility platter and keep warm, reserving the pan juices for the sauce. Set a strainer over a bowl and strain the pan juices from the chicken into a small bowl, scraping all bits from the pan into the strainer. Return the juices to the pan and reduce the liquid over medium-high heat. Make a slurry in a small bowl by adding 1 tablespoon water to the cornstarch. Whisk the slurry into the sauce in the pan. Remove from the heat and whisk in the remaining 2 tablespoons of cubed butter. (Assemble the tarts at the last minute, below.)

Method for the vol-au-vent pastry

While the garlic is in the oven, make the vol-au-vent (tart pastry). Roll out the puff pastry dough and use a 4-inch circle cutter (biscuit cutter, bowl, or plate) to cut out eight 4-inch-diameter dough rounds. Place 4 dough rounds on a lightly greased baking sheet. Using a 3-inch circle or biscuit cutter, cut a concentric circle in the middle of each remaining 4-inch dough round to create a ½-inch-wide circle of dough (reserve the 3-inch circles of dough in the centers for another use). Place one of the ½-inch-wide circles of dough on top of each of the rounds on the baking sheet, matching up the edges. Brush the egg wash over the surface of each of the paired circles and rounds. Use a fork to prick through the dough around the perimeter (that is, *through* each dough circle and into the round beneath it). (Meanwhile, make the paste and start the chicken, above.)

Once you get the chicken cooking, bake the tart shells. The oven should now be at 400°F. Place the sheet of pastry shells into the oven and bake until golden brown, about 20 minutes. (Meanwhile, start the tart filling, below.)

The center of each pastry shell will rise. Remove the pastry shells from the oven and allow to cool slightly.

Method for the tart filling

While the chicken is cooking and the tart shells are baking, begin the filling for the tart. Start with the parsnip puree, which will serve as a binding base for the artichoke tart. Place the parsnips in a deep saucepan with enough water to cover and simmer over medium heat until tender.

Prepare the artichoke hearts to be sautéed by gently pulling the artichoke leaves away from the disk-shaped "hearts," dividing them into two groups on a plate.

While the parsnips are still simmering, in a medium sauté pan, heat the grapeseed oil over medium-high heat. Add the shallot, garlic, basil, marjoram, pine nuts, and artichoke leaves (reserving the artichoke hearts) and sauté until the shallot turns translucent, about 3 minutes.

Reduce the heat to medium-low, add the artichoke hearts to the pan, and gently fold them in so they will pick up the flavors from the pan. Season everything with freshly ground black pepper. Cook for about 5 minutes. Remove from the heat, cover, and set aside.

When the parsnips are tender, drain well and add the butter and salt and pepper to taste. Mash by hand and then transfer to a blender. Add the cream and puree. Cover to keep warm and set aside.

Remove the artichoke hearts from the pan, set them on a small plate, and cover to keep warm. Mix the parsnip puree into the rest of the artichoke mixture a little at a time. (Do not feel compelled to use all the parsnip puree. It is used primarily to bind the mixture in the tart as a creamy base, so don't use so much that it is too runny or overflows the tart shells.) Adjust the seasoning if needed with salt and pepper. Cover and keep warm. (Return to the chicken—remove it to a platter to let it rest and make the sauce.)

Assemble the tarts at the last minute. Break through the center "dome" of each tart shell. (This is where you will spoon the filling.) Fill each tart shell with the parsnip mixture and top with an artichoke heart. Sprinkle with chopped fresh basil.

Presentation

Place the chicken on a serving dish. Spoon the sauce on top and garnish with parsley. Pair with a vegetable tart.

Pork Medallions with Goat Cheese and Apple Cinnamon Raisin Compote

SERVES 6

Amazingly comforting food, especially served with mashed potatoes. The sweet and savory compote is of home and good memories.

INGREDIENTS FOR THE PORK MEDALLIONS

3 pounds pork loin, cut into ¼-inch-thick slices and pounded into ⅛-inch-thick medallions

1½ cups all-purpose flour seasoned with salt, pepper, and paprika

¼ cup grapeseed oil

4 tablespoons unsalted butter

One 3-ounce goat cheese log, crumbled

INGREDIENTS FOR THE APPLE CINNAMON RAISIN COMPOTE

6 Granny Smith apples, peeled, cored, and thinly sliced (Sprinkle with lemon juice to prevent oxidation.)

½ cup golden raisins

½ cup dry white wine

1 cup vegetable stock

1 teaspoon ground cinnamon

4 tablespoons unsalted butter

Salt to taste

TIMELINE

Ingredient prep:
Pound pork medallions .... 5 minutes
Peel, core, and slice apples .... 10 minutes
Season flour and measure out
    ingredients .... 5 minutes
Peel and cut potatoes, if using .... 5 minutes
Total estimated prep time....................**25 minutes**

Boil potatoes, if using (10 minutes)
    Overlaps with:
    Dredge pork (2 minutes)
    Sear pork (4 minutes)
    Sauté apples (3 minutes)..................... 10 minutes
    Cook apples in sauce (5 minutes)
    Overlaps with:
    Mash potatoes (if using) .... 5 minutes
Subtotal active cooking time.............. **15 minutes**

Assembly ....**2 minutes**

Total estimated time ....**42 minutes**

OPTIONAL MASHED POTATO ACCOMPANIMENT: 4 to 6 large white and/or sweet potatoes and/or yams, peeled, cut into 1-inch chunks, boiled, and mashed with ½ cup milk or light cream and 3 tablespoons unsalted butter

Method for the pork medallions

Coat the pork medallions with the flour mixture, shaking off the excess. (If you are serving mashed potatoes as an accompaniment, begin boiling the potatoes.) Heat the grapeseed oil over medium-high heat in a large skillet and melt 4 tablespoons of the butter. Sear the pork medallions, leaving undisturbed for the first 2 minutes to allow the flavors to integrate into the meat and to prevent the flour coating from crusting off. Carefully turn the medallions over and sear the other side in the same way. When both sides of the crust turn golden brown and juices are no longer running from the meat, remove them to a tray. Cover the tray with aluminum foil and keep in a warm place to let rest. (Reserve the oil and pan juices in the skillet for the compote.)

Method for the apple cinnamon raisin compote

To the oil and juices in the skillet, add the apples and raisins and sauté for 3 to 4 minutes over medium-high heat to cook the apples through quickly. Add the wine and simmer until most of the alcohol has evaporated. Add the vegetable stock and cinnamon and cook for about 5 minutes to allow the flavors to integrate. Swirl the remaining 4 tablespoons of butter into the apple mixture. Lower the heat as needed to keep the compote from burning, but keep it high enough to allow the liquid to reduce and thicken. Season to taste with salt and pepper.

Presentation

Spoon some apple compote into the center of each serving plate and place some crumbled goat cheese in the center. Place the pork medallions on top. If using, serve the mashed potatoes on the side.

Sun-dried Tomato Pesto–Crusted Chicken Breast over Creamy Polenta with Cave-Aged Cheddar and Pineapple-Mango Demi-glace

SERVES 6

Cheese is aged in cool, moist conditions, most often in storage rooms where these conditions can be carefully controlled. However, some Cheddar is still cave-aged in locales where such cheese has been made for hundreds of years. Cave-aged Cheddar has a certain *je ne sais quoi,* something special, that is perhaps akin to beer brewed in places where the dust and cobwebs in the rafters are not disturbed for fear of upsetting the "living conditions" of the naturally occurring yeast that gives that beer its character. In reality it's likely a combination of factors that contribute to the specialness of cave-aged Cheddar, including the influence on the source milk of the native grasses on which the artisanal cheesemaker's livestock feed. A number of creameries in Somerset, England, make the genuine article from the original recipe, but excellent domestic Cheddar is made by Grafton Village, Cabot Creamery Cooperative, Sonoma Cheese, and Rogue River Valley.

INGREDIENTS FOR THE PINEAPPLE-MANGO DEMI-GLACE

2 tablespoons grapeseed oil

2 shallots, chopped

2 cups red wine

2 cups beef stock

½ fresh pineapple, skinned, cored, diced small

½ mango, peeled, pit removed, diced small

¼ cup unsalted butter, cut into cubes

Salt and black pepper to taste

INGREDIENTS FOR THE PESTO-CRUSTED CHICKEN

2 cups jarred, oil-packed sun-dried tomatoes

4 garlic cloves, quartered

2 cups packed fresh basil leaves

1 cup grated Parmigiano-Reggiano cheese

Salt and pepper to taste

1½ tablespoons grapeseed oil approximately

2½ to 3 pounds boneless chicken breasts, cut and pounded into twelve 3- to 4-ounce ¼-inch-thick pieces

INGREDIENTS FOR THE POLENTA

2 cups chicken stock

2 cups heavy cream

1 cup cornmeal

1 cup freshly shredded Cheddar cheese, preferably cave-aged

Salt and pepper to taste

Method for the pineapple-mango demi-glace

Heat the oil in a heavy saucepan over medium-high heat. Sauté the shallots until soft, about 2 minutes. Add the wine to the pan and reduce by half. Add the stock and cook until the sauce thickens enough to coat the back of a spoon. Add the pineapple and mango and cook for about 3 minutes, or until softened. Remove from the heat. Puree in a blender (or with an immersion blender if the pot is deep enough) and keep warm until needed.

Just before serving, reheat the demi-glace if necessary and whisk the butter into the sauce. Season to taste with salt and pepper.

Method for the pesto-crusted chicken

Preheat the oven to 375°F.

To make the pesto crust, blend the sun-dried tomatoes, garlic, and basil in a food processor. Stir in the Parmesan cheese, pepper to taste, and salt only if needed. (The Parmesan cheese will lend some saltiness.) Set aside.

Heat the oil in a large skillet over medium heat. Season the chicken with pepper only (the pesto will provide the salt). Cover the curved side of each chicken piece with pesto, pressing to make it adhere. Sear the chicken pieces pesto-side down for 1 or 2 minutes, being careful not to burn it. Using a spatula, carefully flip the chicken over and sear on the other side for 1 minute. (You will probably have to do this in batches.) Transfer the breasts to a large baking dish or roasting pan and roast until fork-tender, 15 to 20 minutes.

Method for the polenta

Combine the stock and cream in a large heavy saucepan. Bring the mixture to a gentle boil over medium heat, being careful not to burn it. Whisking constantly, gradually add the cornmeal. Once the cornmeal is incorporated, lower the heat and continue whisking until the mixture is slightly thickened and creamy, about 10 minutes. Remove the pan from the heat and add the Cheddar, stirring until it is melted. Season with pepper (and salt if needed).

Presentation

Spoon some polenta onto each serving plate, top with 2 pieces of chicken, and spoon some sauce around.

Roasted Cornish Game Hen with Sweet Potato Gnocchi

SERVES 4

Barding (tying) and larding (lacing with lard) lend moisture to lean Cornish game birds. This dish looks wonderful on the plate with its autumnal colors (see the photo!). It is like giving each person his or her own mini-Thanksgiving feast. The gluten-free gnocchi recipe comes compliments of my co-authors, Brian and Virginia.

INGREDIENTS FOR THE SWEET POTATO GNOCCHI

Cloves from 1 roasted head of garlic (see page 137)

1 pound sweet potatoes or yams (approximately 3 or 4 sweet potatoes or 1 or 2 yams), peeled, cut into 1-inch chunks, boiled until very tender, well drained, and allowed to return to room temperature

1 cup white rice flour, plus some to flour the board

¾ cup potato starch

¼ cup cornstarch

¼ teaspoon ground nutmeg

1 tablespoon chili powder

¼ teaspoon freshly ground black pepper

1 teaspoon ground cumin

½ teaspoon dried oregano

1 teaspoon salt

1 tablespoon brown sugar

1 tablespoon unsalted butter, cut into cubes

2 tablespoons grated sharp Cheddar cheese

2 eggs, beaten

INGREDIENTS FOR THE CORNISH GAME HENS AND SAUCE

4 Cornish game hens

Salt and freshly ground black pepper to taste

One 6-ounce package bacon, cut into 2-inch pieces

2 tablespoons grapeseed oil

1 red onion, minced

1 cup dry sherry

1 cup low-sodium vegetable stock

½ cup demi-glace or beef stock, or ½ teaspoon beef base

½ teaspoon tomato paste

4 fresh thyme sprigs

1 bay leaf

1 teaspoon McCormick Hot Mexican Chili Powder

2 tablespoons unsalted butter, cut into cubes

¼ cup minced fresh flat-leaf parsley leaves

Method for the sweet potato gnocchi

Please note: If you've roasted the garlic immediately before starting this recipe, allow the oven temperature to drop down to 400°F. Squeeze the roasted garlic cloves from their papery skins directly into a large mixing bowl and mash the garlic into a paste. To the bowl of garlic, add the sweet potatoes and mash them by hand to break them up and remove any large lumps but still keeping the potato a light fibrous pulp. In a separate large bowl, combine the rice flour, potato starch, cornstarch, nutmeg, chili powder, black pepper, cumin, oregano, and salt, and mix well. Add the brown sugar to the dry ingredients and stir to combine evenly. Transfer the dry ingredients to the bowl of garlic and sweet potatoes and add the cubed butter, cheese, and eggs. Fold the ingredients together to moisten the dry ingredients and mix well, but avoid manipulating the dough too much. (Gnocchi should be light and fluffy; overworking the dough will make them dense.) Knead the dough lightly, divide it into 4 portions, and shape each one into a cylinder without compressing the dough. Place them in a large bowl, cover with a damp towel, and let rest for about 20 minutes. (Begin preparing the game hens, and return to form the gnocchi once the game hens are in the oven and the sauce is underway.)

While the sauce is reducing, use a floured surface (such as a large wooden cutting board) for lightly rolling each portion of dough into a long ropelike cylinder, about ¾ inch in diameter, without overworking the dough. Cut each cylinder into 1½-inch pieces and let rest for about 10 minutes. Bring a large shallow pan of water to a boil and add salt. (Strain the sauce, below.)

TIMELINE

Ingredient prep:
Roast garlic (15 minutes at 500°F, per the
   instructions on page 226)
   Overlaps with:
Peel and cut sweet potatoes (5 minutes)
Boil potatoes (10 minutes)....................15 minutes
Chop onion and herbs .... 3 minutes
Measure ingredients.. 5 minutes
Estimated time for ingredient prep....19 minutes

Mash garlic and potatoes, mix with dry
   ingredients, and knead .... 5 minutes
Let dough rest (20 minutes)
   Overlaps with:
Bard game hens (15 minutes)
Sauté (5 minutes)..................................... 20 minutes
Roasting time for game hens (45 minutes)
   Overlaps with:
Sauté onion for sauce (5 minutes)
Deglaze with sherry and let
   evaporate (5 minutes)
Add stock and seasonings and let reduce
   (20 minutes)
   Overlaps with:
   Roll gnocchi (5 minutes)
   Cut gnocchi (5 minutes)
   Let gnocchi rest (10 minutes)
   Start water boiling
   (5 minutes) ....45 minutes
Remove game hens from oven and let rest
   (5 minutes)
   Overlaps with:
Strain and finish sauce (5 minutes)
   Overlaps with:
   Boil gnocchi (5 minutes) .... 5 minutes
Subtotal active cooking time ....75 minutes

Assembly ....5 minutes

Total estimated time..........1 hour and 39 minutes

Add the gnocchi to the boiling water. As they set up, gently remove them to a utility platter with a slotted spoon, preferably a wooden one.

Method for the game hens

Preheat the oven to 400°F. (Be sure to let the oven temperature drop if you've just roasted the garlic.)

While the gnocchi dough is resting, season the game hens inside and out with salt and pepper. Bard (tie) the game hens, beginning with a 2- to 3-foot length of kitchen string for each bird. Let the center point of the string rest at the opening to the breast cavity. Pull the string taut and loop each end of the string once down and around the narrowest part of the drumsticks as you bring them together. Bring the loose ends up to each wing and loop once back and up around the "elbow" of each wing. Cross the loose ends over the back and bring each end up over the breast again, tying securely. Trim away any extra string. Slip pieces of bacon under the taut string to flavor the game hen and keep it moist.

In a large skillet, heat the grapeseed oil over medium heat. When it begins to shimmer, add the game hens, one bird at a time, and brown on all sides. Transfer the game hens to a roasting pan, reserving the skillet and bacon fat to make the sauce. Cover the roasting pan with foil and roast for 25 minutes. (Once the hens are in the oven, start preparing the sauce, below, and then return to roll the dough into gnocchi.)

Remove the game hens from the oven, cut the strings using kitchen shears, and remove the strings and bacon. Roast the game hens about another 10 to 20 minutes, or until they're fork-tender and the juices run clear (not pink). Test the juices by inserting a knife at the crevice between the breast and the wing. Remove the game hens to a utility platter to let rest. (Start boiling the gnocchi now, above.)

Method for the sauce

While the game hens are roasting, return to the same pan in which you browned them. Pour off any fat in excess of about 2 tablespoons and heat over medium-high heat. Sauté the onion until it turns translucent, about 3 to 5 minutes, then deglaze the pan with the sherry. When most of the alcohol has evaporated, add the vegetable stock, demi-glace (or beef stock, or beef base stirred into ½ cup water), tomato paste, thyme, bay leaf, and chili powder, and cook until it is reduced by half, 10 to 20 minutes. (Meanwhile, begin rolling the dough into gnocchi.)

While the uncooked gnocchi are resting, strain the sauce into a medium bowl and gradually whisk in the butter, allowing each addition to melt before adding the next. Adjust the seasoning with salt and pepper. Set the bowl into a larger bowl of warm water to keep it warm. (Finish the dish by boiling the gnocchi, above.)

Presentation

Transfer 1 game hen to each serving dish. Arrange the gnocchi around the game hen and spoon the sauce on top. Sprinkle the gnocchi with parsley.

Shredded Roast Beef au Jus over Crostini with Horseradish Cream

SERVES 6

When I was a kid, the Reynolds Oven Cooking Bag was a new thing. Well, it's no longer new, but while other cooking shortcuts have come and gone, it's still around and it's still a good thing. It's intended to provide easy cleanup, but because I like to sear the meat beforehand, I'm still left with a pan to scrub. However, I really like the results it produces because it releases enough moisture to give the mouthfeel that only dry heat can impart but holds in enough to make the meat succulent. As a cross between braising and cooking en papillote (in parchment), it's actually fairly unique in the realm of home cooking. This recipe is intended for use at a low temperature with an oven cooking bag. Pop this roast into the oven a few hours before a football game and eat dinner on tray tables in front of the TV. If you don't want to use the bag, you can braise the meat pot roast–style after searing it—the texture of the meat will be more stewlike, but still very pleasant.

INGREDIENTS FOR THE RUB AND BEEF

One 3-pound beef eye roast

2 teaspoons cayenne pepper

2 teaspoons paprika

2 teaspoons chili powder

1½ teaspoons ground cumin

1 teaspoon freshly ground black pepper

1 teaspoon salt

½ teaspoon dried oregano

¼ teaspoon garlic powder

¼ teaspoon onion powder

¼ teaspoon crushed red pepper

1 lemon

1 tablespoon all-purpose flour

1 tablespoon grapeseed oil

INGREDIENTS FOR THE HORSERADISH CREAM

1 cup heavy cream

1 lemon, halved and seeded

¼ cup prepared horseradish

¼ teaspoon salt

⅛ teaspoon white pepper

INGREDIENTS FOR THE CROSTINI

1 loaf Italian bread, sliced lengthwise

SPECIAL EQUIPMENT

1 Reynolds Oven Cooking Bag

Method

Rinse the meat and pat dry with paper towels. To prepare the rub, in a medium bowl, combine the cayenne, paprika, chili powder, cumin, black pepper, salt, oregano, garlic powder, onion powder, and crushed red pepper. Squeeze lemon juice into the bowl and stir to make a paste. (If you keep the sliced side of the lemon against your palm while you squeeze, the seeds will remain in the rind. Of course, you can also use a juicer.) Rub the paste over the entire eye roast. Let sit for 1 hour.

Place the oven rack at a low position so that the cooking bag has enough room not to touch any oven surface. Preheat the oven to 325°F.

To prepare the horseradish cream, beat the heavy cream with an electric mixer until stiff peaks form. Squeeze in lemon juice, half a lemon at a time, and beat until incorporated. Gradually beat in the horseradish, salt, and pepper. Chill for about an hour before serving.

Shake the flour in the oven cooking bag (to keep it from bursting) and place the bag in a roasting pan that is at least 2 inches deep.

Heat the oil in a large sauté pan over medium-high heat until it shimmers. Sear the beef on all sides. Transfer the beef to the oven bag, add ¼ cup water, seal the bag with the provided twist tie, tuck the end under the beef, and make 6 slits in the bag.

Roast until the beef is very tender and can be shredded with a fork. A boneless cut of meat is used here, but if it weren't, you would want the meat to be at the stage where it is falling off the bone. This will take about 1 hour per pound at this oven temperature—about 3 hours in total. (To check for doneness, carefully release the resealable tie from the bag, protecting your face from the escaping steam and ensuring that no juices escape.) When the meat is suitably fork-tender, remove the meat from the oven and bag and set it on a platter to rest.

Pour the juices from the oven bag into a pan (be careful about the slits) and add 1 cup water to make a thin "gravy." Set it aside.

If you want the bread toasted, place it on a baking sheet in the still-warm oven for about 5 minutes. Cut it into 3- to 4-inch lengths and place on serving dishes.

Using two forks, shred the rested beef with the grain and place some on top of the bread. Spoon the sauce over the beef and top with horseradish cream.

Porcini-Dusted Pork Chops with Cremini Mushrooms and Golden Raisins over Horseradish-Scented Potatoes

SERVES 4

In *Mission: Cook* and on TV, I've said that it's a good idea to have a coffee grinder dedicated to the grinding of your own spices. Now is the time to get serious and listen! (Eat your fruits and vegetables, too, while you're at it!) I personally believe that spices should be kept no longer than four weeks—how's that for being a freshness nut? I know there are those of you who right now have spices in your cabinets that have been there for four years and you're still using them. Stop it. When you taste the difference of freshly ground spices, not to mention the aroma in the kitchen when you grind them, you'll love grinding your own. For a recipe like this, the dedicated grinder is indispensable because you'll need to grind dried mushrooms. That's not to say you can't find ground dried mushrooms, but for a relatively small amount of money, save yourself the trouble and get yourself the grinder, which you will then have for other recipes. If you thought your mother's pork chops with cream of mushroom soup was a memorable dish, prepare yourself for a new daydream: porcini-dusted pork chops!

INGREDIENTS FOR THE PORK CHOPS

2 ounces dried cremini mushrooms, or 1 pound fresh

1 ounce dried porcini mushrooms

Four 6-ounce (about 1½ pounds) center-cut pork chops or eight 3-ounce chops (if using thin chops, allow 2 per person)

Salt and freshly ground black pepper

2 tablespoons unsalted butter

2 tablespoons canola oil

INGREDIENTS FOR THE SAUCE

1 teaspoon dried thyme, or 1 tablespoon minced fresh

½ cup golden raisins

Salt and pepper to taste

SPECIAL EQUIPMENT

Electric coffee grinder dedicated to grinding spices

INGREDIENTS FOR THE HORSERADISH-SCENTED POTATOES

2 pounds potatoes (about 4 large potatoes)

2 tablespoons unsalted butter

½ cup light cream or milk

1 tablespoon prepared horseradish

Salt and pepper to taste

Method

If you're using dried cremini mushrooms, in a small bowl, cover the mushrooms with 2 cups hot water. Let stand 25 minutes to rehydrate the mushrooms. Meanwhile, grind the porcini mushrooms to a powder using a coffee grinder dedicated to spices. Rinse the pork chops and pat dry with paper towels. Add salt and pepper to the porcini powder to make a rub and rub it into all the surfaces of the pork chops, reserving any extra rub. Set the chops aside.

Peel and cut the potatoes into 1-inch chunks, immediately placing them into a large saucepan of cold water; boil them until tender. Drain and keep warm.

If you're using dried cremini mushrooms, save their soaking liquid. Place a paper towel inside a strainer fitted over a small bowl. Drain the cremini soaking liquid into the bowl and reserve it. Remove the cremini mushrooms to a plate or bowl and discard the paper towel. Place the rehydrated mushrooms back in the strainer, rinse briefly, and set aside. If you are using fresh cremini mushrooms, whisk any leftover pork chop rub into 1 cup of warm water and set aside.

If you're using thicker pork chops, preheat the oven to 375°F.

Melt 1 tablespoon of the butter in 1 tablespoon of the oil over medium-high heat in a large skillet with an oven-safe handle. Sear the pork chops, leaving them undisturbed for 3 to 4 minutes to let the seasonings and porcini powder integrate into the surface of the meat and to prevent it from "crusting off." After about 3 minutes, you will see the edges of the chops beginning to turn golden. Add the rest of the oil and butter to the pan and flip the chops to sear the other side in the same way. If you are using thin-sliced chops, remove them to a utility platter and keep warm. The pork will continue to cook

```
TIMELINE

Ingredient prep:
Peel and cut potatoes and herbs...............7 minutes

Rehydrate cremini mushrooms (25 minutes)
    Overlaps with:
    Grind porcini mushrooms (5 minutes)
    Season and rub pork chops (4 minutes)
Let pork chops sit with
    seasonings (19 minutes) ........................25 minutes

Boil potatoes (10 minutes)
    Overlaps with:
    Drain cremini mushrooms to reserve soaking
        liquid (2 minutes)
    Preheat oven and sear pork chops
        (8 minutes) .............................................10 minutes

Finish pork chops in oven (variable)
    Overlaps with:
    Add soaking liquid to pork pan along with
        cremini mushrooms, mushroom powder,
        thyme, and raisins, and let reduce (10 minutes)
    Overlaps with:
    Mash/whip potatoes (5 minutes) ....... 10 minutes

Assembly ................................................ 2 minutes

Total estimated time,
start to finish ......................................54 minutes
```

for a few minutes after you have removed them from the pan (this is called carry-over cooking). Thin-sliced chops will most likely be cooked enough. Larger chops should be transferred to a baking sheet and finished in the oven to an internal temperature of 180°F. But be careful not to overcook them—pork chops can quickly become tough.

To the pan in which you cooked the pork chops, add the soaking liquid from the cremini mushrooms, the rehydrated cremini mushrooms, leftover mushroom powder, thyme, and golden raisins. (If you're using fresh cremini mushrooms, add the mushrooms, the rub/water mixture, and the thyme and golden raisins.) Over medium-high heat, allow the liquid to reduce by half, about 8 to 10 minutes.

Meanwhile, finish the mashed potatoes. Add the butter to the drained potatoes and mash by hand. Add the cream or milk and horseradish and season with salt and pepper to taste. Whip the potatoes with an electric beater and keep warm.

Season the mushroom-raisin sauce with salt and pepper as needed.

Presentation

Spoon some of the potatoes onto a serving plate. Top with one 6-ounce chop or two 3-ounce chops and spoon the mushroom-raisin sauce on top and around.

Garlic and Herb Pesto-Crusted Lamb Chops

SERVES 4

This recipe isn't deceptively easy—it's just easy! Pesto delivers a wallop of flavors without investing a lot of time and effort, but you still get all the credit.

INGREDIENTS

6 to 8 large garlic cloves, quartered

½ cup fresh flat-leaf parsley leaves

Leaves from 3 fresh rosemary sprigs

½ cup fresh basil leaves

¼ cup fresh thyme leaves

¼ cup fresh oregano leaves

5 or 6 fresh sage leaves

½ cup pine nuts

¼ to ½ cup olive oil

Salt and freshly ground black pepper to taste

8 loin lamb chops

Method

Preheat the oven to 350°F. Place the garlic, parsley, rosemary, basil, thyme, oregano, sage, and pine nuts in a food processor and pulse. Remove the herb mixture to a bowl, stir in enough of the olive oil to moisten the mixture to a pastelike consistency without making it too loose, and season to taste with salt and pepper. Press into the surface of the lamb chops and place the chops on a foil-lined baking sheet. Roast until fork-tender, to an internal temperature of 145°F for medium rare or 160°F for medium, about 15 to 25 minutes.

Roasted Chicken Thighs with Black Cherry Chutney and Sweet Potato Cakes

SERVES 4

There's something about a good chutney that stirs my English soul. This is a lovely variation on the theme that makes great use of the intense flavor of dried black cherries.

INGREDIENTS FOR THE SWEET POTATOES

1 pound sweet potatoes (about 4), peeled and cut into 1-inch chunks

4 tablespoons unsalted butter

¼ teaspoon allspice

⅛ cup light cream or milk

Salt and freshly ground black pepper to taste

1 tablespoon grapeseed oil

INGREDIENTS FOR THE CHICKEN

2 tablespoon grapeseed oil

8 boneless chicken thighs (about 2 pounds)

Salt and freshly ground black pepper to taste

2 teaspoons garlic powder

INGREDIENTS FOR THE BLACK CHERRY CHUTNEY

1 teaspoon grapeseed oil

1 shallot, minced

1 large orange, zested, with the skin sliced off just below the pith and the orange cut into ½-inch pieces

1 cup orange juice

1 tablespoon balsamic vinegar

1 teaspoon minced fresh thyme leaves

½ cup dried black cherries

Pinch of freshly ground black pepper

2 tablespoons tawny or ruby port wine

1 teaspoon cornstarch, made into a slurry with 1 teaspoon water

Method for the sweet potatoes

In a medium saucepan of salted water, boil the sweet potatoes until tender. Drain, return to the pan, and add the butter, allspice, cream or milk, and salt and pepper. Mash by hand and set aside to cool while you start the chicken and chutney.

Form the sweet potatoes into 4 patties. Heat the oil in a skillet over medium heat. Add the potato patties and cook until you see the edges begin to turn golden brown. Leave undisturbed for a few minutes to allow the patties to "set up," about 4 minutes, then flip them and cook the other side the same way. Remove from the pan and keep warm.

Method for the chicken

Heat the oil over medium-high heat in a large sauté pan with an oven-safe handle. Season the chicken thighs with salt, pepper, and garlic powder and sear beginning with the curved "outside" part of the thighs first, leaving undisturbed to allow the seasonings to integrate into the surface of the chicken and to allow the caramelization process to begin, about 3 minutes. Flip the chicken and sear the other side the same way, then transfer to the oven and roast until fork-tender, about 25 to 35 minutes. (Meanwhile, begin the chutney.) Remember to use an oven mitt on the hot handle of the pan when it comes from the oven.

Method for the black cherry chutney

Heat the oil over medium-high heat in a small saucepan until it begins to shimmer. Add the shallot and sauté until it begins to turn translucent, being careful not to burn it. Add the orange zest, orange pieces, orange juice, balsamic vinegar, and thyme and allow the liquid to reduce by half, about 5 minutes. (Meanwhile, begin sautéing the sweet potato patties.) Stir in the cherries and drizzle with the port wine to allow them to cook until they rehydrate and plump up a bit but still retain their rich color, about 5 minutes. Then whisk in the slurry and reduce the heat to allow the mixture to thicken, about 5 minutes. Remove the chutney from the heat, stir in the orange segments, and set aside.

TIMELINE

Ingredient prep:
Peel sweet potatoes...3 minutes
Measure ingredients.......................................5 minutes
Chop shallot and herbs.................................2 minutes
Zest and segment orange..........................4 minutes
Prepare cornstarch slurry............................1 minute
Subtotal for ingredient prep................15 minutes

Active cooking time:
Boil sweet potatoes (10 minutes)
  Overlaps with:
Season and sauté chicken
  (7 minutes)...10 minutes
Oven roasting time for chicken (35 minutes)
  Overlaps with:
  Chutney cooking time (15 minutes)
  Potato patty sautéing
    time (8 minutes)...................................25 minutes
Subtotal for cooking time....................35 minutes

Assembly ....5 minutes

Total estimated time ....55 minutes

Presentation

Place a sweet potato patty on each serving dish. Arrange a chicken thigh on either side of the patty (2 thighs per person). Spoon the chutney over the chicken.

Thyme-Roasted Pork Chops with White Wine Reduction, Crisp BBQ Wontons, and Roasted Root Vegetables

SERVES 6

This is one of those great meals where you can do a lot in advance to bring your actual crunch-time preparation down to only 35 minutes. Follow the timeline up to "add wine and allow to reduce," then bring everything to room temperature, cover, and refrigerate until needed. Just before mealtime, microwave the root vegetables to reheat and gently reheat the wine reduction on the stovetop. (This will take about three minutes total.) Then pick up where you left off on the timeline, and in another thirty-two minutes . . . voilà!

INGREDIENTS FOR THE ROASTED ROOT VEGETABLES

½ large red onion, cut into medium dice (use the other ½ onion below)

1 large garlic clove, lightly crushed with the side of a knife blade and minced

Leaves from 3 large fresh oregano sprigs, minced

1½ carrots, peeled and cut into medium dice (use the other ½ carrot below)

¾ celery root (celeriac), peeled and cut into medium dice (use the other ¼ root below)

3 large potatoes, peeled and cut into medium dice

⅛ cup grapeseed oil

Kosher salt and freshly ground black pepper

INGREDIENTS FOR THE WHITE WINE REDUCTION

1 cup beef stock

½ large red onion, cut into medium dice

1 garlic clove, lightly crushed with the side of a knife blade and minced

½ carrot, cut into medium dice

2 large fresh parsley sprigs

3 large fresh thyme sprigs

1 fresh rosemary sprig

1 bay leaf

1 cup dry white wine

½ stick (4 tablespoons) unsalted butter, cubed

Salt and freshly ground black pepper to taste

INGREDIENTS FOR THE CRISP BBQ WONTONS

6 wonton skins

2 tablespoons grapeseed oil

1 large red bell pepper, cut brunoise (cut julienne, then crosswise)

1 ounce (about a 1-inch piece) fresh gingerroot, covering scraped off with the tip of a spoon, minced

Salt and freshly ground black pepper to taste

1 tablespoon molasses

1 to 2 tablespoons unsalted butter, or as needed to sauté

INGREDIENTS FOR THE PORK CHOPS

½ cup all-purpose flour

Salt and freshly ground black pepper to taste

Six 6-ounce pork chops (about 2 ¼ pounds)

2 tablespoons unsalted butter

2 tablespoons grapeseed oil

3 large fresh thyme sprigs, stripped from stems and chopped

TIMELINE

Ingredient prep:
Cut vegetables and herbs......................... 20 minutes
Measure ingredients....................................... 5 minutes
Subtotal ingredient prep...................... 25 minutes

Active cooking time:
Coat root vegetables with oil and roast,
   covered (40 minutes)
  Overlaps with:
  Assemble and cook stock and
    vegetables for sauce (25 minutes)
  Overlaps with:
  Lay out wontons, sauté filling,
    fill wontons, and boil (20 minutes)
  Overlaps with:
  Return to stock, add wine,
    and allow to reduce
    (15 minutes) .... 40 minutes
Assemble and sauté pork chops.............. 12 minutes
Remove cover from roasted
  vegetables in oven and add pork
  chops to oven to finish (10 minutes)
  Overlaps with:
  Strain sauce (5 minutes)
  Sauté wontons (5 minutes)................... 10 minutes
Rest time for pork (5 minutes)
  Overlaps with:
  Finish sauce (5 minutes) .... 5 minutes
Subtotal active cooking time .... 67 minutes

Assembly and presentation....................5 minutes

Total estimated time .... 1 hour and 37 minutes

Method for the roasted root vegetables

Preheat the oven to 375°F, making sure there will be room in the oven for both the vegetables and (later) the pork chops. Add the onion, garlic, oregano, carrots, celery root, and potatoes to a small roasting pan. Coat with oil (using your hands to toss is easiest) and season with salt and pepper. Cover the pan with a lid or foil, place the vegetables in the oven, and roast until tender, about 40 minutes. (Meanwhile, begin the stock and vegetables for the wine reduction.)

Remove the cover from the vegetables and roast, uncovered, until golden for about 10 minutes.

Method for the white wine reduction

Heat the beef stock in a large saucepan over medium-high heat and add the onion, garlic, carrot, parsley, thyme, rosemary, and bay leaf. To intensify the flavor, boil vigorously, uncovered, until the stock is very nearly evaporated, but do not allow it to burn. It could take 20 minutes or more at a rolling boil. (Meanwhile, begin the filling for the wontons.)

Add the wine to the stock mixture and cook over medium heat until it is reduced by half, 10 to 15 minutes. (Meanwhile, start on the pork chops and continue with the sauce when they are in the oven.)

Remove the sauce from the heat and strain it through a chinois (a conical strainer) or some cheesecloth. Use a wooden spoon to squeeze the vegetables against the strainer to extract the liquid into the bowl. Set aside in a warm place until needed.

If necessary, reheat the sauce before serving. Remove from the heat and whisk in the butter to make the texture smooth and silky. Taste the sauce and add salt and pepper only if needed.

Method for the crisp BBQ wontons

Bring a shallow pan of water to a boil and lay out the wonton skins. Heat 1 tablespoon of the oil in a sauté pan over medium heat. Sauté the pepper and ginger until they begin to soften, about 5 minutes. Remove from the heat, stir in the molasses, and season to taste with salt and pepper. Spoon a little of the mixture onto each wonton skin. Fold over and seal by moistening the seams with a little water, making sure that no mixture oozes out. Add the wontons to the boiling water and cook for 1 or 2 minutes, or until the dough sets up and is no longer fragile. With a slotted spoon, preferably a wooden spoon, set them aside to drain and rest. (Meanwhile, add the wine to the reduction and put the pork chops in the oven to finish.)

Rinse and/or wipe out the same sauté pan and melt the butter over medium heat. Gently pan-fry the wontons for about 2 minutes, or until just golden, and remove to a utility plate.

Method for the pork chops

While the wine in the sauce is reducing and the boiled wontons are resting, begin preparing the pork chops. The oven should already be at 375°F, with the vegetables roasting inside.

Season the flour with salt and pepper and lightly dredge the pork chops in the flour, allowing any excess flour to fall away. In a large skillet with an oven-safe handle over medium-high heat, melt 1 tablespoon of the butter in 1 tablespoon of the oil over medium-high heat. Sprinkle some thyme into the pan in the spots where you are going to place the chops and immediately place the chops onto the thyme. Sear the pork chops, leaving them undisturbed for about 3 minutes to let the thyme and flour integrate into the surface of the meat and to prevent it from "crusting off." After about 3 minutes, you will see the edges of the chops beginning to turn golden. Add the rest of the oil and butter to the pan and flip the chops to sear the other side in the same way.

Transfer the entire pan to the oven to finish the chops to an internal temperature of 165°F, about 8 to 10 minutes. (This may also be the time to remove the foil from the root vegetables to allow them to brown while you are finishing the pork.) Be careful not to overcook the pork chops—they can become tough quickly. (Meanwhile, strain the sauce and finish the wontons.)

Transfer the pork chops to a utility platter to let rest and carry-over cook for 5 minutes.

Presentation

Place some roasted vegetables in the center of individual serving plates and top with a pork chop. Spoon some sauce on top and garnish with a wonton.

Blue Cheese Filet Mignon with Turnips, Parsnips, and Potatoes Anna

SERVES 4

I did an episode of *Dinner: Impossible* where my challenge was to prepare trompe l'oeil ("fool the eye") food for the attendees at a magicians' convention. I learned some amazing things that day from a man who has made it his life's work to devise ways to make foods do what you didn't think they could. It got me thinking about doing the unexpected in cooking to avoid the possibility of monotony in our dishes.

Potatoes Anna can best be described as a potato upside-down cake. The classic is wonderful, but this version lends a twist that's especially fun for your palate. Layered in with the potatoes are sliced turnips or rutabagas, which are peppery sweet, and parsnips, which have a spicy finish. I've paired them here with blue cheese filet mignon, which serves as a delicious counterpoint. But do not hesitate to make Root Vegetables Anna on their own, say, for Sunday brunch.

INGREDIENTS FOR THE ROOT VEGETABLES ANNA

⅜ cup clarified butter (start with ½ cup or 1 stick butter if you are clarifying your own, see page 116)

1 large potato (about 3 or 4 ounces), peeled and sliced ⅛ inch thick with a mandoline or the slicing disk of a food processor

1 large parsnip (about 3 or 4 ounces), peeled and sliced ⅛ inch thick with a mandoline or the slicing disk of a food processor

Salt and freshly ground black pepper to taste

1 turnip or rutabaga (about 3 or 4 ounces), peeled and sliced ⅛ inch thick with a mandoline or the slicing disk of a food processor

4 tablespoons crème fraîche or sour cream

INGREDIENTS FOR THE BLUE CHEESE FILET MIGNON

Six 4–ounce beef tenderloins (filet mignon)

Salt and freshly ground black pepper to taste

3 ounces blue cheese

¾ cup breadcrumbs

About ⅛ cup grapeseed oil

2 tablespoons minced fresh parsley leaves

SPECIAL EQUIPMENT

8-inch cast-iron pan or other heavy-bottomed 8-inch skillet with a lid (or aluminum foil to cover)

Flat lid or heavy dish that will fit into the skillet to compress the vegetables

Mandoline or a food processor with a ⅛-inch slicing blade

Kitchen torch (such as the ones used for crème brûlée) or a stainless steel platter

Method for the root vegetables Anna

Preheat the oven to 400°F. Set an 8-inch skillet over low heat and pour in clarified butter to about a ¼-inch depth. Using the most attractive slices, arrange the bottom layer with potato slices in an overlapping pattern of concentric circles. Take the most care with this layer

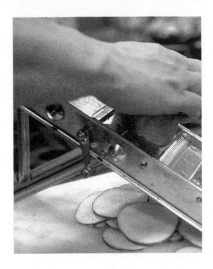

since you will be inverting the assembly after it is baked and this will be your top layer. Next add a layer of parsnip slices drizzled with a teaspoon of butter and seasoned with salt and pepper. Finish with a final layer of turnip or rutabaga slices, also drizzled with a teaspoon of butter and seasoned with salt and pepper. (Note: It is important to put the layers in this order because the respective densities of each will enable them to bake best this way.) Use a flat pot lid or heavy dish that fits inside the skillet to firmly press down the vegetables. Cover the vegetables with a lid or foil and roast for about 40 minutes, then uncover and roast for about another 15 minutes, or until the top layer is nicely golden brown. (Meanwhile, prepare the filets.)

Let the vegetables rest for 5 minutes. (Meanwhile, transfer the filets to the oven to finish.)

Hold a plate against the edges of the pan and carefully invert the root vegetable "cake" onto it. Use a kitchen torch to brown the top. If you have a stainless steel platter, you can place the "cake" in the broiler to brown it. Cut it into 4 wedges.

Method for the filet mignon

Season the filets with salt and pepper. In a mixing bowl, crumble the blue cheese into the breadcrumbs and set aside. When the vegetables are at the stage of roasting uncovered, heat a sauté pan with oven-safe handles over medium-high heat, adding just enough oil to coat the bottom. Cook the filets for approximately 2 to 3 minutes on one side, then turn and continue the searing process on the other side for another 2 to 3 minutes. Press a ¼- to ½-inch-thick layer of the blue cheese mixture on each of the filets. Place them into the oven (still heated from the vegetables) for 6 to 8 minutes, depending on the thickness of the steaks. (Only you know your oven and your own preference for doneness. For medium rare, a meat thermometer will read an internal temperature of 115°F.) Set the filets aside to rest (they will continue to cook for another 5 minutes). (Meanwhile, brown the root vegetable cake.)

Presentation

On each serving plate, arrange a wedge of root vegetable cake topped with a dollop of crème fraîche or sour cream alongside a steak and garnish with parsley.

Lamb Racks with Peach-Mint Polenta and Rosemary Reduction

SERVES 4

When I cooked at Resorts Hotel and Casino in Atlantic City, this was one of my specialties.

INGREDIENTS FOR THE PEACH-MINT POLENTA

2½ cups chicken stock

2 garlic cloves, minced

1 cup polenta (cornmeal)

1 stick (½ cup) unsalted butter

3 tablespoons mascarpone cheese

1 peach, peeled, poached for 5 minutes in boiling water, and diced, or ⅓ cup diced canned peach

1 tablespoon chopped fresh mint leaves

⅛ cup chopped fresh chives

INGREDIENTS FOR THE SAUCE

1 tablespoon grapeseed oil

1 large red onion, minced

1 large carrot, diced small

¼ cup fresh rosemary leaves

1 cup chicken stock

Salt and freshly ground black pepper to taste

2 tablespoons unsalted butter, cut into cubes

INGREDIENTS FOR THE LAMB

⅛ cup grapeseed oil

4 half racks of lamb (4 bones per serving), silver skin removed, rinsed and dried with paper towels, seasoned with salt and pepper, and allowed to rest for 1 hour

Kosher salt and freshly ground black pepper to taste

¼ cup (½ stick) unsalted butter

3 garlic cloves, minced

2 tablespoons minced fresh thyme (from 4 to 6 large sprigs)

2 tablespoons minced fresh rosemary (from about 3 to 5 sprigs)

INGREDIENTS FOR THE VEGETABLES

2 carrots, peeled and cut julienne

2 turnips, peeled and cut julienne

1 small celeriac, peeled and cut julienne

4 baby bok choy, halved lengthwise

4 tablespoons unsalted butter

TIMELINE

Cooking time for cornmeal for polenta
Overlaps with:
Cooking sauce..........................15 minutes
Cooling time for cooked cornmeal
Overlaps with:
Sear time for lamb (6 minutes)
Roast time for lamb (6 minutes)......15 minutes
Rest time for lamb (5 minutes)
Overlaps with:
Cooking time for
vegetables (5 minutes)
Cutting and sautéing of
polenta cakes (5 minutes)............5 minutes

Total cooking time...........................35 minutes

Method for the polenta

Have a pan ready, such as a 9×12-inch pan, that will allow the polenta to settle at an even thickness of 1½ to 2 inches. Bring the stock and garlic to a boil in a medium saucepan over medium-high heat. Add the polenta and return to a boil, then reduce the heat to low and simmer for 10 to 15 minutes, or until the polenta is thick and smooth, stirring occasionally. (Meanwhile, prepare the sauce, below.)

Remove the polenta from the heat and stir in 4 tablespoons of butter (reserving the rest of the butter to sauté), the mascarpone, peach, mint, and chives. Pour the polenta mixture in an even layer into the pan you have waiting and set it aside to cool and set up. (Meanwhile, begin searing the lamb, below.)

While the lamb is resting, use a 3- or 4-inch circle cutter or biscuit cutter to cut out 4 polenta cakes. Heat the remaining 4 tablespoons of butter over medium heat in a large sauté pan and use a spatula to transfer the polenta cakes to the pan. Sauté each side of the polenta cakes until golden, about 3 to 4 minutes per side. Remove to paper towels to absorb the grease and set aside in a warm place.

Method for the sauce

While the polenta is simmering, start the sauce. In a large sauté pan over medium-high heat, heat the grapeseed oil. Add the onion and carrot and sauté until they are tender, about 5 to 8 minutes. Add the rosemary and gently cook for 1 minute. Add the stock, season with salt and pepper, and allow to reduce by half. Remove from the heat and whisk in the butter. Strain and adjust the seasoning with salt and pepper as needed. Keep warm until needed. (Return to the polenta.)

Method for the lamb

While the polenta is cooling, begin the lamb. Preheat the oven to 375°F.

In a large sauté pan with oven-safe handles over medium-high heat, heat the grapeseed oil. Sear the lamb, fleshiest side down first, leaving undisturbed for about 2 or 3 minutes to let the flavors integrate into the surface of the meat and to allow caramelization to begin. Flip and sear the other side, being careful not to overcook. Remove the lamb to a utility platter. Pour off most of the fat from the pan, leaving only a coating. Return the lamb to the pan, place an even amount of butter on top of each rack, and rub the butter into the meat. Combine the garlic, thyme, and rosemary in a small bowl and press an even amount of the mixture onto each rack. Roast until the lamb reaches an internal temperature of 140°F for medium rare or 155°F for medium, about 15 minutes. (Meanwhile, bring a pot of water to a boil for the vegetables, below.)

Remove the lamb from the oven and let it rest and carry-over cook for 3 to 5 minutes. (Meanwhile, cut and sauté the polenta.) For ease of eating, use a knife to gently loosen the lamb chops from the bone before serving a rack to each guest.

Method for the vegetables

Bring a medium saucepan of water to a boil. Add salt and boil the vegetables until tender, about 5 minutes. (Do not overcook.) Drain and toss with butter. Set aside in a warm place.

Presentation

Place a polenta cake, lamb rack, and vegetables on each serving plate. Spoon the sauce over the lamb. (See the photo for visual reference.)

Venison Potatoes Brandade

SERVES 6

I urge you to experience the use of game meats in your cooking. Venison should be available in a well-stocked supermarket or butcher shop, and you can have it ground there if necessary. If you are using fresh or frozen hunted venison, soak the meat in white vinegar and salt overnight in the refrigerator, then rinse before grinding it for this recipe. Alternatively, ground beef can be used.

INGREDIENTS

1 pound ground venison

2 garlic cloves, finely chopped

1 medium onion, finely chopped

1 tablespoon chopped fresh rosemary

Salt and freshly ground black pepper to taste

2 ½ pounds potatoes (about 5 large potatoes)

½ cup (1 stick) unsalted butter

½ cup grated Parmesan cheese

2 tablespoons chopped fresh chives

3 to 4 liters canola oil, or as needed for deep-frying

1 cup all-purpose flour, or as needed to coat the brandade

3 to 4 eggs, lightly beaten, or as needed for breading

1 to 2 tablespoons milk, or as needed for breading

1 cup fine breadcrumbs, or as needed to coat the brandade

SPECIAL EQUIPMENT

2½-inch circle or biscuit cutter

Deep fryer

Method

Bring a pot of water to boil for the potatoes.

In a hot sauté pan, brown the venison with the garlic, onion, and rosemary. Drain the extra juices off, season with salt and pepper to taste, and set aside to cool.

Peel the potatoes, cut into 1-inch chunks, boil, drain well, and mash with the butter. Stir in the Parmesan cheese and chives and let cool.

Heat the oil in a deep fryer to 325°F (or the temperature suggested by the manufacturer of your deep fryer for similar foods). Combine the venison with the potatoes. When the mixture is cool enough to handle, you can shape with a mold (such as a 2-inch cookie cutter) as I prefer to do, or make patties, logs, or small spheres. Bread the brandade in a three-step process: Roll in flour (or use a sifter if the shape is not conducive to rolling), then dip in egg mixed with milk, then coat with breadcrumbs. Fry until golden brown in the deep-fryer. Serve warm.

6. BOUNTY OF THE SEA: FISH AND SHELLFISH

There was a time when to fully experience the joys of seafood, you had to live near the sea. Today, given advanced modes of transportation, flash-freezing techniques, and modern fishing and handling methods, it's easy to get great-tasting fish most everywhere. The test of a good seafood dish, in my opinion, is whether it gives you that immediate feeling of being near the water, whether it captures that sudden clarity, that snap of freshness in the air that makes you catch your breath and inhale just a bit more deeply.

The best thing you can do with a beautiful fresh piece of fish is to get out of its way.

An overcooked piece of fish is ruined in my opinion. Good rule of thumb: If you are cooking fish and it looks like it's done to you, you probably should have taken it off the heat thirty seconds ago. This is an instance where carry-over cooking (see page 23) can be your best friend or your worst enemy. The tastes and textures of fish are best described as delicate. If you respect this fact, the bounty of the sea will translate into joy in your kitchen.

One of the toughest tests in a classic brigade system is the assumption of the position of *poissonier*, or the fish station. That is mainly because your timing must be dead-on accurate at all times. You have some leeway when you're grilling a nice thick steak, but a thin, flaky fillet of Dover sole will not forgive the extra twenty seconds you took wiping your brow or pan-frying the trout at the other end of the station. It will dry or break on you and humiliate you.

The same largely applies with shellfish. The gentle hand is the most successful. Shrimp, lobster tail, crawfish—all require only the briefest introduction to heat to render the best they have to offer. Overcook them and they will shrink, toughen up, and abandon their flavor, leaving you with nothing but a chewy and expensive little ball of muscle. Clams, mus-

Lamb Racks with Peach-Mint Polenta
and Rosemary Reduction (page 162)

Citrus-Braised Lobster Tails over Savory Corn "Cake" (page 170)

Blue Cheese Filet Mignon with Turnips, Parsnips, and Potatoes Anna (page 160)

Lobster Napa Cabbage Wraps (page 198)

Ocean Perch over Herbed Couscous with Baby Bok Choy
and Lemon Horseradish Sauce (page 179)

Crispy Crab and Smoked Salmon Cakes with
Baby Arugula and Mango Aioli (page 172)

Pan-Seared Salmon and Lemon Confit over
Sage Ratatouille (page 182)

Sea Scallops over Leeks with
Mango Curry Chocolate Sauce (page 191)

Wasabi Honey-Crusted Black Cod and Green Apple–
Red Cabbage Slaw with Curry Oil (page 168)

Braised Asian Pear with Roquefort
and Sweet Port Wine Dressing (page 224)

Pineapple and Artichoke Pasta with Pine Nuts (page 232)

Cornish Pasties (page 252)

Chicken Pot Pie in a puff pastry crust (page 238)

Sweet and Savory Crepes:
Banana Chocolate–Hazelnut (page 240)

Cranberry Clafoutis (page 266)

Almond Rochers (page 258)

sels, and oysters are also very simple organisms. They are not turkeys or chickens. Their top halves do not cook at a different rate from their "walking around" halves. Essentially, once they're heated through, they're finished. Don't let them toughen up through neglect. Keep your eye on them and err on the side of pulling them sooner rather than later.

The key to fish dishes is to showcase their elegant flavors whilst providing counterpoints, elements of balance that complement but do not overwhelm.

One other important note: I believe that the more aware we are of the foods we eat, where they come from and how they are produced, the better for all involved. This is especially true when we are talking about fish and seafood because of the issues of overfishing and sustainability. Populations of certain types of fish, especially those that take longer to grow and mature, can be threatened when too many are "harvested," usually in response to market demand. Most responsible restaurateurs and fishmongers are aware of what species are threatened at any given time and will gladly offer alternative suggestions to you. This is an instance where personal awareness and changing one's habits, even temporarily, can have a beneficial effect on the environment, help to guarantee the health of the food business, and guarantee the availability of a great variety of healthy, fresh seafood for future generations.

Wasabi Honey-Crusted Black Cod and Green Apple–Red Cabbage Slaw with Curry Oil

SERVES 6

This recipe includes a homemade curry oil that needs to sit for a while and is best made at least a day in advance. The oil is delicious and versatile. It will keep well for a few weeks and would also be tasty in a chicken salad, over a garbanzo bean salad, or with couscous or a similar dish.

INGREDIENTS FOR THE CURRY OIL

1 teaspoon curry powder

⅓ cup canola oil

INGREDIENTS FOR THE SLAW

6 tablespoons apple cider vinegar

2 teaspoons packed brown sugar

½ teaspoon freshly ground black pepper

1 teaspoon salt

1 tablespoon (½ ounce) juice from a jar of pickled ginger

¼ cup canola oil

1 Granny Smith apple, skin left on, cored, sliced, and coated with lemon juice to keep it from browning

10 ounces shredded red cabbage, from about ½ cabbage (The medium slicing blade on the food processor does this beautifully.)

¼ cup pickled ginger from a jar

1 seedless cucumber, peeled and sliced into thin disks using a mandoline if you have one

2 ounces snow peas, julienned

2 ounces (about ¼ cup) canned bamboo shoots, rinsed to remove any tinny taste

INGREDIENTS FOR THE FISH

1 tablespoon wasabi paste (along with some prepared wasabi for the wasabi lovers at the table)

¼ cup honey

2 tablespoons unsalted butter, plus extra for the baking rack

2 cups panko (Japanese breadcrumbs)

Salt and pepper to taste

Six 6-ounce cod fillets

SPECIAL EQUIPMENT

Baking rack placed on a baking sheet

Method for the curry oil

Put the curry powder in a mixing bowl. Stir in a teaspoon at a time of the oil until the oil uniformly darkens and the mixture is the consistency of a crumbly paste. Add the remaining oil, stir well, and transfer to a mason-type jar. Seal the jar and let sit for 8 hours. This will keep up to 1 month in a cool, dry place.

Method for the slaw

Stir together the vinegar, brown sugar, pepper, salt, pickled ginger juice, and oil in a large bowl. Add the apple, cabbage, pickled ginger, cucumber, snow peas, and bamboo shoots and toss. Adjust the seasoning with salt and pepper as needed.

TIMELINE

Measure ingredients .... 5 minutes
Cut apple and toss with lemon juice .... 2 minutes
Shred cabbage in food processor .... 2 minutes
Cut cucumber and peas .... 2 minutes
Subtotal estimated prep time ....11 minutes

Pre heat oven, then:
Mix curry oil .... 3 minutes
Toss dressing together with slaw
    ingredients .... 3 minutes
Mix coating for fish .... 2 minutes
Bread fish .... 5 minutes
Bake fish in oven ....12 minutes
Subtotal active cooking time .... 25 minutes

Assembly .... 5 minutes

Total estimated time,
start to finish .... 41 minutes

Method for the fish

Move an oven shelf to the top level and preheat the oven to 400°F. Mix together the wasabi, honey, butter, panko, and salt and pepper. Place the fish on a buttered baking rack on a baking sheet. Press the panko mixture onto the surface of the fish. Bake on the top rack of the oven until the fish is just cooked through, about 12 to 15 minutes. The timing depends entirely on the thickness of the fish and your oven. Do not overcook. The fish is done when it springs back upon gentle pressing.

Presentation

Place the apple/cabbage slaw in the middle of a serving plate. Top with the crusted fish. Drizzle the curry oil on and around the fish. (See the photo for visual reference.)

Citrus-Braised Lobster Tails over Savory Corn "Cake"

SERVES 4

Using a binding agent such as cheese or mashed potatoes, which will enable you to mold other vegetables such as corn or beans into "cakes," is a great way to elevate your presentation to a new level.

INGREDIENTS FOR THE CORN

½ cup grapeseed oil

1 large red onion, diced

2 garlic cloves, chopped

¼ cup chopped fresh tarragon

¼ cup chopped fresh thyme

1½ pounds fresh corn kernels, from about 6 ears (or use frozen corn; canned corn will become gummy)

2 teaspoons salt

½ teaspoon freshly ground black pepper

3 ounces Boursin cheese

¼ cup chopped fresh chives

INGREDIENTS FOR THE LOBSTER AND BRAISING LIQUID

2 lemons

⅛ cup grapeseed oil

½ cup (1 stick) unsalted butter, melted

6 celery ribs, diced medium

2 large onions, diced medium

4 lobster tails

2 cups dry white wine

½ teaspoon salt

⅛ teaspoon freshly ground black pepper

2 tablespoons OLD BAY Seasoning

4 tablespoons (½ stick) unsalted butter, cut into cubes

TIMELINE

Ingredient prep:
Chop onion, garlic, herbs, corn,
    and celery .... 10 minutes
Sauté onion, garlic, herbs, and corn........ 5 minutes
Roasting time for corn mixture (35 minutes)
    Overlaps with (during last 20 minutes
        of roasting time):
    Microwave lemons (2 minutes)
    Sauté celery and onion for
        braising liquid (3 minutes)
    Place lobster tails, add wine,
        squeeze lemons, add seasonings,
        and cook until opaque (5 minutes)
    Remove lobster to rest, strain braising liquid,
        and return to pan to reduce (10 minutes)
    Overlaps with:
    Slice lobster ....35 minutes
Stir Boursin cheese into corn
    to let melt (2 minutes)
    Overlaps with:
    Finish sauce with butter (2 minutes).... 2 minutes
    Form corn cakes (5 minutes)
        and assemble .... 7 minutes

Total estimated time,
start to finish .... 59 minutes

Method for the corn

Preheat the oven to 375°F. In a large oven-safe skillet, add ¼ cup of oil and heat the pan over medium-low heat. Add the onion, garlic, tarragon, thyme, corn, salt, and pepper and sauté until the corn feels cooked to the bite, about 5 minutes. Place in the oven and roast until the corn is light golden brown, about 30 to 45 minutes (some ovens may need longer than others). (During the last 20 minutes of roasting time, start to prepare the braising liquid, below.)

Remove the corn mixture from the oven and adjust the seasoning with salt and pepper as needed. Crumble the Boursin cheese onto the corn and set it aside to melt. The cheese will bind the corn together so that it can be easily molded into rounds. When the cheese has melted a bit, stir it into the corn. (Meanwhile, whisk the butter into the sauce to finish, below.)

Method for the lobster and sauce

While the corn is roasting, prepare the braising liquid. Place the lemons in a small bowl and microwave them for a minute or so to release the essential oils. They will be hot, so set them aside just until they are cool enough to handle. (If you let them cool too long the oils will be reabsorbed.) In a large lidded sauté pan deep enough to accommodate the lobster tails when covered, heat the oil and butter over medium-high heat. Add the celery and onions and sauté until the onions are translucent, about 5 minutes. Place the lobster tails in the pan and pour the white wine over them. Cut the lemons in half and squeeze them over the lobster, tossing the rinds into the pan. Season the lobster with the salt, pepper, and OLD BAY Seasoning, cover, and cook until the shells are red and the meat is opaque, about 5 minutes.

Remove the lobster to a utility platter, cover to keep warm, and let rest.

Strain the pan liquids into a bowl, return them to the pan, and reduce the liquid by half over medium-high heat, about 8 to 10 minutes.

Meanwhile, remove the lobster from the shells and slice the meat into ¼-inch-thick disks.

Remove the pan of reduced liquid from the heat and whisk in the butter to make a sauce. Cover and keep warm.

Presentation

Fill a 4-inch circular pastry cutter with the corn mixture in the center of each plate and carefully remove the cutter. Place slices of lobster tail on top and around the corn. Spoon the sauce around the corn. Sprinkle with the chives and serve. (The finished dish is shown in the photo insert.)

Crispy Crab and Smoked Salmon Cakes with Baby Arugula and Mango Aioli

SERVES 4

These cakes can be made with less expensive backfin crabmeat so you can make fresh crab cakes without worrying about exceeding your budget. Despite this, even crab cake connoisseurs will agree that these are exceptional.

INGREDIENTS FOR THE MANGO AIOLI AND ARUGULA

½ large ripe fresh mango, peeled, pitted, and sliced

3 tablespoons mayonnaise

2 tablespoons finely chopped cilantro, plus 6 small sprigs for garnish

Salt and white pepper to taste

2 cups baby arugula, soaked in salt water to remove grit, thoroughly rinsed, dried in a salad spinner, tender parts of leaves torn into bite-size pieces

INGREDIENTS FOR THE CRAB AND SALMON CAKES

8 ounces (½ pound) cooked fresh backfin or lump crabmeat, such as Graham and Rollins Old Point Comfort brand (avoid using canned)

2 tablespoons scallions, white and tender green parts only, cut into thin diagonal slices

1 tablespoon capers

1 tablespoon chopped fresh parsley leaves

Finely grated zest of 1 lemon

¼ cup whipped cream cheese

¼ teaspoon salt

⅛ teaspoon ground black pepper

¾ pound smoked sliced salmon, cut into ½-inch pieces

1 cup panko (Japanese breadcrumbs)

2 tablespoons grapeseed oil

Method for the mango aioli

Add the mango, mayonnaise, and cilantro to a food processor or blender and blend until smooth. Season with salt and white pepper to taste. Refrigerate until needed.

Method for the crab and salmon cakes

Preheat the oven to 350°F. Carefully examine the crabmeat without breaking up the lumps, removing any bits of shell or cartilage. Gently squeeze the crabmeat to remove any excess liquid, but it should still be moist. Place the scallions, capers, parsley, lemon zest, cream cheese, salt, and pepper in a medium bowl and combine well. Then fold the crabmeat and salmon into the mixture so that it's just combined and the crab is not broken or mashed. Divide the mixture into 4 portions and shape into cakes about 2 to 3 inches in diameter and 1½ inches high. Pat the panko onto the tops and bottoms of the cakes. Heat the grapeseed oil in an ovenproof skillet over medium-high heat. Add the crab and salmon cakes and cook undisturbed for about 2 minutes, or until golden on one side. (To keep the cakes from breaking apart, it is important to let them sear long enough to achieve some integrity on the cooked surface. But watch carefully so that they don't burn.) Flip the cakes over and put the skillet into the oven for 3 to 8 minutes to allow them to set up. Remove the crab cakes and let them rest briefly.

Presentation

Arrange the arugula on a serving plate, top with a crab and salmon cake, spoon the mango aioli around, and garnish with a cilantro sprig. (The finished dish is shown in the photo insert.)

Tuna with Portobello Mushrooms and Ruby Port Reduction over Citrus Rice

SERVES 6

This is staggeringly easy to make, and staggeringly delicious.

INGREDIENTS FOR THE CITRUS RICE

1 cup long-grain white rice

Zest of 1 large orange

1 large orange, peeled and cut into ½-inch
    segments without any pith

1 tablespoon unsalted butter

1 teaspoon salt

¼ teaspoon cracked black pepper (such as
    McCormick brand)

**INGREDIENTS FOR THE PORTOBELLO
MUSHROOMS AND RUBY PORT REDUCTION**

½ cup (1 stick) unsalted butter

2 shallots, minced

6 portobello mushrooms, cleaned with a soft
    brush, gills removed with the tip of a
    kitchen spoon, and sliced into ¼-inch-
    thick strips

1 cup ruby port

1 cup chicken stock

Salt and pepper to taste

INGREDIENTS FOR THE TUNA

2 tablespoons unsalted butter

Six 6-ounce tuna steaks

1 tablespoon lemon pepper

Salt to taste

6 small parsley sprigs

TIMELINE

Ingredient prep:

Grate orange zest .... 2 minutes

Segment orange .... 2 minutes

Brush portobello mushrooms,
    remove gills with tip of teaspoon,
    and slice into strips .... 10 minutes

Measure ingredients .... 2 minutes

Boil rice with orange zest
    and segments (20 minutes)
    Overlaps with:
    Sauté shallots for
        mushroom/sauce (2 minutes)
    Cook portobellos until
        softened (8 minutes)
    Deglaze mushroom pot with port
        and allow to evaporate (8 minutes)

Add chicken stock to mushrooms and allow to
    reduce (7 minutes)

Remove rice from heat and let stand (5 minutes)
    .... 25 minutes

Season tuna, heat pan, and
    sear tuna steaks .... 5 minutes

Allow to rest to carry-over cook .... 5 minutes

Assembly .... 5 minutes

***Total estimated time,
start to finish*** .... **56 minutes**

Method for the rice

Bring 2½ cups water to a boil in a medium saucepan over medium-high heat. Stir in the rice, orange zest and pieces, butter, salt, and pepper. Return to a boil, cover, reduce the heat to low, and cook for 20 minutes, leaving the lid undisturbed. Remove from the heat and let sit 5 minutes.

Method for mushrooms and reduction

Melt the butter over medium heat in a saucepan or skillet and sauté the shallots until translucent, 1 or 2 minutes. Add the portobello mushrooms and cook until they begin to release their juices and lightly caramelize, about 8 to 10 minutes, stirring often to keep them covered with butter and to make sure the butter does not burn. Deglaze the pan with the port. When most of the alcohol has evaporated and you see just a light coating of the port left on the bottom of the pan, about 8 to 10 minutes, add the chicken stock and simmer until the liquid has reduced by half, another 8 to 10 minutes or so. Season to taste with salt and pepper.

Method for the tuna

I usually cook the tuna medium rare; however, if you like the tuna well done (cooked through instead of dark pink), preheat the oven to 375°F. Melt the butter over medium-high heat in another large skillet with an oven-safe handle. Season the tuna with the lemon pepper and salt and sear each side for about 2 minutes undisturbed, to allow the surface to caramelize and for the flavors to integrate into the surface of the fish. Remove to a utility platter and let the tuna carry-over cook to medium rare. However, if you want the tuna to be well done, transfer the entire pan to the oven to finish for about 5 to 8 more minutes. (The fish is done when the surface springs back upon being lightly prodded. *Do not overcook it.*) If you have the pan in the oven, *make sure you use an oven mitt to remove it and keep that volcanically hot handle covered until it cools off.*

Presentation

Spoon some citrus rice onto the center of a serving plate. Top with a tuna steak and spoon some mushrooms around. Drizzle the port sauce on top. Garnish with a parsley sprig.

Herb-Steamed Halibut Fillet with Rock Shrimp Sauce, Braised Greens, Plum Tomatoes, and Chive Essence

SERVES 6

Garlic, dark green leafy vegetables, fresh tomatoes, and herbs with fish—if we ate like this every day, we'd probably add ten years to our lives!

INGREDIENTS FOR THE GREENS, TOMATOES, AND SAUCE

1 head of garlic

2 tablespoons grapeseed oil

1 cup long-grain white rice

1 teaspoon salt

1 tablespoon butter

1 bunch broccoli rabe (about 1 pound), soaked in salt water to remove grit, tough stems removed, and torn into bite-sized pieces

1 cup vegetable stock

Salt and freshly ground black pepper to taste

6 fresh plum tomatoes, skins scored lengthwise with 4 evenly spaced slashes

2 cups dry white wine

Six 4- to 6-ounce halibut fillets

3 tablespoons finely chopped flat-leaf parsley leaves (from about 8 or 9 sprigs)

6 large fresh thyme sprigs, leaves stripped from the stems and minced

3 ounces fresh garlic chives (about a handful)

½ pound 31-40-size shrimp, deveined, peeled, tails removed, and chopped into small pieces (This size is economical, yet still easy to peel.), or rock shrimp

TIMELINE

Preheat oven to 425°F, slice root end off head of garlic, wrap in heavy foil, pour oil over, and roast (30 minutes)
Overlaps with:
Boil rice (20 minutes)
Overlaps with:
Rinse and cut broccoli rabe and herbs (5 minutes)
Cook broccoli rabe in stock (7 minutes)
Boil water and blanch tomatoes (3 minutes)
Cut and remove seeds from tomatoes (2 minutes)
Add wine to stock and let reduce (15 minutes)
Overlaps with:
Remove rice from heat and let stand (5 minutes)
Season and steam fish (6 minutes)
Steam garlic chives (3 minutes) .... 30 minutes
Remove garlic from oven and foil, and let cool (2 minutes)
Overlaps with:
Cook shrimp in sauce (2 minutes) .... 2 minutes
Squeeze garlic cloves into greens/ tomatoes and toss .... 3 minutes

Assembly .... 3 minutes

Total estimated time, start to finish .... 38 minutes

Method for the greens, tomatoes, and sauce

Preheat the oven to 425°F. Slice the root end off the entire head of garlic and turn it upside down, wrapping it in aluminum foil and molding the foil so it allows the cut end to stand upright in the oven. Pour 1 tablespoon of the oil on the garlic so it slips between the skin and the cloves and enclose the garlic head with the foil and place in a baking pan. Roast until sweet and tender, about 30 minutes.

To make the rice, bring 2½ cups of water to a boil over medium heat. Add the rice, salt, and butter and return to a boil. Lower the heat, cover, and boil undisturbed for 20 minutes.

While the rice is cooking, add the broccoli rabe and vegetable stock to a medium saucepan. Season with salt and pepper and cook, covered, over medium-high heat until tender but still bright green, about 7 to 10 minutes.

While the broccoli rabe is cooking, bring a pot of salted water to a boil and blanch the tomatoes for about 1 minute. Slip off the skins, cut off the stem ends, and halve lengthwise. Scrape out the seeds if there are a lot of them and discard, and place the tomatoes in a large mixing bowl.

Use a slotted spoon to remove the broccoli rabe to the bowl with the tomatoes and set aside in a warm place, leaving the juices in the pot. Then add the white wine to the vegetable stock in which the broccoli rabe was cooked to make a sauce. Turn the heat to medium and let reduce by half, about 10 to 15 minutes. Set the pan aside in a warm place.

Remove the rice from the heat and let stand, covered, for 5 minutes. (Meanwhile, begin the fish and chive essence, below.)

Remove the garlic from the oven and set it aside until it is cool enough to handle.

While the garlic chives are steaming, bring the sauce to a simmer again over low heat, stir in the shrimp, and remove the pan from the heat when they turn pink.

Gently squeeze the roasted garlic cloves directly from their papery skins into the bowl of broccoli rabe and tomatoes, keeping the sweet cloves somewhat intact. Toss together gently and season to taste with salt and pepper.

Method for the fish and chive essence

Season the halibut fillets with salt and pepper. Fill a large skillet with about an inch of water. Set a rack in or over the skillet, with the surface not touching the water, and lay the fillets on the rack. Sprinkle some parsley and thyme on each fillet. Cover the rack and pan with a lid of foil, bring the water to a boil over medium heat, and steam the fish until fork-tender, about 5 minutes.

While the fish is steaming, steam the garlic chives until tender in a separate pot fitted with a steamer. Remove the garlic chives to a plate until just cool enough to handle. Mince the steamed garlic chives, place them in a small bowl, and mash them into a paste with the back of a spoon (or with a mortar and pestle), seasoning with salt and pepper to taste.

Presentation

Fluff up the rice using a small bit of water if necessary to remoisten it. Place some rice in the center of each serving plate and spoon some of the broccoli rabe mixture around it. Top the rice with a fish fillet and spoon some shrimp sauce over the fish. Finish with a small dollop of the chive paste.

Ocean Perch over Herbed Couscous with Baby Bok Choy and Lemon Horseradish Sauce

SERVES 4

The test of a well-developed palate is the ability to recognize and appreciate the subtle and delicate flavors in addition to the more prominent ones. This dish is like a meditation. The texture and flavors are quiet and poignant on one hand, with a burst of inspiration from the horseradish on the other.

INGREDIENTS FOR THE BABY BOK CHOY

4 baby bok choy

2 tablespoons unsalted butter

Pinch of nutmeg

2 teaspoons sugar

INGREDIENTS FOR THE COUSCOUS

I cup couscous

4 tablespoons unsalted butter (2 tablespoons for the herbs, 2 tablespoons for the couscous)

1 shallot clove, minced

1 tablespoon minced fresh flat-leaf parsley

1 tablespoon minced fresh tarragon

Salt and freshly ground black pepper to taste

INGREDIENTS FOR THE OCEAN PERCH

Four 4- to 6-ounce ocean perch fillets (also delicious with tilapia)

1 cup milk, or as needed for breading

1 cup fresh breadcrumbs, or as needed for breading, seasoned with salt and pepper

2 tablespoons grapeseed oil

INGREDIENTS FOR THE LEMON HORSERADISH SAUCE

1 lemon

⅛ cup prepared horseradish

¼ cup white wine

4 tablespoons unsalted butter, cubed

Salt to taste

White pepper to taste

Method for the baby bok choy

Steam or boil the baby bok choy in salted water until just tender, about 5 minutes. (Meanwhile, start the couscous, below.)

Remove the bok choy from the heat and set aside until needed in a colander placed over a plate to drain well. (Start the herbs for the couscous, below.)

Using the same skillet you used for the herbs for the couscous, add the butter and melt over medium heat. Slice the bok choy in half lengthwise so that you have 8 pieces and sprinkle the cut sides with nutmeg and sugar. Add the baby bok choy to the pan, sliced-side down, and cook until the cut side has caramelized, about 3 to 5 minutes, taking care not to burn the butter or the bok choy. Remove to a utility platter, cover, and set aside. (Use the same skillet to sauté the fish now.)

Method for the couscous

As the bok choy is steaming, bring 2 cups of water to a boil in a medium saucepan. Add the couscous, return to a boil, cover, and remove from the heat. Let stand for 5 minutes. (Meanwhile, remove the bok choy from the heat.)

Melt 2 tablespoons of butter over medium heat in a large skillet. Sauté the shallot, parsley, tarragon, and salt and pepper until the shallot turns translucent, about 2 minutes. Stir the herbs into the pot of couscous, reserving the sauté pan. Cover the couscous and keep it warm. (Sauté the drained bok choy now.)

Just before serving, stir in a bit of water to refresh/rehydrate the couscous, along with the remaining 2 tablespoons of butter.

Method for the ocean perch

Moisten the fish fillets in the milk, then roll them in breadcrumbs seasoned with salt and pepper, pressing to make the breadcrumbs adhere.

Using the same pan you used for the bok choy and herbs, add 1 tablespoon of grapeseed oil over medium-high heat (reserving the rest of the oil for when you flip the fish fillets). When it begins to shimmer, add the breaded fillets and let sear for a few minutes *undisturbed* to allow the seasonings to integrate into the surface of the fish and prevent "crusting off." When you see the edges beginning to brown, add the rest of the oil to the pan if needed, flip the fillets, and cook the other side undisturbed in the same way.

Perch is a delicate fish that cooks quickly. Because of carry-over cooking, the fillets will continue to cook for a few minutes even after you remove them from the pan and will most likely be done by the time you finish the sauce. (If not, you can always put them in a 375°F oven for a few minutes to finish.) Transfer the fish to a platter, cover to keep warm, and use the same pan to make the sauce.

Method for the lemon horseradish sauce

Squeeze the juice from the lemon into the hot pan and add the horseradish. Return to medium-high heat and, stirring constantly, add the white wine to deglaze the surface of the pan and combine the flavors. Increase the heat to medium-high and allow the liquid to reduce quickly, about 2 minutes. Season with salt and pepper, remove from the heat, and strain into a small bowl. Gradually whisk in the butter to finish. (Finish the couscous now.)

Presentation

Spoon about ½ cup of herbed couscous into the center of each serving plate. Top with a perch fillet and spoon 1 or 2 teaspoons of the sauce over the fish. Arrange 2 bok choy halves on the plate, seared-side up, flanking the couscous. (The finished dish is shown in the photo insert.)

Pan-Seared Salmon and Lemon Confit over Sage Ratatouille

SERVES 6

This dish is a veritable celebration of herbs and might inspire you to plant an herb garden, even if it's only on the windowsill.

INGREDIENTS FOR THE RATATOUILLE

12 small red potatoes (about 1 pound), well scrubbed and sliced ¼ inch thick (The slicing blade of a food processor works well.)

⅛ cup grapeseed oil

1 shallot, diced small

1 head of fennel, sliced ¼ inch thick (The slicing blade of a food processor works well.)

½ pound haricots verts, trimmed and sliced to 1 or 1½ inches in length

1 small or medium zucchini, skin on, sliced into ¼-inch-thick disks

2 tablespoons minced fresh sage (from about 4 to 6 leaves)

2 teaspoons minced fresh oregano, or ½ teaspoon dried

1 tablespoon minced fresh thyme, or 1 teaspoon dried

1 teaspoon minced fresh rosemary, or 1 pinch dried, ground to a powder with a mortar and pestle

2 tablespoons tomato paste

1 cup dry red or white wine

1 teaspoon dried lavender (such as McCormick brand), ground to a powder with a mortar and pestle

Salt and freshly ground black pepper to taste

4 tablespoons Boursin cheese

8 snipped fennel fronds, for garnish

INGREDIENTS FOR THE LEMON CONFIT

½ cup sugar

⅛ teaspoon salt

½ teaspoon xanthan gum, optional (usually sold with the dietetic foods or gluten-free flours)

1 tablespoon cornstarch, made into a slurry with ¼ cup water

Zest and juice of 3 lemons

1 tablespoon honey

2 egg yolks

2 tablespoons unsalted butter, cut into small chunks

INGREDIENTS FOR THE SALMON

1 to 2 tablespoons grapeseed oil, or as needed to sear the fish

Six 6-ounce salmon fillets

Salt and freshly ground black pepper to taste

1½ teaspoons dried dill

6 small fresh dill sprigs, for garnish

SPECIAL EQUIPMENT

Candy thermometer

Method for the ratatouille

Parboil the potatoes for 5 minutes in a small saucepan of water. Meanwhile, in a large sauté pan or skillet with a cover, heat the oil over medium heat. Sauté the shallot, fennel, haricots verts, zucchini, sage, oregano, thyme, and rosemary until the shallot becomes translucent, about 2 to 3 minutes. Stir in the tomato paste and fold in the potatoes. Pour the wine into the pan and season with the lavender and salt and pepper. Allow to cook until all the vegetables are tender, about 35 to 40 minutes, being careful not to overcook. (Meanwhile, make the lemon confit, and start on the salmon when the ratatouille has 15 minutes more to cook.)

When the salmon has been cooked, remove the vegetables from the heat and crumble the Boursin cheese on top. Cover and let sit to rest and to allow the cheese to melt.

Method for the lemon confit

While the vegetables are cooking, whisk together the sugar, salt, xanthan gum, and cornstarch slurry in a medium saucepan until well mixed. Blend in the lemon zest and juice and honey. Whisk in the egg yolks until no yellow streaks remain. Add the butter and whisking constantly bring the mixture to 160°F (as measured with a candy thermometer) over low heat. Simmer for 1 minute and remove from the heat. Place a sheet of plastic wrap directly on the surface of the sauce and set aside until needed.

Method for the salmon

In the last 15 minutes of cooking time for the ratatouille, preheat the oven to 325°F. Heat the oil in a large skillet with oven-safe handles over medium-high heat. Season the salmon fillets with salt and pepper and dried dill, and sear the fish on both sides, leaving each side undisturbed for the first 2 minutes so that the seasonings integrate into the surface of the fish and the caramelization process begins (which will keep the fish from tearing). Transfer the

TIMELINE

Ingredient prep:
Dice shallot and trim haricots verts......... 5 minutes
Slice fennel, zucchini, and potatoes
   in food processor.. 4 minutes
Mince herbs .... 2 minutes
Grate lemon zest and juice lemons........... 5 minutes
Measure ingredients .... 5 minutes
Estimated prep time for ingredients ... 21 minutes

Active cooking time:
Parboil potatoes.. 5 minutes
Sauté vegetables .... 5 minutes
Add tomato paste, fold in potatoes,
   and add wine and seasonings................ 3 minutes
Cooking time for ratatouille (35 minutes)
  Overlaps with:
  Make lemon confit (10 minutes)
  Sear both sides of salmon (6 minutes)
  Finish salmon in oven (8 minutes) .....35 minutes
Allow Boursin cheese to melt...................... 2 minutes
Subtotal active cooking time .... 45 minutes

Assembly ....5 minutes

Total estimated time .... 1 hour and 11 minutes

pan to the oven to finish for about 5 to 8 minutes, taking care not to overcook the fish. (It's done when the surface of the salmon springs back upon being lightly prodded.) (Meanwhile, finish the ratatouille.)

Presentation

Place some ratatouille in the center of a serving plate, sprinkle with fennel fronds, and top with a salmon fillet. Spoon some lemon confit on the salmon. Garnish with a dill sprig. (The finished dish is shown in the photo insert.)

Thyme-Roasted Sea Bass
with Shrimp Fritters, Sweet Corn, and Roasted Garlic Essence

SERVES 4

This recipe goes more quickly if you have roasted garlic on hand; roasted garlic lasts in the refrigerator for a number of weeks.

INGREDIENTS FOR THE CORN

1 head of garlic

¼ cup grapeseed oil (1 tablespoon for the garlic, 3 tablespoons for the corn)

1 pound fresh corn kernels, from about 4 to 6 ears (or 1 pound frozen corn; do not use canned because it becomes gummy)

Salt and freshly ground black pepper to taste

INGREDIENTS FOR THE SHRIMP AND SAUCE

Four U-10–size (very large) shrimp, deveined, with shells and heads on, if possible

1 tablespoon grapeseed oil

1 cup fumet (fish stock) or seafood stock (such as Kitchen Basics brand)

1 tablespoon unsalted butter, plus 1 stick cold unsalted butter, cut into ½-inch pieces

2 tablespoons chopped shallot

¼ cup dry white wine

1 large thyme sprig

Kosher salt and freshly ground black pepper to taste

INGREDIENTS FOR THE FRITTER BATTER

¾ cup all-purpose flour

1 teaspoon baking powder

⅛ teaspoon salt

4 teaspoons canola oil (plus 1 to 4 liters as needed for frying or deep-frying)

¾ cup milk

1 egg

Freshly ground black pepper to taste

INGREDIENTS FOR THE SEA BASS

1 cup all-purpose flour

Kosher salt and freshly ground black pepper to taste

Four 4-ounce sea bass fillets, skin on

½ cup milk, or as needed to moisten the fish fillets

4 tablespoons (½ stick) unsalted butter

4 tablespoons grapeseed oil

¼ cup chopped fresh thyme (from about 12 sprigs)

1 lemon, cut into 4 wedges

SPECIAL EQUIPMENT

Deep fryer (optional)

Method for the garlic essence and sweet corn

For this recipe, the garlic is roasted a bit first and then the corn is added to continue roasting. Preheat the oven to 425°F. Slice the root end off the entire head of garlic and turn it upside down, wrapping it in aluminum foil and molding the foil so it allows the cut end to stand upright in the oven. Pour 1 tablespoon of oil on the garlic so it slips between the skin and the cloves, and enclose the garlic head with the foil. Roast the garlic about 15 minutes. Lower the oven temperature to 350°F and set the garlic aside until it is cool enough to handle.

In a large oven-safe skillet, heat 3 tablespoons of the grapeseed oil over medium heat. Add the corn, stir to coat with oil, and cook until the corn feels cooked to the bite, about 5 minutes. Gently squeeze the roasted garlic cloves into the pan with the corn. Season with salt and pepper and gently toss together. Making sure the oven has had time to lower in temperature to 350°F, roast the corn/garlic mixture until pleasantly golden, about 25 minutes.

Method for the sauce

While the corn and garlic are roasting, peel the shrimp to obtain the shells and heads and return the shrimp to the refrigerator. Heat 1 tablespoon of grapeseed oil in a skillet over medium-high heat. Add the shells and cook for about 2 minutes, or until they turn pink, then add the fumet. Simmer until the liquid has reduced by half. Strain into a bowl, discarding the shells and reserving the liquid. Melt the tablespoon of butter over medium heat in the same pan. Add the shallot and cook for 1 minute. Add the wine, thyme sprig, and reduced fumet and cook until again reduced by half. (This intensifies the flavor.)

TIMELINE

Preroast garlic cloves (15 minutes)
Overlaps with:
Ingredient prep: Strip corn kernels from cobs
   (unless using frozen)................................. 5 minutes
Chop shallots and herbs.............................. 2 minutes
Measure ingredients...................................... 2 minutes
Subtotal prep time ....**9 minutes**

Sauté corn... 5 minutes
Remove garlic from oven, add to corn,
   and roast (25 minutes)
Overlaps with:
   Peel shrimp (2 minutes)
   Cook shells (2 minutes)
   Reduce fumet (10 minutes)
   Strain sauce (2 minutes)
   Sauté shallots (1 minute)
   Reduce wine (5 minutes)
   Whisk in butter and strain (3 minutes)
   Set bowl in hot water to keep warm (1 minute)
   Remove corn/garlic from oven and
      cover to keep warm...........................25 minutes
Make fritter batter... 2 minutes
Dredge sea bass... 2 minutes
Sauté sea bass.. 6 minutes
Place sea bass in oven
   Overlaps with:
   Deep-fry shrimp .... 2 minutes
Subtotal active cooking time.............. **42 minutes**

Assembly ....**5 minutes**

Total estimated time (5 minutes
less with frozen corn)........................**56 minutes**

Turn the heat down to low and whisk in the stick of butter a piece at a time, adding each piece only after the previous one has melted. Strain through a fine-mesh sieve into a small bowl and season with salt and pepper. Set the bowl into a small saucepan of hot water to keep warm.

Method for the fritter batter

Combine the flour, baking powder, and salt in a large bowl. In a smaller bowl, whisk together the oil, milk, egg, and black pepper. Add the egg mixture to the flour mixture and combine until all the dry ingredients are moistened. Heat the oil in a sauté pan over medium-high heat until it shimmers, or in a deep fryer to 325°F, or as suggested by the manufacturer for similar foods. (Meanwhile, start to prepare the sea bass fillets.)

Method for the sea bass

Preheat the oven to 375°F. Season the flour with salt and pepper, moisten the sea bass fillets with the milk, and lightly dredge them in the flour mixture, allowing any excess to fall away. In a large ovenproof skillet over medium-high heat, melt 2 tablespoons of butter in 2 tablespoons of grapeseed oil (reserving the rest of the butter and oil). Sprinkle some thyme into the pan where you are going to place the first fillet and immediately place a fillet onto the thyme, flesh-side down. Working quickly, do the same with the remaining fillets. Allow the fish to cook for about 3 minutes undisturbed to allow the thyme to integrate into the surface of the fish and avoid tearing the fish. Add the remaining oil and butter to the pan. Lift a fillet, sprinkle a little more thyme in the pan, and flip the fillet onto the thyme to cook the other side. Repeat with the other fillets and cook for 2 to 3 minutes more. If the fish does not spring back when lightly prodded, place it in the oven for 2 minutes or so to finish, but do not overcook.

Method for the shrimp fritters

While the fish is cooking, place each shrimp on a slotted spoon, and holding over the bowl of fritter batter, ladle enough of the batter over it to coat. Deep-fry in hot oil until golden brown, about 2 to 3 minutes, and drain.

Presentation

Place some of the corn and garlic mixture in the center of a serving plate. Top with the fish and spoon the sauce over and around. Place a shrimp fritter on the fish. Garnish with a wedge of lemon (for squeezing onto the shrimp).

Seared Sea Scallops
with Shelling Bean Salad

SERVES 4

As the fruits of bean plants, beans in their pods go through levels of maturation before they're mature seeds. Young beans are eaten in their tender pods, the way we're familiar with eating string beans. Mature beans, those capable of germination, are dried, and if they're to be consumed as food, need to be cooked slowly. In between those two stages are the shelling beans, which—in a typical growing season—are available in late summer. They are semi-mature beans that are "shelled" from their pods. I acknowledge that it's not always easy to obtain fresh shelling beans, but I'd hate to think you'll miss out on this beautiful dish because the elements aren't in season. I would advise using canned beans in varieties that complement each other in color and shape, maybe butter beans with small red beans or fava beans with cannellini beans. But if at all possible at the end of the summer, do the Tom Sawyer thing, sit out on the back porch, and enjoy the pleasure of popping some fresh shelling beans out of their pods.

INGREDIENTS FOR THE SHELLING BEAN SALAD

1 carrot, peeled, quartered lengthwise, and cut crosswise into ¼-inch-thick pieces

1 celery rib, cut crosswise into ¼-inch-thick slices

1 small onion, diced

1 bay leaf

1 tablespoon fresh thyme leaves (stripped from about 2 or 3 fresh sprigs)

2 cups mixed "shelling beans," such as borlotti, cannellini, cranberry, garbanzo, and/or flageolet beans (about 2 pounds, shelled and kept separate by variety), or the equivalent amount of canned beans

Kosher salt

2 tablespoons olive oil

¼ cup finely diced shallots

½ teaspoon minced garlic

1 tablespoon chopped fresh flat-leaf parsley leaves

Freshly ground black pepper

½ cup finely diced Manchego cheese

INGREDIENTS FOR THE SCALLOPS

8 large dry-packed sea scallops (U-10 size, about 1½ ounces each)

Kosher salt and freshly ground black pepper

2 tablespoons olive oil

2 thinly sliced avocados (about 20 slices, 5 per plate)

Spanish smoked paprika

Unfiltered olive oil or any artisanal extra virgin olive oil

Aged Spanish sherry vinegar

Method for the shelling bean salad

To cook canned beans, combine the carrot, celery, onion, bay leaf, thyme, and beans with about 4 tablespoons of their liquid in a 2 to 2½-quart saucepan. Cook over medium heat until the vegetables are soft and the flavors integrate, about 15 to 20 minutes.

To cook fresh shelling beans, put the carrot, celery, onion, bay leaf, thyme, and enough water to cook the beans (about 8 cups) into a large pot and bring to a boil on medium-high heat. Decrease the heat to medium-low (or whatever setting on your stove enables you to maintain a simmer (just below a boil) and cook for 30 minutes. Strain the cooking liquid into a large bowl, discard the solids, and wash out and dry the pot. Return the vegetable liquid to the saucepan and bring to a boil over medium-high heat. (Meanwhile, wash and dry the bowl so that it will be ready for each variety of beans as it is finished, and prepare a large bowl of ice water for shocking the beans.) Cook the beans in the vegetable liquid one variety at a time, so that you can monitor when each type is tender to the bite and no hard or chalky core remains. Bring each variety to a boil and skim off and discard the foam. Decrease the heat to maintain a simmer and cook for 10 to 20 minutes, depending on the kind of bean. Use a slotted spoon to scoop out the beans into a strainer and plunge the strainer full of beans into the bowl of ice water. Transfer the beans to the waiting bowl and proceed with cooking the next bean variety. (You can refrigerate the beans in their cooking liquid for up to 4 days. If you choose to do this, remove the pot of cooking liquid from the heat when all the beans have been cooked and season it well with salt. When the liquid has cooled, add the beans back to the pot.)

To prepare the bean salad, heat the oil in a large sauté pan or skillet over medium heat. Add the shallots and garlic and cook for 1 minute. Add the beans and 2 tablespoons of their cooking liquid and warm through, stirring occasionally for 2 to 3 minutes. Remove from the heat, add the parsley, and season to taste with salt and pepper. Toss the cheese with the warm beans.

```
┌─────────────────────────────────────────┐
│                TIMELINE                   │
│                                           │
│ Ingredient prep:                          │
│ Chop carrot, celery, onion, shallots,     │
│    and garlic ...................... 10 minutes │
│ Mince herbs ......................... 5 minutes │
│ Slice avocados ...................... 5 minutes │
│ Dice cheese ......................... 2 minutes │
│ Estimated subtotal for                    │
│    ingredient prep ............. 22 minutes │
│                                           │
│ Cook time for vegetables and beans ..... 15 minutes │
│ Sauté shallots and garlic; mix with beans │
│    and cheese to make warm salad ...... 5 minutes │
│ While cheese is melting, cook scallops .. 8 minutes │
│ Let scallops rest while you               │
│    begin assembly ................... 5 minutes │
│                                           │
│ Total estimated time ............ 55 minutes │
│                                           │
│ Add time to shell fresh beans             │
│ at summer's end (+45 minutes)             │
│                                           │
│ Additional cooking time for               │
│ fresh beans (+50 minutes)                 │
└─────────────────────────────────────────┘
```

Method for the scallops

Season the scallops with salt and pepper. Heat a large skillet over high heat, add the oil, and heat for a few seconds more until it shimmers. Add the scallops and cook undisturbed until you see the edges begin to turn golden brown, about 4 minutes. This will let the seasonings integrate into the scallops and allow the surface to caramelize slightly to prevent tearing. Turn the scallops over and cook the other side the same way. The scallops should be 90 percent opaque on the inside—just check the opacity on the side of the scallop as it cooks. Remove the pan from the heat and let rest. Because of carry-over cooking, the scallops will continue to cook and are less likely to overcook.

Presentation

For each serving, arrange the avocado slices in a ring in the center of a dinner plate, leaving a space in the center. Mound the beans in the center and place 2 scallops on top of the beans. Dust with paprika and drizzle with some unfiltered or artisanal oil and sherry vinegar.

Sea Scallops over Leeks with Mango Curry Chocolate Sauce

SERVES 4

This recipe is an opportunity for chocolate lovers to use one of their favorite foods as an ingredient in a savory meal. I had the opportunity to film an episode of *Dinner: Impossible* at the famed Hershey headquarters in the Pennsylvania town named for the company and its founder. My challenge was to use chocolate in all the courses of a meal prepared for a group of chocolate experts. Since then I've had a lot of people ask me for nondessert chocolate-based recipes, and I think you'll enjoy this entrée served over rice or rice noodles.

This dish exemplifies the use of carry-over cooking—the fact that all foods will continue to cook even after you've removed them from the heat—to one's advantage. You can train yourself to master the timing of carry-over cooking so that it takes over and finishes the cooking process to perfection. Large scallops—such as the ones used here—are good test subjects for this course in Carry-over Cooking 101 because you can very easily see how opaque (done) a scallop is by looking at its side. You leave the scallop to sear undisturbed for the first couple of minutes *on each side* to allow the seasonings to adhere to the surface and to achieve a nice finish that prevents the fish from tearing. Then—when both sides are seared—you're free to turn the scallop to allow it to cook further. When the scallops look opaque about a third of the way in from both the top and bottom, set them aside, covered with a pot lid, to allow carry-over cooking to take over and finish the job for you. The goal is to have a completely opaque scallop that's not dry inside and hasn't split.

INGREDIENTS

3 tablespoons grapeseed oil (1 tablespoon for the leeks, 1 tablespoon for the onion and garlic, and 1 tablespoon for the scallops)

4 tablespoons (½ stick) unsalted butter (1 tablespoon for the leeks, 1 tablespoon for the scallops, and 2 tablespoons for the sauce)

4 leeks, white and tender greens parts only, soaked in salt water to remove the grit and sliced on the bias into ½-inch pieces

1 onion, peeled and thinly sliced into rings

1 garlic clove, peeled and thinly sliced

2 cups mango-peach juice (preferably with no sugar added)

2 tablespoons mild curry paste

½ cup Hershey's Special Dark Chocolate Chips

1 pound rice noodles or 1 cup white rice (cooked with 1 tablespoon butter and 1 teaspoon salt) as an optional accompaniment

Eight U-10–size sea scallops

2 teaspoons chili powder

2 teaspoons Hershey's Cocoa Special Dark Chocolate

Salt and freshly ground black pepper to taste

¼ cup sour cream

Method

Heat 1 tablespoon of grapeseed oil over medium heat in a large sauté pan and melt in 1 tablespoon of butter (reserving the rest of the oil and butter). Reduce the heat to low and slowly cook the leeks until tender, stirring occasionally, about 30 minutes.

While the leeks are cooking, start the mango curry chocolate sauce. In a medium saucepan, heat 1 tablespoon of oil over medium heat and sauté the onion and garlic until the onion becomes translucent, about 5 minutes. Add the mango-peach juice and curry paste and let reduce by two thirds. Reduce the heat to low, whisk in the chocolate chips, and cook for about 5 minutes to melt the chocolate and integrate the flavors.

If you'll be serving rice noodles as an accompaniment, begin cooking the pasta in boiling water. If you're serving with rice, bring 2½ cups water to a boil and add the rice with 1 tablespoon butter and 1 teaspoon salt. Return the rice to a boil, reduce the heat to low, and cook undisturbed for 20 minutes.

While the sauce is cooking, dust the scallops on both sides with chili powder and cocoa powder and season with a little salt.

Return to the saucepan and put ¼ cup of the hot sauce into a separate bowl. Gradually mix the sour cream into the hot sauce a spoonful at a time to temper the sour cream and keep it from breaking.

Gradually whisk the tempered sour cream into the sauce and allow the mixture to thicken, about 5 more minutes, stirring often. Adjust the seasoning as needed with salt and pepper.

Meanwhile, check on the leeks. When they're done, transfer them to a utility platter, cover, and keep warm. In the same pan, heat the remaining 1 tablespoon oil over medium-high heat and melt in 1 tablespoon of butter (reserving the rest of the butter). Sear the scallops on

TIMELINE	
Ingredient prep:	
Soak leeks	5 minutes
Slice leeks, onion, and garlic	5 minutes
Subtotal for ingredient prep	**10 minutes**
Slowly cook leeks (30 minutes)	
Overlaps with:	
Sauté onion and garlic (5 minutes)	
Reduce mango juice/curry paste (20 minutes)	
Add chocolate to sauce and cook	
(5 minutes)	30 minutes
Begin cooking rice or	
rice noodles if serving	
Season scallops/dust with cocoa	2 minutes
Temper sauce	2 minutes
Allow sauce to thicken (5 minutes)	
Overlaps with:	
Sear scallops (4 to 5 minutes)	5 minutes
Finish scallops	4 minutes
Allow scallops to carry-over cook	
while resting	5 minutes
Assembly	**2 minutes**
Total estimated time,	
start to finish	**1 hour**

both sides, leaving each side undisturbed for the first 2 minutes or so to let the caramelization process begin. (This will prevent tearing and allow the seasonings to cook into the flesh.) Further cook the scallops until you see from the side that they're beginning to turn opaque. When the opacity extends about a third of the way in on both sides of the scallops, remove them to a plate and cover them with a pot lid to allow carry-over cooking to take over and avoid overcooking the scallops.

Presentation

Place about 1 cup of cooked noodles (if you're serving them) in the center of each serving plate. Spoon some leeks onto the noodles, top with 2 scallops, and spoon some curry sauce around. (See the photo for visual reference.)

Pan-Seared Scallops with Saffron Broth and Tomato Relish

6 APPETIZERS

This utterly simple appetizer course will make any meal seem elegant.

INGREDIENTS FOR THE SCALLOPS

2 cups low-sodium vegetable stock or chicken stock

1 pinch of saffron

Six U-10–size scallops

Salt and freshly ground black pepper to taste

2 tablespoons grapeseed oil

2 tablespoons unsalted butter

INGREDIENTS FOR THE TOMATO RELISH

1 fresh plum tomato (preferably Roma), cut into ¼-inch cubes, seeded if desired

2 teaspoons capers

1 shallot clove, cut into ⅛-inch dice

½ teaspoon balsamic vinegar

Salt and freshly ground black pepper to taste

1 teaspoon extra virgin olive oil

INGREDIENTS FOR THE GARLIC BREAD

1 baguette loaf, cut evenly into ¾- to 1-inch-thick slices

2 large garlic cloves, crushed with the side of a knife blade and finely minced

Freshly ground black pepper to taste

2 tablespoons olive oil

TIMELINE

Ingredient prep..................................	10 minutes
Overlaps with:	
Warm the stock (2 minutes)..................	2 minutes
Preheat the oven for the garlic bread	
Stir saffron into warm stock to bloom (10 minutes)	
Overlaps with:	
Make tomato relish (5 minutes)	
Season and sear scallops (5 minutes)..............................	10 minutes
Reduce saffron broth and carry-over cook scallops	
Overlaps with:	
Prepare and toast garlic bread (5 minutes).................................	5 minutes
Assembly..	5 minutes
Total estimated time	**32 minutes**

Method for the scallops and saffron broth

Heat the stock in a small saucepan just until it is warm, about 2 minutes. Transfer ¼ cup of the warmed stock to a small bowl, add the pinch of saffron, and let it stand 10 minutes to allow it to bloom. (Meanwhile, prepare the tomato relish, below.)

Season the scallops with salt and pepper. In a large sauté pan, melt the butter in the oil over medium-high heat and sear both sides of the scallops, leaving each side undisturbed until you see the edges begin to turn golden brown, about 2 to 4 minutes, to let the seasonings integrate into the scallops and allow the surface to caramelize (which will prevent tearing of the flesh). Check the sides of the scallops for opacity as they cook, a sign of doneness. When they are opaque about one-third of the way in from each flat side, transfer them to a utility plate, cover with foil, and set aside for about 5 minutes to carry-over cook. (They will continue to cook when removed from direct heat, but are less likely to overcook.)

Meanwhile, return the bowl of bloomed saffron to the rest of the stock, pour it into the same sauté pan over medium-high heat, and allow it to reduce by about half, about 5 minutes.

Method for the tomato relish

In a small bowl combine the tomato, capers, shallot, vinegar, salt, pepper, and extra virgin olive oil. Set the mixture aside while you cook the scallops, above.

Method for the garlic bread

Preheat the oven to 375°F. Place the slices of bread on a baking sheet, sprinkle them with even amounts of garlic, grind black pepper over them, and drizzle them with the olive oil. Toast the bread lightly, 2 to 5 minutes.

Presentation

Spoon some saffron broth onto individual salad plates. Place a scallop in the center of the broth and top with a small amount of the tomato relish. Serve with garlic bread to dip into the saffron broth.

Olive and Sun-dried Tomato-Stuffed Black Bass over Braised Potatoes with Tomato Broth

SERVES 6

Stuffed fish over potatoes is an old-world classic.

INGREDIENTS

One 3- to 4-pound whole black bass, cleaned, rinsed, and dried with paper towels (also delicious with haddock)

Salt and freshly ground black pepper

2 tablespoons grapeseed oil (1 tablespoon for the fish and 1 tablespoon for the vegetables)

2 shallot cloves, diced medium

2 garlic cloves, lightly crushed with the side of a knife blade and minced

2 large celery ribs, well scrubbed and sliced into ⅛-inch slices

½ cup oil-packed sun-dried tomatoes (or if dehydrated, soaked in water to rehydrate), cut into ½-inch pieces

¼ cup green olives with pimientos, sliced crosswise

¼ cup pitted black olives, sliced crosswise

3 or 4 large thyme sprigs, leaves stripped off and minced

1 teaspoon very finely minced fresh rosemary leaves, or ¼ teaspoon dried, ground into a powder with a mortar and pestle

1 teaspoon minced fresh oregano leaves, or ¼ teaspoon dried

3 fresh sage leaves, minced, or ¼ teaspoon dried

½ cup white wine

One 29- to 32-ounce can plum tomatoes in juice

8 small potatoes (about 2 pounds), cut into ⅛- to ¼-inch-thick slices

1 tablespoon finely minced fresh dill

Method

Season the fish with salt and pepper inside and out and brush or rub with 1 tablespoon of oil (reserving the other tablespoon). In a lidded sauté pan large enough to accommodate the entire stuffed fish when covered, heat the remaining 1 tablespoon oil over medium-high heat. To make the stuffing, add the shallots, garlic, celery, sun-dried tomatoes, green olives, black olives, thyme, rosemary, oregano, and sage. Stir to combine and coat with the oil and cook until the shallots turn translucent, about 3 minutes. Deglaze the pan with wine and allow most of the wine to evaporate, about 5 minutes. Transfer this stuffing mixture to a bowl. Add the plum tomatoes and their juice to the pan. Add the potatoes, distributing them around the pan so they'll cook evenly, and season with salt and pepper. Cover, increase the heat to high, and bring to a boil.

Spoon the stuffing mixture into the fish and secure with kitchen twine or skewers. Place the fish over the bed of potatoes in tomato broth, cover, and reduce the heat to low. Cook until the fish flakes with a fork, about 20 minutes.

Finish and presentation

Remove the fish to a utility platter and let rest. Place some potatoes in the center of each serving dish, taking care to keep them intact (a flat wooden spatula or paddle works well for this purpose), and arrange some of the plum tomatoes around them. Slice the fish to reveal the stuffed interior and place a piece on top of the potatoes and tomatoes. Strain the tomato broth from the pan and spoon some over and around the fish and vegetables. Garnish with minced dill.

Lobster Napa Cabbage Wraps

SERVES 4

This is a fun dish that beautifully features lobster. If you're looking for a special dish for date night, your in-laws' visit, or an intimate dinner party, this is it. Be sure to check out the photo in the insert!

INGREDIENTS FOR THE LOBSTER/SHRIMP FILLING

1 pound (4 sticks) unsalted butter

Two 4-ounce lobster tails

½ pound 21-30–size shrimp, deveined

2 shallots, chopped

8 scallions, white and tender green parts only, chopped

INGREDIENTS FOR THE NAPA CABBAGE WRAPS

8 to 12 napa cabbage leaves

INGREDIENTS FOR THE SAUCE

1 cup milk or light cream

1 small onion, finely chopped

1 bay leaf

3 whole cloves

¼ teaspoon ground nutmeg (optional)

1½ teaspoons cornstarch

¼ cup grated Parmigiano-Reggiano cheese

¼ cup Cognac

White pepper to taste

Salt, if needed

INGREDIENTS FOR THE TOPPING

⅛ to ¼ cup grated Parmigiano-Reggiano cheese

1 tablespoon minced fresh dill

TIMELINE

Ingredient prep:
Chop shallots, scallions, onion,
   and dill.. 8 minutes
Separate cabbage leaves, rinse
   and dry .... 4 minutes
Grate Parmigiano-Reggiano cheese .... 5 minutes
Subtotal, estimated prep time............. 17 minutes

Poach lobster and shrimp...........................15 minutes
Cool lobster and shrimp (5 minutes)
   Overlaps with:
   Heat milk (4 minutes) .... 5 minutes
Remove lobster and shrimp from
   shells and add shells to milk .... 5 minutes
Steam cabbage leaves
   (8 minutes, approximately)
   Overlaps with:
   Slice lobster and shrimp (4 minutes)
   Remove shells from milk and add
      onion and seasonings (2 minutes)
   Sauté shallots/warm scallions
      (2 minutes) .... 8 minutes
Remove cabbage leaves to cool (1 minute)
   Make cheese slurry for sauce
      (2 minutes), temper slurry (1 minute),
      and add remaining sauce
      ingredients (1 minute) .... 5 minutes
Cook sauce .... 10 minutes
Assemble filling and wraps .... 5 minutes
Bake wraps .... 10 minutes
Subtotal active cooking time .... 63 minutes

Assembly .... 5 minutes

***Total estimated time,
start to finish*** .... 1 hour and 25 minutes

Method for the lobster filling

Melt the butter in a sauté pan that is just large enough to accommodate the lobster tails. The butter should be very hot but not sizzling (165° to 180°F). Add the lobster tails to the pan, meat-side down and shell-side up, and poach until the meat is opaque and the shells are red, about 15 minutes. Add the shrimp to the pan and poach until the shells are pink and the meat is opaque, about 3 to 5 minutes. Remove the lobster and shrimp to a utility platter and let cool. Pour the melted butter into a bowl for use in other elements of this recipe and keep the pan handy. (Meanwhile, begin heating the milk for the sauce, below.)

Remove the lobster meat and shrimp from the tails and shells. (Add the shells to the milk, below, and then start steaming the cabbage leaves as directed.)

As the cabbage is steaming, slice the lobster tail meat lengthwise down the middle and into 4 slices crosswise, and the shrimp crosswise into 4 slices. Cover and set aside. (Remove the shells from the milk below while continuing to monitor the cabbage leaves.)

As the sauce continues to warm, return 2 tablespoons of the reserved melted butter to the same sauté pan in which you poached the lobster and sauté the shallots until translucent. Add the scallions at the end to heat for just a minute. Set aside and finish the sauce as the cabbage leaves cool.

Method for the sauce

While the lobster and shrimp are cooling, above, add the milk to a heavy-gauge, noncorrosive saucepan and place the pan over low heat. When you've separated the meat from the shells, add the lobster and shrimp shells to the milk and continue to warm over low heat, about 5 minutes. (Meanwhile, start steaming the cabbage leaves, below.)

While keeping tabs on the status of the steamed cabbage, use a slotted spoon to remove the shells from the milk and discard them. Add the onion, bay leaf, cloves, and nutmeg to the saucepan and continue to warm over low heat. (Meanwhile, sauté the shallots and scallions, above, and set the cabbage leaves aside to cool.)

Spoon 2 tablespoons of the reserved melted butter into a heat-resistant bowl and create a slurry with the cornstarch, then whisk in the Parmigiano-Reggiano cheese. Pour a small amount of the hot milk mixture into the slurry, stirring until the milk is thoroughly blended in. Return this to the milk in the pan, add the Cognac, and simmer, stirring frequently until the flavors are integrated and you can taste that the alcohol in the Cognac has dissipated, 5 to 10 minutes. Remove the saucepan from the heat and season the sauce to taste with white pepper and salt if needed. Remove and discard the bay leaf and cloves. Immediately put a sheet of plastic wrap on top of the sauce to prevent a skin from forming and keep warm (see Note).

Method for the cabbage wrapper

While the milk for the sauce is heating, steam the cabbage leaves until tender but not mushy, about 5 to 8 minutes, but use your judgment to determine when the leaves are pleasantly softened but still firm enough to support the lobster filling. (Meanwhile, slice the lobster.)

Remove the steamed cabbage leaves from the heat and let cool until cool enough to handle. (Return to the sauce to add the cheese.)

Method for the assembly of the lobster wraps

Preheat the oven to 350°F. In a mixing bowl, gently fold the lobster/shrimp and shallot/scallion mixtures together with just enough of the sauce to bind it. (Reserve the rest of the sauce.) If the filling seems loose, stir in more Parmesan. (You don't want the filling to be too runny.) Lay the cabbage leaves out and remove or slit any ribs or spines of the leaves if they seem too stiff to roll (be sure to leave enough of the leaf to be able to roll it shut). Spoon 3 or 4 tablespoons of the lobster/shrimp mixture onto each leaf. Fold in the sides of leaves and roll up. Layer some of the remaining sauce on the bottom of an ovenproof dish (such as a Corning pie plate) and carefully nestle the cabbage rolls, seam-side down, in the dish so they won't unroll. Sprinkle with a little of the cheese. Bake for 10 minutes, or until the cheese is melted.

Presentation

Spoon some of the sauce onto each serving plate. Place a lobster wrap in the center of the plate and slice it in half to reveal the interior. Serve garnished with fresh dill and with the remaining lobster sauce on the side.

Note: Here's a handy method to keep sauce warm without overcooking it: Put the sauce in a small bowl and nest it in a slightly larger bowl filled with warm water, being careful not to splash any of the water into the sauce. Cover the two bowls with plastic wrap.

7. PASTA AND RICE AND EVERYTHING NICE

Back in the good old days, when the typical home-cooked meal consisted of a protein on the plate in the 3 o'clock position and a veggie at 12, you could always count on a warm, filling, comforting starch at 9 o'clock: rice, potatoes, or macaroni of some description. It was usually the most abundant item on the plate, and you could usually have as much as you wanted. Personally I think of potatoes as more of a stand-alone item—a side dish, whether baked, mashed, or gratinéed—so this chapter is about just pasta and rice, which are among the most reliable and versatile ingredients a cook has to work with.

Pasta and rice are found in one shape or form or another in virtually every cuisine in the world. In some places, they're staple subsistence foods, in the same way that bread has been throughout history. Their flavor and texture are consistent, with only the slightest variations—maybe in the case of freshly made pasta versus dried, medium-grain versus long-grain rice versus Arborio rice, and so on. They cook quickly, with a minimum of fuss and bother. Whether you're cooking a pot of rice in Japan, South America, Savannah, or Beijing, you know what you'll end up with after about twenty minutes. Their flavors are very subtle on the palate. In some ways, they function as a blank canvas does for a painter.

Sometimes the quickest way to getting dinner on the table is to build a meal around pasta or rice. It's easy to change their characters with different toppings and preparations, but you can count on ending up with a filling dish that provides energy from carbohydrates and will more often than not form the basis for future reminiscences about comfort food.

Some simple guidelines for pasta: Do not overdress your pasta; it should be adorned with sauce, not swimming. If you'll be mixing the pasta into a sauté, add a ladleful of the pasta cooking water to the mixture for flavor and texture. Cook both pasta and rice al dente; individual grains or strands should be firm to the bite, neither crunchy nor too mushy.

Because of their neutrality, pasta and rice dishes reflect the sensibilities and moods of their creators. Pasta with olive oil, garlic, and parsley is a perfected dish, as is a bowl of rice with green scallion and ginger and a little soy sauce. I would describe these as quieter dishes. But you can also make boisterous jambalayas and colorful primaveras, a mélange of exotic Asian stir-fries, Indian curries, Cajun gumbos, and Italian classics featuring fresh vegetables, succulent meat, and fish and tantalizing sauces. With these versatile ingredients as a foundation, you can make some serious noise.

Smoked Salmon Pillows
with Black Beans and Yogurt Sauce

SERVES 6 (APPROXIMATELY 6 TO 8 RAVIOLI EACH)

Making your own pasta "pillows" is an investment of time, much of which is for the dough-resting time. As long as you keep the pasta from drying out, you can break the preparation time down into its component parts and do it in increments around your schedule. The thing about this dish is that it's *so* delicious you'll find yourself looking for an excuse to make it.

INGREDIENTS FOR THE PASTA DOUGH

4 cups all-purpose flour

4 eggs, at room temperature

2 teaspoons olive oil

INGREDIENTS FOR THE SALMON FILLING

1 cup whipped cream cheese

2 teaspoons minced fresh dill

One 4-ounce package smoked salmon, cut into ½-inch pieces

One 3-ounce jar capers

INGREDIENTS FOR THE BLACK BEANS

2 tablespoons olive oil

2 shallot cloves, minced

Two 16-ounce cans black beans, drained

INGREDIENTS FOR THE SAUCE

1 cup plain yogurt

Juice of 1 lemon

Salt and freshly ground black pepper to taste

6 to 8 scallions, white and tender green parts only, sliced on the diagonal

SPECIAL EQUIPMENT

Pasta maker

TIMELINE
Ingredient prep .... 10 minutes
Active pasta making .... 30 minutes
Rest pasta .... 30 minutes
Assemble ravioli .... 50 minutes
Rest ravioli (2 hours) .... 120 minutes
Cook ravioli (5 minutes)
Overlaps with:
Cook beans (3 minutes)
Assemble sauce (2 minutes) .... 5 minutes
Total time .... **4 hours and 5 minutes**

Method for the pasta

Mound the flour in the center of a clean, room temperature work surface, such as a large wooden cutting board. Create a crater in the center of the mound. Crack the first egg into the center of the crater and add ½ teaspoon of oil. With a fork, gently begin to scramble the mixture within the confines of the crater, integrating the flour from the sides of the crater as you carefully beat the egg. When the first egg is mostly mixed in, shore up the sides of the mound with flour to maintain the crater shape. Repeat with the second egg and ½ teaspoon of oil, and again in turn with the third and fourth eggs and remaining oil in ½-teaspoon increments. Start kneading the dough with your palms, allowing the warmth of your hands to impart elasticity to the dough. Knead for a count of about 400 strokes, or until you feel you have created a cohesive mass. Wrap the dough in plastic and allow it to rest for about 30 minutes.

When the dough is rested and ready for you to begin making the salmon cheese pillows, have a bowl of water handy to moisten and seal the dough. Divide the dough in thirds. (You will be working with a third of the dough at a time, keeping the rest wrapped in plastic to keep it from drying out.) Divide the first third of the dough in half. Use a pasta machine to gradually roll down each piece of dough, successively reducing the setting on the machine until it is at its thinnest. Sprinkle flour on your work surface and lay the sheet of pasta down. Spoon ½ teaspoon of cream cheese at 4-inch intervals on the pasta dough and top with a sprinkle of dill, 1 teaspoon salmon, and 2 or 3 capers. Dip your fingers into the bowl of water and moisten the dough surrounding the salmon and cheese filling. Cover the filling with the other rolled-out sheet of dough and press gently around the filling to seal, being careful not to flatten the filling or tear the dough. Using a pizza cutter, cut the filled dough into ravioli squares. Remove each ravioli to a floured surface, pressing the edges firmly together as you do so. Cover the ravioli with a towel and proceed with the other 2 dough balls. Set the covered ravioli aside for 2 hours.

Bring a large shallow pan of water to a boil.

Heat the grapeseed oil over medium heat in a saucepan and gently sauté the shallots. Stir in the black beans and cook to let the flavors integrate, about 3 minutes. Remove from the heat and keep warm.

To make the sauce, in a medium bowl, fold the yogurt and lemon juice together and season to taste with salt and pepper. (If you're squeezing the lemon juice by hand, keep the sliced side of the lemon against your palm to keep the seeds in the rind.)

Salt the boiling water, add the ravioli in batches so they are not crowded in the pot, reduce the heat, and cook very gently, just until the dough sets up and the filling is heated through, about 2 to 4 minutes. Remove the ravioli with a slotted spoon and transfer them to a platter. (Allow the water to come back up to boiling before cooking each batch.)

Presentation

Place about 6 to 8 ravioli on each individual serving plate. Spoon the beans over the ravioli, top with the yogurt sauce, and sprinkle with scallions.

Linguine Serrano with Tequila, Red, Green, and Yellow Bell Peppers, and Sautéed Shrimp

SERVES 6 TO 8

This is a playful dish that features a little spice. While some hand protection is better than none at all, it's best to use disposable plastic gloves rather than Latex. The Latex polymer used to make gloves is highly variable in size and distribution, and it won't resist the capsaicin molecules in hot peppers as well as most vinyls.

INGREDIENTS

2 pounds linguine

2 pounds 21-25–size shrimp, deveined

1 tablespoon grapeseed oil

1 cup seafood stock (such as Kitchen Basics)

1 shallot clove, minced

1 serrano pepper, seeded and thinly sliced
(Use disposable plastic gloves to handle
these and all hot peppers; protect your face
and eyes, and avoid breathing in the fumes.)

1 red bell pepper, seeded and cut brunoise
(julienne, then crosswise)

1 green bell pepper, seeded and cut brunoise

1 yellow bell pepper, seeded and cut brunoise

2 tablespoons minced fresh cilantro leaves
(1 tablespoon for the sauce, 1 tablespoon
for garnish)

½ teaspoon crushed red pepper

2 cups tequila, such as Sauza or Jose Cuervo

2 teaspoons OLD BAY seasoning (or as needed
to season the shrimp)

Salt and freshly ground black pepper

TIMELINE

Ingredient prep:
Cut vegetables..................................... 10 minutes

Active cooking time:
Clean shrimp....................................... 10 minutes
Sauté shells, reduce stock,
    and strain into bowl.................... 12 minutes
Sauté vegetables .... 7 minutes
Reduce tequila and seafood stock
    Overlaps with:
    Cook pasta....................................... 10 minutes
Cook shrimp... 4 minutes
Combine pasta with shrimp and sauce.... 2 minutes

Assembly.. 2 minutes

***Total estimated time,
start to finish*** .... **57 minutes**

Method

Bring a large pot of water to a boil for the linguine.

Peel the shrimp, reserve the shells and tails, and refrigerate the shrimp. In a large sauté pan deep enough to accommodate the cooked pasta, heat the grapeseed oil over medium-high heat. Add the shrimp shells and tails and cook for 2 minutes, or until they turn pink, then add the seafood stock. Simmer until the liquid has reduced by half. Strain the liquid into a bowl, discarding the shells. In the same pan, sauté the shallot until it turns translucent. Add the serrano and bell peppers, 1 tablespoon of cilantro, and the crushed red pepper and cook until the peppers begin to soften, about 3 minutes. Add the tequila and the reserved seafood stock and cook until the sauce is reduced by half, about 10 minutes over medium-high heat.

Meanwhile, cook the linguine and drain well.

Season the shrimp with the OLD BAY seasoning and salt and pepper, and stir them into the sauce. Cook just until the shrimp turn pink, remove the pan from the heat, and let stand until the shrimp are opaque. Set aside 1 shrimp per serving to use as a garnish, then fold the linguine into the pot with the sauce, coating well.

Presentation

Transfer the pasta and sauce to serving dishes. Top each serving with 1 shrimp and a bit of cilantro.

Porcini Mushrooms with Potato Gnocchi, Truffle Olive Oil, and Mushroom Sauce

SERVES 4 TO 6 (MAKES ABOUT 6 DOZEN GNOCCHI)

For my friends the noncarnivores out there, this is a vegetarian and gluten-free recipe.

INGREDIENTS FOR THE GNOCCHI

2 pounds potatoes (about 4 or 5 medium potatoes), peeled, cut into 1-inch chunks, and placed in a pot of enough water to cover

1 cup white rice flour, plus extra to flour the board

¾ cup potato starch

¼ cup cornstarch

1 teaspoon salt, plus extra for the water

1 tablespoon unsalted butter, cubed

2 tablespoons grated Parmigiano-Reggiano cheese

2 eggs, beaten

¼ cup truffle olive oil

Freshly ground black pepper

INGREDIENTS FOR THE MUSHROOMS AND SAUCE

1 stick (8 tablespoons) unsalted butter

2 cups (about 6 to 8 ounces) white mushrooms, cleaned, trimmed, and sliced

½ pound (about 1½ cups) fresh porcini mushrooms (or 2 ounces dried porcini mushrooms, soaked in hot water to rehydrate and remove grit)

Salt and pepper to taste

2 cups dry white wine

¼ cup minced fresh flat-leaf parsley

TIMELINE

Ingredient prep:
Rehydrate porcini mushrooms (20 minutes)
Overlaps with:
Peel and cut potatoes .... 3 minutes
Measure ingredients .... 5 minutes
Mince herbs .... 2 minutes
Clean/trim mushrooms .... 10 minutes
Estimated prep time .... 20 minutes

Boil potatoes.. 10 minutes
Mash potatoes, mix gnocchi dough,
and let rest (25 minutes)
Overlaps with:
Sauté mushrooms in butter for sauce
(8 minutes)
Add wine and let reduce (12 minutes)
Begin boiling water and finish sauce
(5 minutes) ....25 minutes
Form gnocchi .... 5 minutes
Boil gnocchi .... 5 minutes
Active cooking time .... 45 minutes

Assembly .... 5 minutes

Total estimated time .... 1 hour and 10 minutes

Method for the gnocchi

Boil the potatoes until very tender but not mushy, about 10 minutes. Drain them well, and set aside to cool. In a large bowl, combine the rice flour, potato starch, cornstarch, and salt and mix well. Mash the potatoes by hand in a separate large bowl, keeping them fluffy without breaking up the potato fibers too much. Fold the dry ingredients as well as the butter, cheese, and eggs into the potatoes. Mix well to moisten the dry ingredients but do not overwork the dough. (Gnocchi should be light and fluffy rather then dense.) Knead just lightly and divide the dough into 4 portions. Cover the bowl with a damp towel and let the dough rest for about 20 minutes. (Meanwhile, start on the mushroom sauce, below.)

Bring a large shallow pan of water to a boil and add salt. On a floured surface (such as a large wooden cutting board), roll each dough portion into a long cylinder, about ¾ inch in diameter. Cut the cylinders into 1-inch pieces and add them to the boiling water. They will puff up when they cook. As they set up, use a slotted spoon to remove them to a large bowl. Gently toss the gnocchi with the truffle olive oil and season with pepper.

Method for the mushroom sauce

While the gnocchi dough is resting, begin the mushroom sauce. (If you're using dried mushrooms, carefully remove them from their soaking liquid so that all the grit remains at the bottom. If you wish, you can strain the soaking liquid through cheesecloth and use it to replace up to half the wine in the recipe.) In a large sauté pan over medium-low heat, melt 2 tablespoons of butter, reserving the other 6 tablespoons for the sauce. Add the white and porcini mushrooms and season with salt and pepper to taste. Cook the mushrooms, stirring occasionally, until they give up their juices and are tender. Remove the mushrooms to a utility plate in a warm place. To the pan juices, add the white wine (and mushroom-soaking liquid, if using) and let reduce by two thirds. (Meanwhile, start cutting and cooking the gnocchi, above.) When the mushroom sauce has reduced, remove it from the heat and whisk in the rest of the butter. Season to taste with salt and pepper. Return the mushrooms to the pan of sauce and toss together.

Presentation

Place some gnocchi on a serving plate, spoon the mushrooms and sauce on top, and sprinkle with parsley.

Chicken and Shrimp Jambalaya

SERVES 6

Everyone appreciates New Orleans more since we almost lost it. What better way is there to celebrate the culinary gifts the area has given the world than with a good old-fashioned jambalaya?

INGREDIENTS

1 teaspoon grapeseed oil

½ pound andouille sausage

4 boneless chicken thighs, halved (about 1 pound)

Salt and freshly ground black pepper to taste

1 white onion, diced small

1 green bell pepper, seeded and diced

2 celery ribs, diced

2 tablespoons chopped fresh flat-leaf parsley leaves

1 tablespoon minced fresh thyme leaves

1 bay leaf

One 29- to 32-ounce can crushed tomatoes

1 quart (4 cups) chicken stock

¼ teaspoon crushed red pepper

1 teaspoon cayenne pepper (optional)

2 cups white rice

1 pound 21-25–size shrimp, deveined and shells and tails removed

1 lemon

6 scallions, white and tender green parts only, sliced on the bias

Method

In a large sauté pan (about 8 quarts) with a lid, heat the grapeseed oil over medium-high heat and sauté the sausage until browned. Remove to a cutting board and cut into 1- to 1½-inch slices. Season the chicken with salt and pepper, add it to the pan, and brown it on all sides, about 2 to 3 minutes per side. Remove the chicken to a utility platter.

Add the onion, bell pepper, celery, parsley, thyme, and bay leaf to the drippings in the pan and sauté over medium-high heat until the onion begins to turn translucent, about 3 minutes, stirring frequently to prevent burning. Add the crushed tomatoes, chicken stock, crushed red pepper, and cayenne pepper (if using) and bring to a boil. Stir in the rice and return to a boil. Return the sausage and chicken to the pan, cover, and reduce the heat to low. Cook undisturbed for 20 minutes. Lay the shrimp on top of the jambalaya, cover, and cook until pink, about 5 minutes. Remove from the heat and uncover. Let rest for 5 minutes.

Presentation

Remove some of the shrimp to a plate. Transfer the jambalaya to a serving bowl, lay the shrimp on top, and squeeze lemon juice on top. (If you hold the sliced side of the lemon against your palm while squeezing, the seeds usually stay in the rind.) Sprinkle with scallions and serve with a crisp white wine, such as a chardonnay.

Spaghetti and Smoked Salmon Carbonara with Caramelized Lemon

SERVES 4

This recipe is a twist on an all-time Italian classic. The smoked salmon both complements and takes the essential flavor of the bacon in this recipe to new heights. The element of caramelized lemon balances them out perfectly.

INGREDIENTS

2 tablespoons unsalted butter

1 teaspoon dried thyme

1 lemon, cut crosswise into ¼-inch-thick slices and seeded

1 teaspoon dried dill

4 eggs, beaten

6 ounces smoked Norwegian salmon, cut into 1-inch pieces

1 cup grated Pecorino Romano cheese

2 pounds spaghetti

8 bacon strips, cut into ½-inch pieces

2 garlic cloves, minced

½ teaspoon crushed red pepper

Salt and freshly ground black pepper to taste

Method

Bring a large pot of water to a boil for the pasta.

In a large skillet, melt the butter over medium heat. Distribute even pinches of thyme into the pan and place a lemon slice directly over each "pinch." Cook for 2 to 3 minutes undisturbed to let the seasonings integrate into the surface of the lemon. Then distribute even pinches of dill in the pan near each lemon slice and flip the slices onto the dill, again cooking undisturbed for 2 or 3 minutes. When the lemon slices begin to caramelize, use a slotted spatula to move them to a utility platter to cool.

In a large mixing bowl, combine the eggs, salmon, and cheese.

Salt the pot of water for the pasta and cook the spaghetti until al dente.

Using the pan from the lemons, cook the bacon over medium heat until the fat is rendered and the bacon is crispy. Remove the bacon to paper towels to drain and pour all but 1 tablespoon of the fat from the pan. Add the garlic and crushed red pepper and sauté over low heat until the garlic is golden, taking care not to burn it. Add the bacon and garlic to the bowl with the salmon mixture. Reserve 4 caramelized lemon slices for garnish. Cut the rest of the caramelized lemon into small pieces and add them to the salmon mixture as well.

Drain the spaghetti and gently toss with the ingredients in the large mixing bowl. Season to taste with salt and pepper. Transfer to a serving dish and garnish with the reserved caramelized lemon slices.

Chicken Stroganoff with Fried Heirloom Tomatoes

SERVES 4

Stroganoff is like a hug on a plate. Paired with the tang of fried tomatoes, it's like a hug and a kiss!

INGREDIENTS FOR THE CHICKEN AND SAUCE

1 pound wide egg noodles

2 pounds boneless chicken breasts, cut into 1-inch cubes

1 teaspoon paprika

Salt and freshly ground black pepper

1 tablespoon unsalted butter

1 tablespoon grapeseed oil

1 small white onion, minced

2 tablespoons Wondra flour

1 cup chicken stock

½ cup sour cream

2 tablespoons minced fresh parsley leaves

INGREDIENTS FOR THE FRIED TOMATOES

2 or 3 large firm but ripe heirloom tomatoes, cut into ½-inch-thick slices

½ cup all-purpose flour seasoned with salt and pepper

1 tablespoon unsalted butter

1 tablespoon grapeseed oil

Method for the chicken

Bring a large pot of salted water to a boil for the noodles and cook them while you're preparing the chicken.

Season the chicken cubes with the paprika and salt and pepper. In a large sauté pan over medium-high heat, melt the butter in the oil and sauté the chicken until it is browned on all sides and cooked through, about 8 to 10 minutes. With a slotted spatula or spoon, remove the chicken to a utility platter, cover, and keep warm.

In the same pan, sauté the onion over medium-high heat until translucent, stirring constantly to prevent burning, about 3 to 5 minutes. Whisk in the Wondra flour to make a roux and cook, stirring constantly, until it emits a nutty fragrance but is not yet browned, about 3 minutes. Gradually whisk in the chicken stock and let it reduce by half, about 10 minutes.

Meanwhile, drain the noodles and transfer to a large bowl. Toss with freshly ground black pepper, cover, and set aside in a warm place. While the sauce is reducing, fry the tomatoes.

Method for the tomatoes

Dredge the tomato slices in the seasoned flour. Melt the butter and the oil in another large skillet over medium heat and sauté the tomatoes, leaving each side undisturbed for 1 or 2 minutes to let the seasoned flour cook into the surface and prevent it from "crusting off." Remove the tomatoes to paper towels to absorb any grease.

When the sauce has reduced by half, remove the pan from the heat and whisk in the sour cream. Season to taste with salt and pepper and gently fold in the chicken to reheat it.

Presentation

Place some noodles in the center of each serving dish. Spoon some chicken in the stroganoff sauce on top. Sprinkle with parsley and arrange tomato slices around the plate.

8. FINISH YOUR VEGETABLES (AND FRUIT, TOO!)

If variety is the spice of life, then even I have to admit that Mother Nature might very well be a vegetarian. The colors, flavors, textures, and sheer variety of the edible vegetables and fruits available on planet Earth are truly awe-inspiring. The seemingly limitless range of what's available to the modern cook these days, in season or out, sourced indigenously or internationally, fresh or fresh frozen, everyday or exotic, is breathtaking.

One reason people who love to cook often get bored with vegetables may be due to a lack of new ideas for their preparation. It may also simply be because fresh fruits and vegetables are so nutritious and so good when prepared as closely to their natural states as possible. You can stick just about any vegetable in simmering water for a few minutes or roast it in the oven, stick it on a plate, and throw some salt, pepper, and butter on it and it will be really delicious. Most fruits and vegetables can also happily be eaten raw or close to raw, and when you can just pluck something off a bush or a tree or yank it out of the ground and eat it, the cook may find him- or herself elbowed out of the equation.

For many cooks (unless they happen to be vegetarian), vegetables and fruits are sometimes an afterthought, confined to side dishes and salads. I am a carnivore, or at least an omnivore with carnivorous leanings, and I generally like to feature proteins as the centerpiece of my entrées. I'll use vegetables as a base or to surround the protein, integrate them into a mélange in stews and curries, or use them to top the main protein. But I love their flavors and textures, which offer so many more choices in variety of taste, shape, and color than meat, fish, and poultry.

Some recipes in this chapter consider the vegetable as side dish, to be used as part of an entrée, as an accent on the plate, or served family style in friendly serving bowls. Others can stand alone as a main dish. Some contain both savory and sweet elements and could equally be served as a dessert or a light midday meal.

The two broad concepts to keep in mind on this subject are seasonality and restraint. First, even though modern transportation and preservation techniques allow an amazing level of access to fruits and vegetables from just about anywhere year-round, keep in mind *where* you are and *when* you are when putting your dishes together. This applies more to vegetables and fruits than to most ingredients and preparations. I recently took a trip to Hawaii and took a chance on the lunch special, listed as "roast pork." I had just completed a challenge on *Dinner: Impossible* to cook an authentic Hawaiian luau to be presided over by Sam Choy, my good friend and an island legend. One part of the day had me sweating my pants off, up to my knees in blazing hot river rocks and black volcanic sand preparing, burying, and excavating Kalua pig. At the subsequent banquet, I served the cheek meat historically reserved for the king to Sam along with poi that David Britton made by hand in the traditional manner. It was a great day and a terrific show, but as usual I didn't get to eat anything beyond the smallest tastes, so the next day, I was hungry for some regional fare—something that would taste like pure Hawaii.

The plate that came to me was oven-roasted pork drenched in a thick brown gravy with mashed potatoes and peas. I was crestfallen. This might have been great diner fare in Minnesota on a cold winter's day, but it was a ridiculous choice for a place that touted the authentic flavors of Hawaii in the front window. No doubt someone had good intentions in preparing something that would be considered what an Englishman would eat. However, despite any nods to my native land, when you're dressed in shorts and wandering the street in a hot, sunny climate, you want fresh, clean, spicy flavors, not ones that are rich, overly filling, and calorie-laden. This was food fit for an Eskimo, not a native Hawaiian or anybody who wanted to feel like one, at least for a day.

The lesson here? Be aware of your surroundings and circumstances when you cook. If you're near the beach and you're cooking seafood, make sure your fruits and veggies are lightly cooked, local, and seasonal. If you're in Scotland and there is a nip in the air, you want leek and potato soup on the menu, not gazpacho. If you find yourself in an eatery in the French countryside and fall is turning to winter, order the ratatouille, which ideally will be warm and satisfying, and will feature appropriately seasonal vegetables freshly harvested from the garden. Fresh corn is good in the summer, pumpkin in the fall, potatoes in the winter, and asparagus in the springtime. There's a season to everything, including your natural appetite, so it's best to pay attention to it.

Fruits and vegetables are best when they're kept close to their natural states. Even if you're cooking them down in a pie or a compote, you want to preserve their flavors, not obliterate them. Peach preserves should put you in mind of biting into a fresh peach, not eating baby food. A brussels sprout should be firm to the tooth, with a rich, intense, cabbagey taste. It should not look and taste like gray mush. Many recipes for haricots verts call for blanching the green beans, then shocking them in cold water to stop overcooking them. This allows for proper cooking to develop their flavor, stopped at the right moment in order to preserve their natural texture and color. In the world of cooking beautiful natural produce, limp and colorless is bad; vibrant and al dente is good.

Cauliflower Huevos Salad

SERVES 8

Since raw cauliflower is very crunchy, it's lightly steamed for this salad to preserve vitamins while giving it a mouthfeel that's more in line with the other textures so they're not overshadowed. It's also a very "pretty" salad, with the play of dark and shiny olives against the light cauliflower and hard-boiled eggs.

INGREDIENTS

2 cauliflower heads, cleaned and cut into medium florets

¼ cup apple cider vinegar

2 tablespoons fresh lemon juice

2 teaspoons minced garlic (from about 2 cloves)

3 tablespoons chopped fresh parsley, plus 8 small sprigs for garnish

1 cup olive oil (preferably extra virgin)

Salt and freshly ground black pepper to taste

4 hard-boiled eggs, peeled (easier when they're still warm) and cooled

1 cup sliced black olives

Method

Steam the cauliflower florets until half cooked (about 4 to 5 minutes), drain, and set aside to cool.

Through the feed opening of a running blender, add one at a time the vinegar, lemon juice, garlic, and chopped parsley. With the blender still running, add the olive oil in a thin stream. Season to taste with salt and pepper.

Chop 2 eggs and cut the other 2 into wedges for garnish. In a large bowl, toss the cauliflower, chopped eggs, and black olives and add enough of the dressing to coat. Cover and refrigerate for 2 hours to marinate. Transfer to a serving dish and garnish with the egg wedges and parsley sprigs. Serve the rest of the dressing on the side.

Brussels Sprouts with Dijon Mustard Sauce

SERVES 6

Brussels sprouts have gotten a bad rap. I understand that they may be an acquired taste for some, but given a little help, such as that provided by the sauce in this recipe, even the most stalwart sprouts haters may be surprised at how pleasant and flavorful they can be.

INGREDIENTS

1 cup vegetable stock
    (such as Kitchen Basics brand)

1 large garlic clove, minced

1 bay leaf

¼ teaspoon ground white pepper

¼ teaspoon freshly grated or ground nutmeg

2 tablespoons unsalted butter

2 tablespoons Wondra flour

2 cups (about 8 ounces) fresh or thawed frozen
    brussels sprouts, tough outer leaves removed

2 teaspoons Dijon mustard

Salt and white pepper to taste

Method

To make the sauce, combine the stock, garlic, bay leaf, white pepper, and nutmeg in a saucepan over medium heat. In a separate small pan, melt the butter and gradually stir in the flour until it emits a nutty aroma (without browning). Remove from the heat. Pour a small amount of the hot stock mixture into the flour mixture, stirring until it is thoroughly blended. Return this to the remaining broth mixture and simmer for a few minutes to let the flavors integrate, stirring frequently.

Meanwhile, steam the brussels sprouts until tender but still bright green, about 8 minutes. Place the brussels sprouts into a mixing bowl.

Remove the sauce from the heat, discard the bay leaf, and whisk in the mustard. Season to taste with salt and pepper if needed. Fold the sauce into the steamed brussels sprouts and serve.

Ginger Vichy Carrots

SERVES 4

Kids *love* Vichy carrots. Big kids too.

INGREDIENTS

4 tablespoons (½ stick) unsalted butter

2 tablespoons finely chopped fresh parsley

1 pound baby carrots, or regular carrots cut into ¼-inch-thick by 2-inch-long strips

Salt and freshly ground black pepper to taste

1 teaspoon ginger powder

One 12-ounce can ginger ale or lemon-lime soda

Method

In a medium saucepan over medium heat, melt the butter. Add the parsley and cook about 1 to 2 minutes, just to soften the parsley and let the flavors integrate. Add the carrots and stir to coat with the butter and parsley. Season to taste with salt and pepper and add the ginger, then add the ginger ale or soda. Bring to a boil, reduce the heat to low, and simmer until the liquid is reduced by half and the carrots are tender, about 8 minutes.

Sour Cream Mashed Potatoes with Tomato Caper Chutney

SERVES 6

Sometimes if one orders baked potatoes in a restaurant, the wait person will ask "Do you want butter or sour cream with that?" My default response, "Both," sometimes elicits a dirty look. Here's a way of having both butter and sour cream with your potatoes.

INGREDIENTS FOR THE MASHED POTATOES

6 large potatoes, peeled and cut into chunks just before use

2 bay leaves

¾ cup butter (1½ sticks), cut into small chunks

1 cup sour cream

Salt and ground white pepper to taste

1 or 2 tablespoons heavy cream, or as needed

INGREDIENTS FOR THE CHUTNEY

1 ripe medium tomato, seeded and cut into small dice

1 small red onion, cut into small dice

1 tablespoon minced garlic chives

1 tablespoon capers

1 tablespoon fresh lemon juice

Salt and freshly ground black pepper to taste

Method

In a medium saucepan over medium-low heat, boil the potatoes with the bay leaves until the potatoes are tender, about 10 to 15 minutes. Drain the potatoes and discard the bay leaves. Using a potato masher, mash the potatoes by hand, then stir in the butter and sour cream. Season with salt and white pepper, then beat until creamy using an electric beater.

To prepare the chutney, combine the tomato, onion, garlic chives, capers, and lemon juice in a small bowl. Season to taste with salt and pepper and set aside.

Spoon the mashed potatoes into a pastry bag fitted with a star tip (if the potatoes are too thick to pipe, remove them and stir in a tablespoon or two of heavy cream). Pipe the potatoes onto a serving plate and garnish with the chutney.

Ragout of Brussels Sprouts, Roasted Shallots, Navy Beans, and Tiny Carrots

SERVES 2 AS AN ENTRÉE OR 4 AS A STARTER OR SIDE DISH

I have a personal passion for brussels sprouts and am always looking for new ways to feature them. This recipe can easily make for a great vegetarian main course.

INGREDIENTS

4 whole shallots

¼ cup grapeseed oil

Salt and freshly ground black pepper to taste

1 pint brussels sprouts, tough outer leaves removed, halved from top to bottom

1 pound small baby carrots, or regular carrots cut into ¼-inch-thick by 2-inch-long strips

2 tablespoons (¼ stick) butter

2 garlic cloves, lightly crushed with the side of a knife and minced

1 cup white wine

One 16-ounce can navy beans, drained

Method

Preheat the oven to 500°F. Slice the root end off the shallots and wrap them in heavy-duty aluminum foil so the cut end stands upright. Coat them with grapeseed oil so that the oil flows between the skin and the shallots, season with salt and pepper, and place the shallots in a roasting pan. Roast until tender, about 15 minutes. Let cool just enough to be able to handle.

Steam the brussels sprouts until they just begin to get tender but are still bright green, about 8 to 10 minutes. Remove from the heat and set aside.

Boil the carrots in salted water until just tender, about 5 minutes or so; do not overcook. Remove from the heat, drain, and set aside.

In a large skillet or sauté pan, heat the butter over medium heat. Add the garlic and sauté until tender, taking care not to burn it. Deglaze the pan with the wine and stir in the navy beans. Slip the roasted shallots from their skins directly into the beans. Fold in the brussels sprouts and carrots, gently stirring to coat with the juices. (The finished dish is shown in the photo insert.)

Braised Asian Pear with Roquefort and Sweet Port Wine Dressing

SERVES 4

Chef David Britton worked with us in cooking the food for the photo shoot for this book's recipes. He's the one who prepared the gorgeous rendition of this dish that you will see in the accompanying pictures. You may not know that the chefs who act as my *sous* chefs on my TV show are executive chefs in *real life*. In fact, some people are surprised to hear that we all have to keep our regular jobs. This is why Big George and Little George can't work with me on every challenge, and why David Britton became the third person in the regular rotation. All these men have big jobs with big responsibilities and demanding schedules that don't always allow them to be free to work on a given challenge being filmed for an episode. If you've read my first book, you already know a little about the Georges, and I should tell you a little about David, too. For several years Chef Britton has been the chef/owner of Springwater Bistro near Saratoga, New York, the home of polo in America, legendary racetracks, and the site of a battle in which you Yanks gained the upper hand in the Revolutionary War. He has an eclectic style based on his classical French training and a wide range of experiences in the Hawaiian Islands, the southwestern United States, southern Europe, eastern Asia, and his continuous travel throughout the world to expand his culinary horizons. A strong advocate of the use of organic foods and local ingredients, he's a good friend and a valuable member of the team.

Professional chefs are trained to measure in pounds and ounces or grams and kilograms. It's commonplace in Europe to find recipes with ingredients listed by weight instead of volume. But one of the parameters for writing recipes for American home cooks is using measuring cups and spoons to describe the amounts of ingredients. However, David Britton can often be heard saying, "Weigh it" or "Use the scale," which I consider to be wise advice. Having a kitchen scale at your disposal can be immensely helpful. It doesn't have to be an expensive one; you can even go to an office supply store and buy a postal scale. There will come a time when you've bought an ingredient in bulk, like potatoes, and will want to be able to weigh it, especially when cooking for a crowd. As always, plan ahead and you'll be ready—take David's advice.

INGREDIENTS

4 Asian pears, top halves sliced off crosswise, bottom halves cored

1 stick (8 tablespoons) butter, melted

¼ cup walnut halves

1 cup ruby port wine

½ cup crumbled blue cheese (about 4 ounces)

1 tablespoon minced fresh mint leaves

1 bottle dry Champagne (optional)

Method

Find a covered pan that is large and deep enough to hold all the pears when standing upright. Over medium-high heat, pour about 1 tablespoon of melted butter (reserving the other 7 tablespoons of butter) into the bottom of the pan. Arrange the bottom halves of the cored pears upright in the pan and stuff some walnuts down the center of each. Pour about half the remaining melted butter in and over the pear bottoms (reserving the rest of the butter) and replace the top halves. Cover the pan, reduce the heat to medium, and cook until the pears are half cooked, about 5 minutes. Uncover the pan and deglaze it with the port wine, pouring some over the pears as you do so. Continue cooking until the port is reduced by half and the pears are tender, about 5 to 8 minutes. Using tongs and a slotted spatula, carefully remove the pears to a platter. Whisk the blue cheese into the pan to encourage the melting process to begin, but then remove the pan from the heat, whisk the cheese until smooth, and then whisk in the last of the melted butter to smooth out the sauce.

Presentation

Place a walnut-stuffed pear on each individual serving plate, drizzle with blue cheese and port dressing, and sprinkle with mint. Serve with dry Champagne.

Allium Tossed Salad

SERVES 4

The allium family is related to the lilies of the field, and includes garlic, onions, shallots, and scallions—all indispensable in the kitchen, and all with the inbred potential to fall within a wide spectrum of flavors, sweet, sharp, and savory, depending simply on how they're cooked. Think of the vast difference in taste between a raw onion and a caramelized one. A sharp-tasting garlic clove is quite another story once it has been slow roasted. Here I'm exhibiting the members of the allium family in all their glory as ingredients in the salad and as the primary element of the dressing.

INGREDIENTS FOR ROASTED GARLIC DRESSING

1 head of garlic

2 shallot cloves

2 tablespoons grapeseed oil

2 tablespoons rice vinegar

1 teaspoon Dijon mustard

2 teaspoons chopped fresh thyme leaves

½ teaspoon salt

⅛ teaspoon freshly ground black pepper

½ cup olive oil

INGREDIENTS FOR THE SALAD

4 cups mixed greens, soaked in salt water to remove grit, stems and tough spines removed, torn into bite-size pieces, and dried in a salad spinner

1 small red onion, chopped

½ cup sliced scallions

1 English cucumber, sliced into ⅛-inch disks

1 pint multicolored baby heirloom tomatoes or grape tomatoes, halved

1 ripe avocado, pit removed, slipped from its skin, and cut into wedges

½ cup green garlic-stuffed olives (available in the deli section)

4 hard-boiled eggs, peeled and cut into wedges

Method

Preheat the oven to 500°F. Slice the root end off the head of garlic and the shallots and turn them upside down, wrapping them in heavy-duty aluminum foil and molding the foil so it allows the cut ends to stand upright in the oven. Pour the grapeseed oil on the garlic and shallots so it slips between their papery skins and the cloves and enclose the garlic and shallots with foil. Place them in a baking pan to insulate them a bit from the high heat. Roast for about 15 to 20 minutes and set aside until they are cool enough to handle. (Be sure to monitor the garlic while it is roasting at such a high temperature. If you have the time, consider roasting the garlic at 350°F for 50 minutes instead.)

Gently squeeze the roasted garlic cloves and shallots from their skins onto a small plate. Through the feed opening of a running blender add, one at a time, the vinegar, mustard, thyme, salt, pepper, roasted garlic, and roasted shallots. Then, leaving the blender running, add the olive oil in a slow stream. Taste the dressing and add salt and pepper as needed.

In a mixing bowl, toss the greens with the onion, scallions, and cucumber. Fold in the tomatoes.

Presentation

Transfer some of the salad to each individual serving dish and top with avocado wedges, garlic-stuffed olives, and hard-boiled eggs.

Louisiana Caviar

SERVES 4 TO 6

Having filmed several episodes of *Dinner: Impossible* in the Deep South, I've heard references to Louisiana caviar many times. I just love the name. There are a number of variations on the recipe and to my knowledge, none of them contains actual caviar. The term refers to the beautiful glistening black of the black-eyed peas or black beans. I've added my own variations to the recipe, and I hope you enjoy it.

Please note the forty-minute roasting time for the peppers, which can be done in advance. The rest of the recipe comes together in a matter of minutes.

INGREDIENTS

1 tablespoon grapeseed oil, or as needed to brush on the peppers

1 red bell pepper, stemmed and seeded but left whole

1 poblano pepper, stemmed and seeded but left whole (Use disposable plastic gloves while handling these and all hot peppers. Protect your face and eyes, and avoid breathing in the fumes.)

2 tablespoons red wine

⅓ cup rice wine vinegar

2 large garlic cloves, lightly crushed with the side of a knife blade and quartered

1 cup olive oil, preferably extra virgin

Two 16-ounce cans black-eyed peas, drained

2 tablespoons sliced scallions, white and tender green parts only (from about 3 scallions)

2 tablespoons chopped fresh parsley leaves

Method

Preheat the oven to 450°F. Brush grapeseed oil on the outside of the peppers and place them on their sides on a piece of heavy-duty aluminum foil (with the edges turned up to avoid drips). Spoon 1 tablespoon of wine into each pepper. Roast for 20 minutes, then use tongs to turn them carefully, trying to keep the wine inside the peppers. Roast until charred, about another 20 minutes, then remove them from the oven and fold the edges of the aluminum foil around the peppers to let them sweat.

Make the vinaigrette just before use. Through the feed opening of a running blender, add the vinegar and garlic. With the blender still running, pour in the olive oil in a slow, thin stream.

Return to the bell peppers and peel off the blackened skin. Slice the flesh of the peppers brunoise (julienne, then crosswise) and place in a mixing bowl. Fold in the black-eyed peas, scallions, and parsley. Stir in only enough of the vinaigrette to coat.

Presentation

Serve family style.

Sprouts, Squash, and 'Shrooms with White Wine and Hoisin Sauce

SERVES 4

If you're looking for a slightly different way to enjoy vegetables, try this variation to fend off boredom. The brussels sprouts are lightly seared to bring out their sugars. White wine lends a delicate flavor to the veggies, with hoisin sauce available on the side for those who like a bolder flavor. This recipe is also delicious served over rice for a light vegetarian entrée.

INGREDIENTS

1 pound baby carrots

1 tablespoon olive oil

1 tablespoon butter

2 shallot cloves, sliced

2 garlic cloves, gently crushed with the side of a knife blade and minced

12 brussels sprouts, tough outer leaves removed and halved from top to bottom

1 cup (about 3 ounces) small white mushrooms, trimmed and cleaned

1 cup (about 3 ounces) large white mushrooms, trimmed, cleaned, and sliced lengthwise

1 cup dry white wine

5 or 6 small pattypan squash, quartered (choose those that are light green but heavy for their size)

⅓ cup hoisin sauce, at room temperature

2 cups cooked rice, as an optional accompaniment for a vegetarian entrée

Method

Parboil the baby carrots in salted water for about 5 minutes. Remove the carrots from the heat, drain, and set aside briefly.

In a large sauté pan, heat the olive oil over medium-high heat and melt the butter in it. Add the shallots and garlic and cook until the shallots are translucent, stirring frequently to prevent burning, about 1 to 2 minutes. Using a slotted spatula or spoon, scoop the shallots and garlic onto a utility platter while you "sear" the brussels sprouts. Place the brussels sprouts, sliced-side down, in the pan to allow their cut surfaces to caramelize a bit, about 3 or 4 minutes. Transfer the brussels sprouts to the utility platter as well. Using the same pan, reduce the heat to medium and cook all the mushrooms until they begin to soften and release their juices, about 8 minutes. Deglaze the pan with the white wine, add the pattypan squash, stir to combine, cover, and cook until it begins to soften, about 10 minutes. Reduce the heat to low and return the brussels sprouts, shallots, garlic, and carrots to the pan. Cover and cook until the squash becomes tender but not mushy and the brussels sprouts are tender but still bright green, about 10 minutes. Do not overcook. Remove from the heat and stir in the hoisin sauce for a bold flavor, or serve on the side as an option for the guests.

Presentation

If you're serving as a vegetarian entrée, place ½ cup white rice in the center of each serving plate and spoon some vegetables over the rice.

Pineapple and Artichoke Pasta with Pine Nuts

SERVES 4 TO 6

Pineapple and pine nuts are not related to each other, and the only thing artichokes have to do with anything that sounds like "pine" is their remote resemblance to pinecones. I first made this recipe when I was trapped in an Ice Hotel and was inspired by the ingredients we had on hand. You may think the combination is a bit unusual, but I assure you, it's a delight for the taste buds that makes you think outside of the box for flavor pairings. It is also really easy to make.

INGREDIENTS

1 tablespoon unsalted butter

1 tablespoon grapeseed oil

3 garlic cloves, lightly crushed with the side of a knife blade and minced

2 shallot cloves, minced

2 cups shiitake mushrooms (about 6 ounces), cleaned, stems trimmed of the woody parts, and sliced

1 jalapeño pepper, stemmed, seeded, and diced small (Use disposable plastic gloves while handling these and all hot peppers. Protect your face and eyes, and avoid breathing in the fumes.)

3 tablespoons chopped fresh cilantro

5 tablespoons chopped fresh flat-leaf parsley (2 tablespoons to mix in, 3 tablespoons for garnish)

1 pineapple, peeled, cored, and cut into medium chunks

1 teaspoon McCormick Mexican Style Chili Powder (a really interesting combination of flavors)

1 teaspoon dried Italian seasoning (or ½ teaspoon each dried thyme and oregano)

2 cups chicken stock

1 pound farfalle pasta

1 cup heavy cream

One 16-ounce can artichoke hearts, quarter cut

½ cup pine nuts

Salt and freshly ground black pepper to taste

1 tablespoon extra virgin olive oil (to toss with the pasta)

Method

Bring a pot of salted water to a boil for the pasta.

In a large sauté pan over medium-high heat, melt the butter in the grapeseed oil. Sauté the garlic, shallots, mushrooms, jalapeño pepper, cilantro, and parsley until the mushrooms give up their juices and the pepper begins to soften, about 5 to 8 minutes. Stir in the pineapple, chili powder, and Italian seasoning and let cook for about 5 minutes. Add the chicken stock and cook until the liquid is reduced by half, about 7 minutes. (Meanwhile, add the farfalle to the pot of boiling water.) Stir the cream into the mixture, add the artichoke hearts and pine nuts, and cook until the flavors are integrated, about 5 more minutes. Season with salt and pepper to taste and remove from the heat.

When the pasta is cooked al dente, drain, coat with the olive oil, and season with freshly ground black pepper.

Presentation

Spoon some farfalle into a serving dish. Top with the sauce and garnish with parsley. (The finished dish is shown in the photo insert.)

9. "I'M NOT A BAKER, BUT . . .": BAKING SAVORY MEALS

I've said it before and I will say it again: I am not a baker.

I am second to none in my admiration for the art of baking. Indeed, one of the best chefs working today is my good friend Michel Richard, and baking is at the very heart of his craft and expertise. For me, it all comes down to method versus madness. Baking reminds me of being at school, with all of the arithmetic and measuring and getting marked down if you get it wrong (try using the wrong proportions in virtually any baking situation and you will immediately see what I mean). You practically need a protractor and a slide rule. I much prefer the free-form method of the kind of cooking I do every day. There are still rules, but you have the freedom to create, to throw ingredients into the mix on sudden inspiration, to react to ideas on the spot, to take outrageous chances and benefit from the madness, usually with delicious results. There is a lot less choreography in my cooking, and a lot more improvisation. I guess that's why I prefer rugby to ballet.

Yet as part of my training, I had to study and become proficient at baking, and in point of fact, I really do enjoy the results. I'm not a baker, but I like pie. I like to feature pastry, tarts, shells, and the like in my dishes a lot more than you might imagine, given my oft-stated inclinations. I have an Englishman's deep appreciation for pies, not only in terms of sweets and dainties, but in savory pies as well, with steak and kidney, lamb and sausages and gravies stuffed in pastry crust. There are echoes of Dickens and Robin Hood, of banquets in medieval castles in this craving, as well as of homely meals served whilst nestled in cozy cottages in the English countryside with a pot of tea, and of pork pies on plank tables washed down with a pint of bitter in pubs and taverns.

This is a category in which I really identify with the home cook and would prefer to buy something premade than go to the painstaking trouble of making it myself. (Although food processors fitted with dough blades have changed everything.) Happily, we live in an age when you can get really nice puff pastry and phyllo dough in the frozen food section of your local grocery. If you master the art of making it yourself, I salute you. You're a better man than I, Gunga Din! But in either case, remember, life is short and we all have only those minutes allotted to us; use yours well and don't make yourself crazy.

When it comes to making cakes and pastry, I really like to keep it simple. I love sponge cake, and I will give you the recipe for light and flaky tart shells, simple and elegant. I have a special prejudice for the kinds of preparations that involve simple batters cooked simply—in the oven, as in Yorkshire pudding, or on the stovetop, as in pancakes, blinis, and crepes. These fully qualify as pastry as far as I'm concerned, even if they don't keep me occupied for hours on end with metric scales and measuring spoons. There are some easy and fun crepe recipes here, and I'll show you how I like to fill mine; fill yours as you like. Their beauty is not only in their ease of preparation, but in the speed at which you can prepare and happily consume them.

Simple Salmon Wellington

SERVES 8 AS AN APPETIZER

Why should beef be the only one that gets a warm, cozy blanket of pastry?

INGREDIENTS FOR THE PUFF PASTRY SHELLS (VOL-AU-VENT PASTRY)

2 puff pastry dough sheets (often sold in 17- or 18-ounce packages containing two 9- or 10-inch-square puff pastry sheets), or alternatively you can purchase frozen prepared shells, such as those made by Pepperidge Farm

1 or 2 eggs, beaten, or as needed for the egg wash

INGREDIENTS FOR THE SALMON

Two 6-ounce salmon fillets

Salt and freshly ground black pepper to taste

2 teaspoons capers

8 very small parsley sprigs (with 1 or 2 leaves on each sprig)

INGREDIENTS FOR THE SAUCE

4 tablespoons (½ stick) unsalted butter

1 shallot clove, minced

¼ cup sherry

1 cup heavy cream

3 egg yolks

Juice of ½ lemon

Salt and freshly ground black pepper to taste

EQUIPMENT

Steaming rack

3-inch circle or biscuit cutter

2-inch circle or biscuit cutter

Method for the puff pastry shells

If you're using premade puff pastry shells, skip to the next paragraph. Preheat the oven to 375°F. Unfold the puff pastry dough, and use a 3-inch circle or biscuit cutter to cut out 8 dough rounds. Place 4 dough rounds on a lightly greased baking sheet. Using a 2-inch circle or biscuit cutter, cut a concentric circle in the middle of the remaining 3-inch dough rounds to create a ½-inch-wide circle of dough. These ½-inch-wide circles of dough are to be used without the 2-inch pieces from the center. Place one of the ½-inch-wide dough circles neatly on top of each of the rounds already on the baking sheet, matching up the edges. Brush egg wash over the surface of each of the paired dough circles and rounds. Then use a fork to prick through the dough around the perimeter of each circle, piercing through to the round underneath.

Bake the egg-washed pastry shells until golden brown, about 20 to 25 minutes; the center of each pastry shell will rise. (Meanwhile, prepare the salmon, below.)

Remove the pastry shells from the oven and allow to cool slightly.

Method for the salmon

Season the salmon fillets with salt and pepper. Place a steaming rack in a wide saucepan and fill the pan with a couple of inches of water. Bring the water to a simmer, place the salmon fillets on the rack, and cover. Steam the salmon until it is about three quarters opaque as seen from the side and the fish is beginning to flake, about 5 to 7 minutes. (Meanwhile, begin the sauce.) Transfer the salmon to a utility platter, cover, and set aside to carry-over cook until it is opaque inside.

Method for the sauce

Melt the butter in a small saucepan over medium heat. Add the shallot and sauté until it is translucent, about 2 to 3 minutes, stirring frequently. Add the sherry and allow it to reduce by half, then reduce the heat to low and whisk in the cream. Stir while the mixture cooks and thickens, about 5 minutes.

In a small bowl, whisk the egg yolks until no streaks remain and the color begins to lighten.

Create a liaison to prevent the eggs from cooking (into scrambled eggs!) when you combine them with the sauce. To do this, remove the cream mixture from the heat and whisk *1 tablespoon at a time* of the warm mixture into the bowl of egg yolks. Do this very gradually, whisking well after each addition, until you've added about half the cream mixture to the egg yolks. Add the remaining cream mixture all at once, whisk well, and return all of the sauce to the pan over low heat, stirring to keep it smooth and integrate the flavors. Remove from the heat, and stir in the lemon juice.

Method to assemble the tarts

Flake the salmon in a small bowl. Do not break up the salmon too much, but keep in mind the size of the pastry shells you will be filling. Gently fold in just enough sauce to coat and hold the mixture together. (You may not need all the sauce.)

Using your fingers, break through the risen center part of each pastry shell. Remove the center portion of each tart to create a cavity to hold the salmon mixture. (Use your own judgment on how much to remove to retain the integrity of the tart and yet have enough room to hold the salmon.) Spoon some salmon mixture into each tart.

Presentation

Place a small spoonful of capers (about ¼ teaspoon) on top of the salmon and add a small parsley sprig.

Chicken Pot Pie

SERVES 6

Timeless comfort food with pearl onions and a puff pastry crust. Again, echoes of being tucked away snugly in that country cottage on a cool autumn evening.

INGREDIENTS

1 cup shelled fresh or thawed frozen peas

4 tablespoons (½ stick) butter

2 tablespoons grapeseed oil

2 carrots, peeled and sliced into ¼-inch-thick rounds

½ pound small potatoes, preferably fingerlings, peeled and cut into ¼-inch-thick rounds

16 pearl onions, blanched for 2 minutes in boiling water, skins slipped off after blanching and then roots sliced off

Salt and freshly ground black pepper

1 pound boneless, skinless chicken breasts, cut into ½- to 1-inch pieces

2 cups (about 4 ounces) white mushrooms, cleaned, trimmed, and cut into halves or quarters if large or left whole if small

2 garlic cloves, peeled, lightly crushed, and quartered

1 teaspoon fresh thyme leaves

1 cup chicken stock

3 puff pastry dough sheets, completely defrosted (often sold in 17- or 18-ounce packages containing two 9- or 10-inch-square puff pastry sheets)

2 eggs, beaten

SPECIAL EQUIPMENT

Six 6-inch diameter ovenproof bowls, such as onion soup bowls or soufflé ramekins

TIMELINE

Cut vegetables and herbs	5 minutes
Blanch and skin onions	3 minutes
Cube chicken	3 minutes
Subtotal ingredient prep	**11 minutes**
Boil peas	2 minutes
Roast carrots, potatoes, and onions (15 minutes) *Overlaps with:* Season chicken and cook with mushrooms, garlic, and thyme (7 minutes)	15 minutes
Combine chicken mixture with roasted vegetables and let rest (5 minutes) *Overlaps with:* Cut pastry circles, fill bowls, and top with crusts	5 minutes
Bake pies	12 minutes
Estimated active cooking time	**34 minutes**
Total estimated time	**45 minutes**

Method

Preheat the oven to 400°F and have a bowl of ice water standing by. Bring a small pot of salted water to a boil and cook the peas until tender but still bright green, 2 to 3 minutes. Drain the peas into a strainer and plunge the strainer into the bowl of ice water to stop the cooking. Drain again and set aside.

In an ovenproof skillet over medium-high heat, melt 1 tablespoon of butter in 1 tablespoon of oil (reserving the rest of the butter and oil). When the butter melts, add the carrots, potatoes, and onions and stir to coat. Season with salt and pepper and put in the oven. Roast until the potatoes are tender, about 15 minutes.

Season the chicken pieces with salt and pepper. While the vegetables are roasting, put the remaining 1 tablespoon oil and another tablespoon of butter in a skillet over medium-high heat. When the butter melts, add the chicken, mushrooms, garlic, and thyme. Cook, stirring occasionally, until the chicken and mushrooms are nicely browned, about 5 minutes. Add the chicken stock and stir to integrate the flavors. Turn off the heat and stir in the remaining 2 tablespoons of butter. Add the roasted vegetables and the peas and let cool to room temperature.

Fold out the pastry dough and, using a cereal bowl or small mixing bowl as a template, cut 6 rounds, each 7 or 8 inches in diameter.

Put the chicken and vegetable mixture into the ovenproof bowls and brush the edges of the bowls with a little egg to keep the pastry from sliding off. Top each with a circle of pastry, draping the crust over the rim. Brush the tops of the pastry with the egg wash and bake until golden, about 12 to 15 minutes.

Sweet and Savory Crepes

SERVES 6

Please make these crepes with whole milk, real butter, and organic eggs, as God and the French intended. You can use flavorful whole ingredients in your cooking; they are quite healthy as long as you do not overindulge. Moderation in all things, my friends, always moderation.

Basic Recipe for Crepes

MAKES 12 CREPES

INGREDIENTS

4 eggs

1½ cups whole milk

1½ cups all-purpose flour

1 teaspoon salt

2 tablespoons (¼ stick) butter

2 tablespoons grapeseed oil

SPECIAL EQUIPMENT

½-cup ladle

10-inch crepe pan

Method for the basic crepes

In a large mixing bowl, whisk together the eggs, milk, flour, and salt until all the lumps are gone.

Use a 10-inch crepe pan (such as the nonstick one made by Calphalon) designed to keep the crepes from sticking. Heat the pan over medium heat and use ½ teaspoon butter melted in ½ teaspoon grapeseed oil for each crepe.

Scoop up batter for the first crepe using a ½-cup ladle, filling the ladle about half full in a quick motion. (In other words, don't fuss over it too much. The natural motion of your arm when you scoop the batter will actually fill it to just where you want it because you will only need about 2 to 3 tablespoons of batter that will be swirled in the pan to make thin crepes about the size of a dinner plate.)

Lift the pan off the heat and quickly pour in the batter to cover the surface of the pan with a thin, even layer, tilting the pan so the batter coats the sides as well. Cook the crepe until it starts to bubble, loosening the edges while it cooks. Flip it over with a thin spatula. Cook the other side just until it is speckled a light brown. Slide the crepe onto a warm plate and make the remaining crepes, remembering to wipe out the pan before cooking each one.

Precook a stack of crepes and serve them with one of the fillings below.

Savory crepes

I offer you two recipes:

- **Traditional Smoked Salmon Crepes with Cream Cheese, Red Onion, Capers, and a Lemon Reduction**

- **Pizza-style Crepes with Fresh Mozzarella, Plum Tomato, Basil, and Shaved Prosciutto**

INGREDIENTS FOR THE SMOKED SALMON FILLING
Makes enough filling for 12 crepes

1 stick butter, softened

1 red onion, peeled and finely sliced

Juice of 2 lemons (about ½ cup)

½ pound smoked salmon, cut into ¼- to ½-inch pieces

8 ounces cream cheese, softened

2 teaspoons small capers

2 teaspoons chopped fresh chives

Method for the smoked salmon filling

In a medium skillet over medium heat, melt the butter. Add the onion and sauté until translucent, about 3 minutes. Add the lemon juice and cook it down until it is reduced to a syrup, about 5 to 8 minutes. Remove from the heat and let cool to room temperature.

Fold the salmon and cream cheese together in a medium bowl.

Heat a clean sauté pan over medium-high heat. Spoon a line of the salmon mixture down the center of each crepe, drizzle some lemon reduction on top, and sprinkle with capers. Fold each crepe in half to secure the filling, then roll up each crepe from the wide side. Add the crepes to the heated pan and warm the crepe through for a few minutes. Serve 2 crepes on each serving plate and sprinkle with chives.

Makes enough filling for 12 crepes

4 prosciutto slices, cut into ½-inch pieces

One 16-ounce can chopped tomatoes

2 ripe plum tomatoes, thinly sliced

½ pound fresh mozzarella, cut into small pieces

6 large fresh basil leaves, minced

Method for the pizza-style filling

In a medium skillet over medium heat, add the prosciutto. Stir in the chopped tomatoes and cook for about 5 minutes to allow the flavors to integrate, then remove from the heat.

Heat a clean sauté pan over medium-high heat. Spoon a line of the tomato mixture down the center of each crepe. Layer slices of plum tomato on top and sprinkle with mozzarella. Fold the crepe in half to secure the filling, then roll up the crepe from the wide side. Add the crepes to the pan and heat through for a few minutes. Serve 2 crepes on each plate and sprinkle with basil.

Sweet crepes

And two sweet recipes:

- **Banana Chocolate-Hazelnut Crepes**

- **Crepes Suzette with Fresh Oranges, Mint, and Crème Fraîche.** (This version is alcohol free.)

Makes enough filling for 12 crepes

1 stick butter, softened

1 cup Nutella chocolate-hazelnut spread

1 cup pure maple syrup

4 bananas, sliced

1 cup confectioners' sugar, as needed to sprinkle on the finished crepes

Method for the banana chocolate-hazelnut filling

Heat a sauté pan over medium heat. In a large bowl, combine the butter, Nutella, and maple syrup. Gently fold in the banana slices. Add the mixture to the pan and cook for a few minutes to integrate the flavors, monitoring to prevent burning. Remove from the heat.

Place a clean 10-inch pan over medium-high heat. Fold one of the crêpes into quarters, add it to the pan, and immediately spoon some of the banana-Nutella mixture over the crepe and allow it to heat through. Slide it onto a plate and top with confectioners' sugar. Repeat for each crepe. (The finished dish is shown in the photo insert.)

INGREDIENTS FOR THE VIRGIN CREPES SUZETTE FILLING

Makes enough filling for 12 crepes

2 teaspoons cornstarch

2 cups freshly squeezed orange juice

4 oranges, segmented

2 teaspoons chopped fresh mint

1 cup crème fraîche

Method for the crepes Suzette filling

Make a slurry by whisking the cornstarch gradually into a small bowl containing a small amount of the orange juice. Pour the slurry into a large bowl with the rest of the orange juice and orange segments and combine.

Place a 10-inch pan over medium-high heat. Fold one of the crepes into quarters, add it to the pan, and immediately ladle some of the orange juice mixture on top and allow it to heat through. Slide the crepe onto a plate and top with fresh mint. Repeat for each crepe. Serve topped with a small dollop of créme fraîche.

Windy City Stovetop Pizza

SERVES 6

Cooking on *Dinner: Impossible* forces me to be resourceful and that's where this dish was born. I hope you feel yourself the beneficiary with the following delicious recipe. It's made entirely on the stovetop, which means you can even make it at a campsite if you bring the ingredients. In fact, a cast-iron pan that you bought for your great-grandchildren to inherit would be perfect for this. The preparation calls for no special equipment, but I list it below in case you're interested in the challenge of campsite cooking. I do recommend premixing the pizza dough if possible!

INGREDIENTS FOR THE PIZZA CRUST

1 tablespoon salt

1 tablespoon sugar

1 packet fast-acting yeast

4 cups all-purpose flour

½ cup cornmeal

1 tablespoon grapeseed oil

INGREDIENTS FOR THE FILLING AND TOPPING

1 tablespoon grapeseed oil

1 medium onion, sliced

2 garlic cloves, minced

1 green bell pepper or banana pepper, stemmed, seeded, and sliced

One 8-ounce can tomato sauce

1 teaspoon Italian seasoning (oregano, thyme, and parsley)

Salt and pepper to taste

¼ pound pepperoni, cut into ⅛- to ¼-inch pieces

½ cup shredded mozzarella

EQUIPMENT

(This is normal stuff around the kitchen, but here's what you need to prepare the dish at a campsite—and it's simpler if you premix the dough and bring it along.)

2-quart mixing bowl

Candy thermometer

Cutting board to stretch out the dough

Heavy 12-inch skillet with a lid (or heavy-duty foil to cover), preferably cast iron

Tongs

Method

Dissolve the salt and sugar in 1½ cups warm water that is between 100°F and 115°F as measured with a candy thermometer, and allow about 15 minutes for the yeast to proof. (Proofing the yeast it testing it for viability. It will develop a foam that looks like the head of a beer. If it doesn't proof, the yeast is dead—discard it and start over with new yeast and water.)

Place the flour in a food processor fitted with a dough blade, and with the food processor running, slowly pour the proofed yeast mixture through the feed tube until the dough comes together and forms a cohesive mass. Transfer the dough to a floured board and knead for about 5 minutes, or until the dough is smooth and elastic. Place the dough in a bowl, cover with a clean dish towel, and set the bowl in a warm place until the dough has roughly doubled in volume, 30 to 60 minutes. The dough has risen enough if you make an indentation with your finger and it does not spring back. Punch the dough down and allow it to rise a second time, about 30 minutes, so that it will have a finer texture. (It won't rise as much the second time.)

For the filling, heat the oil in a sauté pan over medium-high heat and cook the onion until it turns translucent, about 3 to 5 minutes. Add the garlic and pepper and cook until they soften, about 5 more minutes, monitoring to prevent burning. Stir in the tomato sauce and Italian seasoning and season with salt and pepper. Cook for a few minutes to allow the flavors to blend, then remove from the heat and set aside briefly.

On a floured surface, stretch the dough into a 14-inch circle that is thicker around the edges and shake cornmeal over both sides of the dough. (Use your fingertips in a motion that resembles playing chords on a piano to avoid tearing the dough.)

You'll be parbaking the dough on both sides on the stovetop before adding the filling and topping. In a heavy-bottomed, lidded 12-inch skillet, heat a small amount of oil over low heat, swirling the oil to coat the entire inside of the skillet. Transfer the circle of dough to the skillet and cook one side until golden brown (about 5 minutes) before flipping it over with tongs. Spoon the tomato mixture into the center of the lightly browned side of the crust and spread it around, allowing an inch of room around the perimeter. Top the tomato mixture with the pepperoni and mozzarella. Cover the pan and cook for 5 to 8 minutes, or until the sauce is integrated into the surface and the cheese is melted. Serve immediately.

Curry Brandade Pizza

MAKES 6 MINI FLATBREAD PIZZAS

This is a casual and festive way to enjoy fish. The halibut is seared with curry, then mixed with potatoes to make a brandade that serves as the topping. Norwegian salmon and chives are an indulgent garnish topping.

INGREDIENTS FOR THE DOUGH

1 tablespoon salt

1 tablespoon sugar

1 packet fast-acting yeast

4 cups all-purpose flour,
  plus extra for the dough board

¼ cup cornmeal

INGREDIENTS FOR THE BAKED TOPPING

1 tablespoon canola oil

1 garlic clove, minced

1 small onion, minced

2 pounds halibut fillets

Salt and freshly ground black pepper to taste

1 teaspoon curry powder

6 medium potatoes (about 2½ to 3 pounds),
  peeled, boiled, drained well, and mashed
  with 2 tablespoons butter

2 tablespoons olive oil

INGREDIENTS FOR THE GARNISH TOPPING

6 ounces smoked Norwegian salmon, flaked

1 medium red onion, shaved thin with a mandoline

2 tablespoons minced fresh chives

EQUIPMENT

Candy thermometer

Pizza stone

Method

Dissolve the salt and sugar in 1½ cups warm water that is between 100°F and 115°F as measured with a candy thermometer, and allow about 15 minutes for the yeast to proof. (Proofing the yeast is testing it for viability. It will develop a foam that looks like the head of a beer. If it doesn't proof, the yeast is dead—discard it and start over with new yeast and water.)

Place the flour in a food processor fitted with a dough blade, and with the food processor running, slowly pour the proofed yeast mixture through the feed tube until the dough forms a cohesive mass. Transfer the dough to a floured board and knead for about 5 minutes, or until the dough is smooth and elastic. Place the dough in a bowl, cover with a clean dish towel, and set the bowl in a warm place until the dough has roughly doubled in volume, 30 to 60 minutes. The dough has risen enough if you make an indentation with your finger and it does not spring back. Punch the dough down, divide it into 6 equal-size balls, and allow it to rise a second time, about 30 minutes, so that it will have a finer texture. (It won't rise as much the second time.)

While the dough is rising, prepare the pizza topping. Heat the canola oil in a large sauté pan over medium-high heat and sauté the garlic and onion until the onion begins to turn translucent, about 2 to 3 minutes. Season the halibut fillets with salt and pepper and the curry powder and sear them on both sides, leaving each side undisturbed for the first 2 minutes to allow the flavors to integrate into the surface of the fish. Cook until the fish flakes, about another 6 to 8 minutes, and let rest. Flake the fish and fold into the mashed potatoes.

Preheat the oven to 450°F. On a floured surface, stretch the dough into six 6- by 8-inch ovals and shake cornmeal over both sides of the dough. You'll be parbaking the dough on both sides on the stovetop before adding the filling and topping. In a heavy-bottomed, lidded 12-inch skillet, heat a small amount of olive oil over low heat, swirling the oil to coat the entire inside of the skillet. Working one at a time, transfer the ovals of dough to the skillet and allow one side to lightly cook and stiffen up before flipping it over with tongs. When both sides of each oval are parbaked this way, transfer the ovals to a pizza stone. Spoon the potato/fish mixture into the center of the toasted side of each oval, spreading it evenly over the surface. Bake for about 10 minutes, or until the edges of the mashed potatoes begin to turn golden.

Remove the pizzas from the oven and sprinkle them with the salmon, red onion, and chives.

Zucchini and Red Onion Quiche

MAKES 6 INDIVIDUAL QUICHES

This recipe showcases the varying flavors that can be achieved with the same ingredients by using different cooking methods. Compare the taste of the caramelized onions and sautéed zucchini in the topping with the roasted onions and zucchini in the quiche.

As chefs, we start by preparing the items that take longest, which in this case is the pastry for the quiche, followed by the caramelized onions. Because the crusts are prebaked before filling, we use that time for prep work for the topping and filling in order to maximize efficiency and minimize downtime.

INGREDIENTS FOR THE QUICHE PASTRY

1½ cups all-purpose flour

¼ teaspoon salt

½ stick (4 tablespoons) chilled unsalted butter

¼ cup chilled vegetable shortening

1 egg yolk, lightly beaten

INGREDIENTS FOR THE ROASTED ZUCCHINI AND CARAMELIZED ONION TOPPING

1 tablespoon grapeseed oil

½ (cut crosswise) medium red onion (use the other half for the quiche filling, below)

½ (cut crosswise) small zucchini, skin left on (use the other half for the quiche filling, below)

½ teaspoon dried marjoram

½ teaspoon dried thyme

Pinch of dried rosemary (reliable sources describe a pinch as 1/16 teaspoon)

Pinch of dried sage

Salt and freshly ground black pepper to taste

INGREDIENTS FOR THE QUICHE FILLING

½ (cut crosswise) medium red onion

½ (cut crosswise) small zucchini

1 garlic clove, lightly crushed with the side of a knife blade

Salt and freshly ground black pepper to taste

4 eggs

½ cup (4 ounces) ricotta cheese

1½ cups half-and-half

1 tablespoon chopped fresh flat-leaf parsley, plus 4 small sprigs for garnish

2 tablespoons chopped fresh basil leaves

EQUIPMENT

Food processor equipped with a dough blade

Rolling pin (if making your own pastry)

Pastry cloth (if making your own pastry)

Six 4½-inch flan pans (tart tins with removable bottoms)

Pastry weights or dried beans

Parchment paper

A mortar and pestle or coffee grinder dedicated to grinding spices

A thin offset spatula (you can use any spatula, but the way an offset spatula angles away from the handle reduces the likelihood of cracking the baked goods)

Method for the crust

Have a glass of ice water handy. Sift the flour into the bowl of a food processor equipped with a dough blade. Add the salt, butter, and shortening and pulse just until the mixture resembles coarse meal. Add ice water 1 tablespoon at a time through the feed tube, pulsing after each addition. Add just enough water to allow the dough to come together into a cohesive whole, usually between 6 and 8 tablespoons of water. All flours are different, so this amount will vary each time. Transfer the dough to a mixing bowl and form it into a ball. Divide the dough into 6 portions and form them into 6 balls. Flatten the balls slightly and set them aside to rest.

Grease the 6 flan pans well. Using a pastry cloth dusted with just enough flour to keep the dough from sticking, fold the pastry cloth in half over each dough ball, roll each out in turn into a circle 7 or 8 inches in diameter, and ease the dough into a flan pan. Trim the top edge of the dough flush with the top edge of each pan. As you finish each pan, cover it with plastic wrap and set it on a large baking sheet. Preheat the oven to 400°F and place the baking sheet into the freezer for a few minutes while the oven is heating.

Remove the plastic from each pan. Line the bottom of each pastry shell with parchment paper and cover the paper with pastry weights or dried beans. Place the baking sheet of pastries in the oven and blind bake (partially prebake without any filling) until you can see that the dough is beginning to turn golden, about 25 minutes. (Meanwhile, begin the onion for the topping, below.)

TIMELINE

Measure ingredients .... 2 minutes
Prepare pastry dough in food
   processor .... 10 minutes
Grease pans (2 minutes), roll out pastry and
   ease into pans (20 minutes), cover with plastic
   wrap and speed chill in freezer (10 minutes),
   add parchment and weights
   (4 minutes).. 36 minutes

Blind bake crusts (25 minutes)
   Overlaps with:
   Slice onions for topping (5 minutes)
   Begin caramelizing onions (35 minutes)
   Overlaps with:
      Grind dried herbs for topping (5 minutes)
      Julienne zucchini for topping (5 minutes)
      Add zucchini/herbs when onion has
      cooked for 20 minutes (1 minute)
   Remove weights and parchment from
     crusts, prick base of crusts, and
     brush with egg yolks (2 minutes)
   Return crusts to oven to finish
     prebaking (5 minutes)
   Overlaps with:
     Season onion/zucchini/herbs for
     topping and remove from heat
     (5 minutes) .... 35 minutes

Allow crusts to cool (10 minutes)
   Overlaps with:
   Slice onion/zucchini/garlic/herbs
     for filling (5 minutes)
   Beat eggs, ricotta, and
     half-and-half (5 minutes) .... 10 minutes
Layer raw zucchini and onion in
   crusts, pour in custard, and bake ...... 25 minutes
Cool in pan (10 minutes)
   plus assembly (5 minutes) .... 15 minutes

Total estimated time ....2 hours and 13 minutes

Remove the pastry shells from the oven, remove the weights or beans, and prick the base of each shell with a fork. (This "ventilation" will keep the crust from bubbling up in the center.) Brush the shells with egg yolk to impart a glossy finish and prevent the crust from becoming soggy after the filling is added. Return the pastry shells to the oven for 5 minutes to dry out the bottoms of the crusts where they were covered by the pastry weights. (Meanwhile, go back to the topping, below, and add the zucchini and spices.)

Remove the pastry shells from the oven and set them aside to cool. Lower the oven temperature to 375°F. (While the pastry shells are cooling, remove the caramelized onion and zucchini from the heat and begin the filling.)

Method for the topping

While the pastry shells are parbaking (the first time), heat the grapeseed oil in a medium sauté pan over medium-high heat and thinly slice the red onion half. Add the onion to the pan and sauté until it turns translucent, about 5 minutes. Reduce the heat to low and slowly allow the onion to begin to caramelize. (This will take about 35 to 45 minutes altogether, but you will be adding the zucchini and ground herbs to the onion about halfway through the process.) Julienne the zucchini half and grind the marjoram, thyme, rosemary, and sage together into a powder with a mortar and pestle or a spice grinder. (Meanwhile, remove the pastry shells from the oven and prepare them to bake a second time.)

When the onion has been cooking for 20 minutes, add the zucchini to the pan, stir to combine, sprinkle with the ground herbs and salt and pepper, and cook until the zucchini is softened (but not mushy) and the onion is caramelized, another 15 to 25 minutes. (Meanwhile, remove the pastry shells from the oven and allow them to cool.)

Remove the zucchini-onion mixture from the heat, season to taste with salt and pepper, cover, and reserve as the topping.

Method for the quiche filling

The oven temperature should be lowered to 375°F. Line a large baking sheet with foil.

Chop the red onion half and peel and cut the zucchini half into ⅛-inch-thick slices. Mince the garlic. Combine in a mixing bowl.

To make the custard, beat the eggs, ricotta, and half-and-half together in a mixing bowl.

Place the pastry shells on a baking sheet lined with foil. Layer the raw mixture of onion, zucchini, garlic, salt and pepper to taste, parsley, and basil over the bottom of the parbaked pastry shells. Pour the custard on top, taking care to avoid overfilling. Bake until the custard is set and lightly browned, about 25 to 35 minutes.

Remove the quiches from the oven and let cool 10 minutes in the pans, then push the pans up from the bottom to release them from the sides. Use a thin offset spatula to transfer the quiches to serving plates.

Presentation

Spoon some of the zucchini-onion topping in the center of each quiche. Garnish with a sprig of parsley and serve warm.

Cornish Pasties

SERVES 8

"Cornish" refers to Cornwall, England, or to the Celtic language spoken there. The first syllable of "pasties" is like that of the word *past* rather than that of the glue kids use on paper. I think it's one of the world's best finger foods, and I'm sure that Friar Tuck would agree with me.

INGREDIENTS

2 tablespoons grapeseed oil

2 medium carrots, peeled and diced small

1 medium onion, peeled and diced small

1 large potato, peeled and diced small

2 garlic cloves, chopped

1 pound ground beef

Salt and pepper to taste

1½ teaspoons jerk seasoning

3 tablespoons tomato paste

2 puff pastry dough sheets (often sold in 17- or 18-ounce packages containing two 10-inch-square puff pastry sheets)

2 eggs, beaten

Method

Heat the oil in a skillet and sauté the carrots, onion, potato, and garlic until they are softened but still firm. Add the ground beef and brown it. Drain the fat from the pan and season with salt and pepper and the jerk seasoning. Stir in the tomato paste to bind the mixture and set aside to cool.

Preheat the oven to 375°F and lightly grease a large baking sheet. Roll out the puff pastry to a ¼-inch thickness and use a small plate as a template to cut out eight 5-inch circles. Place the dough circles on the baking sheet and place a spoonful of the meat mixture on one side of each circle. Fold the dough over to create half-circles and seal the edges by pinching the dough together. Brush the surface of the pastry with the egg wash. Bake until golden brown, about 15 minutes. (The finished dish is shown in the photo insert.)

10. NEVER SKIP DESSERT!

Aaah . . . dessert. Good old dessert.

I love it.

I would rather go and have dessert than lecture you about how to make it, frankly. I've been known to order an indulgent dessert at a restaurant and rationalize away my "behavior" by claiming that I'm performing professional research.

"I want to see how they make it."

You wouldn't believe some of the looks I've gotten from my companions with that comment. They just don't understand.

My sweet tooth is Herculean and I've learned to accept it. Accept yours. If you don't have one, you have my deepest respect, but also my deepest sympathies, because I can't help but feel you are missing out.

Don't miss out on these.

Enjoy!

Caramel Bananas with Chocolate Espresso

MAKES 24 BANANA TREATS

Since these are the size of hors d'oeuvres, you can still enjoy a treat and yet keep your girlish figure (or manly physique, as the case may be).

INGREDIENTS

48 Nilla wafers (a 12-ounce box)

Two 6-ounce jars caramel topping
(the kind used as an ice cream topping),
at room temperature

Three 12-ounce packages semisweet chocolate
chips

3 tablespoons espresso coffee beans, ground very
fine in a coffee grinder

3 bananas, each sliced crosswise into 8 pieces just
before use

EQUIPMENT

24 foil cupcake liners
(such as Reynolds Foil Bake Cups)

Candy thermometer

Method

Arrange the cupcake liners on a baking sheet or in muffin tins and make room in the refrigerator. Place one Nilla wafer, curved-side down, into each cupcake liner (reserving the other 24 cookies).

Pour 1 jar of the caramel topping (reserving the other jar) into a small saucepan and heat over low heat until it is just softened. Spoon a teaspoon of the softened caramel into each muffin tin on top of the vanilla water. Chill in the refrigerator for 30 minutes.

When the caramel cookies are chilled, the next step is to temper the chocolate. (If chocolate is successively melted and cooled within a certain temperature range—a process known as tempering—it will retain a silky appearance without a chalky finish.) To do this, divide the chocolate chips between 2 stainless steel bowls that will fit over a saucepan in double boiler fashion. When the caramel-topped cookies are chilled—not before—bring an inch or so of water to a boil over medium-high heat in the saucepan and fit one of the bowls of chocolate chips over it. Heat until the chocolate is just melted (about 90°F to 100°F as measured on a candy thermometer) and pour the melted chocolate into the other bowl with the (still solid) chips. Stir to combine, return all the chocolate to the double boiler, and heat to about 120°F.

Remove the chocolate from the heat and immediately whisk in the ground espresso. Pour 1 tablespoon of the espresso chocolate into each muffin tin over each of the chilled caramel-topped cookies. Immediately place a banana slice on top of the melted chocolate, then pour 1 tablespoon espresso chocolate *over* each banana. Let the chocolate harden, then chill in the refrigerator, about 30 minutes.

Heat the other jar of caramel topping over low heat in a small saucepan until it is just softened. Spoon a teaspoon of the softened caramel on top of each chocolate-covered banana and top with a second Nilla wafer.

Chill until the caramel sets up, about 20 minutes.

Presentation

Serve on an hors d'oeuvre tray.

Layered Tropical Fruits with Chamomile Frozen Yogurt

SERVES 6

Low in fat and added sugar, and high in healthful yogurt cultures, the infusion of nerve-soothing chamomile in this creamy concoction layered with vitamin C–laden fruits might just cure what ails you.

I like frozen yogurt best when it's served fresh from the ice cream maker, because once stored it never seems to have exactly that same level of creaminess. In order to achieve that goal, it's easy to make parts of this recipe in advance, such as the steeping of the chamomile tea or the syrup, or both. You can also prep the fruits a bit in advance as long as you keep them from drying out. Of course, the frozen yogurt also keeps well in a plastic container in the freezer if you want to do everything ahead of time or if you have some left over.

INGREDIENTS

6 chamomile tea bags, such as Twinings

6 tablespoons macadamia nuts

½ cup sugar

2 cups plain yogurt

1 mango

2 kiwi fruits

6 large strawberries

6 small mint sprigs

TIMELINE

Boil water and steep tea bags (15 minutes)
Overlaps with:
Crush macadamia nuts
(2 minutes) ....15 minutes
Make chamomile syrup .... 5 minutes
Bring syrup to room temperature .... 30 minutes
Blend yogurt into syrup (2 minutes)
and process in ice cream maker (25 minutes)
Overlaps with:
Peel and slice mango and kiwi
(5 minutes) .... 27 minutes
Assembly...12 minutes

***Total estimated time, start to finish
(including cooling time) ... 1 hour and 29 minutes***

Method

Place the tea bags in a Pyrex bowl or other vessel suitable for steeping tea. Pour 1 cup of boiling water over the tea bags, making sure they are submerged. Let steep for 15 minutes.

Put the macadamia nuts in a plastic bag and lightly crush them with a rolling pin or the side of a meat mallet. Set aside until needed.

Remove the tea bags from the infusion and squeeze them to extract all the brewed liquid. Pour the tea into a small, heavy-bottomed saucepan and add the sugar. Heat over low heat, stirring just until the sugar has dissolved. Remove from the heat and set aside to let cool completely, about 30 minutes.

When the tea syrup has dropped to room temperature, add the yogurt and blend well. Process in an ice cream maker until it reaches the consistency of sherbet, about 25 minutes.

While the yogurt mixture is freezing, peel and slice the mango away from the pit in uniform slices. Peel the kiwi fruits and slice them crosswise into ¼-inch-thick slices.

Presentation

Arrange the mango slices in a vertical overlapping pattern around the bottom of a parfait glass. Spoon about ¼ cup of the frozen yogurt over the mango and top with slices of kiwi. Add a second layer of yogurt and sprinkle with crushed macadamia nuts. Top with a strawberry and mint leaves.

Almond Rochers

MAKES 24 TO 48 COOKIES, DEPENDING ON SIZE

These are light as air, with a satisfying flavor that will make you feel as if you're getting away with something. They are gluten-free, too. In my travels throughout the United States as a chef, I've been amazed at how many people I've met in recent years who have only recently discovered that they have a gluten sensitivity. I feel tremendous empathy for the folks who, had they been diagnosed earlier, could have been spared years of suffering and for kids who might feel left out when it's time for cookies and cakes. So, for all you gluten-free foodies out there, enjoy these wonderful treats!

INGREDIENTS

2 large egg whites, at room temperature

1 cup confectioners' sugar

Pinch of salt

1 cup plus 2 tablespoons sliced almonds (broken into ¼-inch pieces and toasted in a 350°F oven until golden brown, about 7 to 10 minutes)

½ teaspoon vanilla extract

EQUIPMENT

Stand mixer

Pastry bag fitted with a ½-inch tip (optional)

Method

Preheat the oven to 350°F.

Line a baking sheet with parchment paper or a nonstick liner. Pour about 2 inches of water into a medium saucepan and bring to a simmer over medium heat. Combine the egg whites, confectioners' sugar, and salt in the stainless steel bowl of a stand mixer that will rest securely in the rim of the saucepan over, not touching, the water. Whisk the mixture until smooth, then place over the saucepan and continue to whisk until the whites are hot to the touch, about 5 minutes or so. Remove the bowl from over the water and place on the mixer stand. Fit the mixer with the whisk attachment and mix on high speed until the mixture is very thick and holds glossy, stiff peaks when you lift the beater. Fold in the almonds and vanilla with a rubber spatula.

Immediately scoop the meringue into a pastry bag fitted with a ½-inch plain tip and pipe onto the prepared baking sheet, forming kisses about 1 inch in diameter and spacing them about 1½ inches apart. Or you can drop by teaspoonfuls onto the baking sheet.

Place the baking sheet in the oven and keep the door ajar with the handle of a wooden spoon to allow moisture to escape. Bake the cookies until they puff slightly, crack along the sides, and feel dry on the outside but soft to the touch, 15 to 20 minutes. (The finished dish is shown in the photo insert.) Transfer the cookies to a wire rack and let cool.

Brioche Figgy Pudding with Eggnog Ice Cream

SERVES 6 TO 8

This dessert always reminds me of Old Fezziwig's holiday celebration as described in Dickens's *Christmas Carol*.

INGREDIENTS FOR THE EGGNOG ICE CREAM

½ cup golden raisins

3 ounces (6 tablespoons or ⅜ cup) bourbon

4 egg yolks

1 cup sugar

2 cups whole milk

1 cup heavy cream

1 teaspoon freshly ground nutmeg

SPECIAL EQUIPMENT

Candy thermometer

Ice cream maker

INGREDIENTS FOR THE FIGGY PUDDING

1 cup ½-inch brioche bread cubes

1 raspberry Danish, cut into ½-inch cubes to yield 1 cup

1 cup crushed Nilla wafers (from about half a 12-ounce box)

4 large eggs

6 tablespoons sugar

2 cups whole milk

1 cup heavy cream

¾ teaspoon vanilla extract

¼ teaspoon salt

1 pint fresh raspberries

½ pound fresh Mission figs, chopped into ½-inch pieces

½ cup (about 4 ounces) apricot jelly

½ cup whipped cream, for garnish

Method for the ice cream

In a small saucepan, combine the raisins and bourbon. Bring to a simmer over low heat, then set the pan aside to cool completely.

In a large bowl, using an electric beater, beat the egg yolks and sugar until the yolks lighten in color and the sugar is completely dissolved.

In a medium saucepan over medium heat, combine the milk, cream, and nutmeg and simmer to a temperature of 160°F, as measured with a candy thermometer, stirring frequently to keep it from burning. Remove from the heat.

Next, gradually temper the hot milk mixture into the egg and sugar mixture so the eggs don't cook (into scrambled eggs). To do this, create a "liaison" by spooning the hot milk mixture into the bowl of eggs a small amount at a time, mixing well after each addition, until both mixtures are roughly the same temperature. Then combine the two mixtures and stir until a uniform color is achieved.

Return the liaison to the pot and cook over medium heat, stirring constantly, until the mixture reaches 160°F. Remove from the heat and stir in the bourbon and raisins. Pour the mixture into a bowl and let stand until it reaches room temperature, then speed chill in the freezer without actually allowing the mixture to freeze, about 30 minutes.

Process the mixture in an ice cream maker according to the manufacturer's directions, about 25 minutes, and store in the freezer.

Method for the figgy pudding

Preheat the oven to 325°F. Grease a 1½- to 2-quart glass baking dish, eight 6-ounce individual baking dishes, or six 8-ounce individual baking dishes.

In a large bowl, combine the brioche, Danish, and Nilla wafers. In a separate bowl, whisk together the eggs, sugar, milk, cream, vanilla, and salt. Strain this mixture through a conical strainer evenly over the bread mixture and

TIMELINE
Ingredient prep:
Cut bread and cake and crush
wafers for bread pudding .... 3 minutes
Cut figs .... 2 minutes
Measure ingredients .... 5 minutes
Subtotal estimated ingredient
prep time ....**10 minutes**
Grease baking dishes and add bread ..... 2 minutes
Mix eggs, sugar, milk, and cream.
Strain and pour over baked
goods .... 5 minutes
Saturation time for custard (10 minutes)
Overlaps with:
Grind fresh nutmeg (2 minutes)
Bring raisins and bourbon to a
simmer (3 minutes)
Begin warming the cream, milk,
and nutmeg for ice cream (5 minutes)
Overlaps with:
Beat egg yolk, sugar, and vanilla
for ice cream (5 minutes) .... 10 minutes
Prepare bain marie and place
bread pudding in oven .... 5 minutes
Baking time for bread pudding
(60 minutes)
Overlaps with:
Temper egg mixture for ice cream
and cook until thickened (5 minutes)
Cool and chill ice cream
ingredients (30 minutes)
Process ice cream in ice cream maker
(25 minutes) and transfer to
freezer (5 minutes) .... 60 minutes
Allow bread pudding to rest (15 minutes)
Overlaps with:
Spread apricot jelly on bread
pudding (3 minutes)
Prepare whipped cream
(10 minutes) ....15 minutes
Subtotal estimated active
cooking time .... 97 minutes
Assembly ....**5 minutes**
Estimated time,
start to finish ....**1 hour and 52 minutes**

set aside to soak for about 10 minutes. Gently fold in the raspberries and figs. Spread the pudding mixture in the large baking dish or spoon it into individual baking dishes.

Prepare a bain marie by placing the pudding dish or dishes into a larger pan, placing the larger pan in the oven, and then carefully pouring hot water into the larger pan without splashing any into the pudding pan(s). Bake until the pudding firms and puffs up and a toothpick inserted in the center comes out clean, about 1 hour. Remove the larger pan from the oven, remove the pudding pan(s) from the larger pan, and let rest for 15 minutes. Spread a thin layer of apricot jelly over the top of the pudding(s). (The jelly can be slightly thinned with a little warm water if you have difficulty spreading it.)

Presentation

Cut the pudding into wedges or serve in the individual pans. Serve with scoops of eggnog ice cream and whipped cream.

Pecan Bourbon Pralines

MAKES 24 CANDIES, OR ABOUT 36 INDIVIDUAL PRALINES

As if these weren't sinful enough, I like to add bourbon!

INGREDIENTS

2 cups pecan halves

3 cups sugar

1 cup heavy cream

4 tablespoons (½ stick) unsalted butter

¼ teaspoon salt

1 tablespoon blackstrap molasses

2 tablespoons bourbon

EQUIPMENT

Candy thermometer

Method

Preheat the oven to 325°F. Spread the pecans on a baking sheet and toast lightly just until fragrant, about 3 minutes. Let cool completely and reserve them.

Line the baking sheet with parchment paper or a nonstick liner. In a deep, heavy saucepan, combine the sugar, cream, butter, salt, molasses, and bourbon. Place over medium-high heat and cook, stirring with a wooden spoon to break up lumps and dislodge any sugar stuck to the bottom of the pan. Bring to a boil and continue to cook, stirring occasionally, until the mixture registers 240°F on a candy thermometer, 7 to 10 minutes, depending on how vigorously the mixture is boiling. Remove from the heat and let cool to 210°F.

Add the pecans to the sugar mixture and stir vigorously. The mixture will begin to thicken, so you must work quickly. Drop the sugar mixture from a spoon onto the prepared baking sheet, forming circles about 3 inches in diameter, and let cool. Or pour the contents of the pan onto the prepared baking sheet, spread the mixture out, let it cool, and break into pieces with your hands.

Chocolate *Friands*

MAKES 40 MINI-CUPCAKES OR 16 STANDARD CUPCAKES

Friand is the French word for "dainty," as in a tidbit of a dessert, which is what a cupcake is to a cake. The dark chocolate used for *these* cupcakes makes them very satisfying tidbits indeed. Reputed to have aphrodisiac and antidepressant qualities, chocolate can now be purchased with the same attention to detail as a fine wine. You can choose chocolate based on where the cacao bean was grown (South America, Aruba, Santo Domingo), style of preparation (Italian, Swiss, Belgian, American), and reputation of the manufacturer (Ghirardelli, Hershey, Godiva, Lindt). Without getting into too much terminology, which tends to vary anyway, chocolate ranges from a minimum of 10% cacao for milk chocolate, through 30% to roughly 70% cacao for the variously named semisweet or bittersweet chocolates, up to 100% cacao for unsweetened chocolate. By choosing the chocolate you use in a recipe, you have control over the sweetness of the final product. For some of you, the darker the chocolate, the better. This easy recipe is great to try if you want to experiment with your preferences.

INGREDIENTS FOR THE CUPCAKES

6 ounces semisweet or bittersweet chocolate pieces or chocolate squares (between 30% and 67% cacao, depending on the desired sweetness), coarsely chopped (by hand, or dropped through the feed tube of your food processor and pulsed)

2 sticks (1 cup) unsalted butter

1½ cups plus 1 tablespoon sugar

¾ cup all-purpose flour

2 tablespoons cornstarch

¼ teaspoon salt

4 large eggs

INGREDIENTS FOR THE GANACHE

4 ounces semisweet or bittersweet chocolate pieces or chocolate squares (between 30% and 67% cacao, depending on the desired sweetness), coarsely chopped (by hand, or dropped through the feed tube of your food processor and pulsed)

⅔ cup heavy cream

EQUIPMENT

Mini-muffin tins with 1-ounce capacity cups made by Wilton (Avanti), available at fantes.com

Foil muffin liners for mini tins (also available at fantes.com)

264   IMPOSSIBLE TO EASY

Method for the cupcakes

Preheat the oven to 350°F and line the muffin tins with foil liners.

Place the chocolate in a large mixing bowl. In a small saucepan, melt the butter over medium heat until very hot. Pour the butter over the chocolate and whisk or stir until smooth.

In a medium mixing bowl, combine the sugar, flour, cornstarch, and salt and mix well. Add the flour mixture to the chocolate mixture in 3 batches, whisking well after each addition. Add 2 eggs and whisk until combined; then add the remaining 2 eggs and whisk just until incorporated. Be careful not to overmix the batter.

Transfer the batter to a liquid measuring cup for pouring and fill the muffin cups three quarters full. Bake until the cakes just start to crack on top, about 10 to 12 minutes for mini-cupcakes or 12 to 15 minutes for standard cupcakes. Let cool for 10 minutes in the pan, then transfer the cakes to a wire rack to let cool completely before frosting with the ganache.

Method for the ganache

In order to keep the frosting in place, the cupcakes must be completely cooled before dipping them into the ganache. Place the chocolate in a small heatproof bowl. Bring the cream to just under a boil over low heat in a small saucepan. Pour the cream over the chocolate and let sit for a minute or two. Stir gently with a rubber spatula until the chocolate is melted and smooth. If the chocolate is not melting readily, nest the bowl in another bowl of very hot tap water, taking care not to get water into the chocolate.

Dip the cooled cupcakes into the ganache, or spoon the ganache over the cakes.

Cranberry Clafoutis

SERVES 6

For a long while I worked in New Jersey, very close to cranberry country. Chatsworth, a town in the New Jersey Pine Barrens, is the location of many acres of cranberry bogs that supply the Ocean Spray cooperative. Cranberries have been pigeonholed as being only for the holidays, but the fact is, they naturally keep better in their fresh state than many other berries. Their propensity for remaining crisp and firm for extended periods applies to their tenure not only in the growers' coolers, but in your own home refrigerator as well. We photographed the cranberry clafoutis for this recipe in February and had no trouble whatsoever getting fresh cranberries for the purpose in a grocery store in Philadelphia. Ocean Spray is working hard to see that you can get cranberries when you want them. If you can't, be sure to make a point of trying this recipe around the holidays, when *everyone* wants the taste of cranberries.

INGREDIENTS

Butter, for greasing the dishes

4 cups whole milk

1½ cups granulated sugar

1 vanilla bean

Pinch of salt

6 large eggs

⅔ cup all-purpose flour

4 cups fresh cranberries (about a 2-pound bag)

½ cup confectioners' sugar

EQUIPMENT

Six 3- to 4-inch quiche dishes
   or au gratin dishes

Method

Preheat the oven to 425°F. Butter the quiche dishes.

In a medium saucepan, combine the milk, granulated sugar, vanilla bean, and salt. Place over medium heat and stir until the sugar has dissolved (just under a boil).

While the milk mixture is heating, break 2 eggs into a heatproof mixing bowl and whisk until there are no more lumps. Add the remaining 4 eggs and whisk until smooth.

Remove the saucepan from the heat. Gradually temper the hot milk mixture into the eggs in a process known as a "liaison," a procedure that will keep you from ending up with scrambled eggs. Spoon the hot milk mixture into the bowl of eggs a small amount at a time, mixing well after each addition, until both mixtures are roughly the same temperature. Then combine the two mixtures and stir until a uniform color is achieved and whisk in the flour.

Pour the batter into the quiche dishes and distribute the cranberries evenly on top of the batter.

Pour about 2 inches of hot water into a large baking pan. Place the filled dishes into the water to make a bain marie and bake until just set in the middle and slightly puffed out, about 30 to 35 minutes. Remove the baking pan from the oven and remove the clafoutis from the baking pan. Sprinkle some confectioners' sugar on the clafoutis and serve warm. (There is a photo of this dessert for your reference.)

Lemon Cream Tartes

MAKES 6 INDIVIDUAL TARTS

Remember the Bill Cosby routine about his rationalizing giving cake to the kids for breakfast because it contains things that are "good for you," like milk and eggs? It's a funny thing about lemon that the taste of it makes you think it's good for you. Well, it does contain vitamin C and all that! Right?

INGREDIENTS FOR THE PASTRY

2 sticks (1 cup) unsalted butter

1 cup sugar

¼ teaspoon salt

3 large eggs

3 ½ cups all-purpose flour

INGREDIENTS FOR THE LEMON CREAM

⅓ cup fresh lemon juice

3 eggs

2 egg yolks

¾ cup sugar

¼ teaspoon salt

1 stick unsalted butter (½ cup), cut into cubes

Mandarin orange segments, for garnish
Candied orange peel (or your choice of candied
    citrus), for garnish

EQUIPMENT

Stand mixer

Six 4 ½- to 5-inch-diameter tart pans with
    removable bases

Thin offset spatula

Candy thermometer

Method for the pastry

Using a stand mixer with the paddle attachment, mix together the butter, sugar, and salt until the mixture is smooth. Add 1 egg at a time, beating after each addition. Add all the flour at once and mix on low speed until all the flour has been incorporated. Cover the dough and refrigerate it for a couple of hours.

Preheat the oven to 375°F.

Divide the dough into 6 portions. Work with one portion at a time, keeping the rest covered with plastic wrap. For each tart, roll a portion of dough on a floured surface into a circle about 1 inch larger in diameter than the tart pan. Ease the dough into the pans and trim the edges flush with the top edge of the pans. Prick holes in the bottom of the pastry with a fork (to aerate so as to keep the dough from bubbling up). Set the pans on a large baking sheet and bake until golden brown, about 15 to 20 minutes. Let cool 10 minutes in the pans, then press the removable bases up from the bottom to free the tart shells from the sides and use a thin offset spatula to slide the shells off the bases onto a cooling rack.

Method for the lemon cream filling

Fill a medium saucepan with a couple of inches of water and bring to a simmer. In a small stainless steel bowl that will fit comfortably in the saucepan without touching the water (a double boiler), combine the lemon juice, eggs, egg yolks, sugar, and salt. Fit the bowl over the pot of simmering water and whisk the ingredients together, stirring frequently, until the lemon cream mixture thickens and a candy thermometer registers 160°F, about 12 minutes.

Remove from the heat and allow the temperature to drop to 140°F, stirring occasionally while the lemon cream is cooling. Whisk in the butter a little at a time, until smooth.

Spoon the lemon cream into the prepared pastry shells and chill for about an hour to allow the custard to set. Garnish with orange segments and candied peel just before service.

Zucchini and Orange Marmalade Tea Cakes

MAKES 24 TEA CAKES

I'm no different from any other Englishman in that tea has a very special meaning for me. If you have my first book, you may have read about the time I took my mother to afternoon tea at Harrods, a milestone for me as a young man. I also have very stringent guidelines about how I like my tea, as anyone who has ever worked for or with me—or even brought me tea in a restaurant—will attest. And I have an incurable sweet tooth. So, here's a fine combination: tea *and* cake. What could be better? (No need to answer—it was clearly a rhetorical question!)

INGREDIENTS FOR THE CARAMELIZED CITRUS FRUIT

2 tablespoons butter

1 tablespoon granulated sugar

1 orange, peel left on and cut into six ¼-inch-thick slices (minus the ends)

48 tiny fresh mint leaves

INGREDIENTS FOR THE ICING

1½ sticks (¾ cup) butter

1½ teaspoons orange marmalade

6 cups confectioners' sugar

¾ to 1 cup warmed orange juice (not from concentrate)

INGREDIENTS FOR THE CAKE

3 cups flour (preferably cake flour), sifted to aerate

1½ teaspoons baking soda

1½ teaspoons baking powder

½ teaspoon ground cinnamon

¼ teaspoon ground cloves

¼ teaspoon ground nutmeg

¼ teaspoon ground allspice

¼ teaspoon ground ginger

¼ teaspoon salt

1½ cups granulated sugar

¾ cup packed dark brown sugar

¾ cup canola oil

1½ sticks (¾ cup) butter, melted

3 eggs, beaten lightly

2 zucchini, peeled and chopped in a food processor (1½ cups chopped zucchini)

1 large carrot, peeled and chopped in a food processor (¾ cup chopped carrot)

¾ cup golden raisins

1 tablespoon ground walnuts

Method for the caramelized citrus fruit

In a medium skillet, melt the butter over low heat. Distribute 6 pinches of sugar in the pan, spaced so that you can place an orange slice directly over each pinch. Lay the orange slices over the sugar and cook until they begin to caramelize, about 4 minutes per side, leaving undisturbed for the first couple of minutes to let the sugar integrate into the slices. Use a slotted spatula to remove the orange slices to a utility platter to cool. Cut each slice into 4 wedges.

Method for the cake

Preheat the oven to 375°F. Butter and flour a 9×13×2-inch cake pan and line it with parchment paper.

Into a large mixing bowl, sift together the flour, baking soda, baking powder, cinnamon, cloves, nutmeg, allspice, ginger, and salt.

In a separate large mixing bowl, combine the granulated sugar, brown sugar, oil, melted butter, and eggs and beat with a mixer until the mixture begins to fluff up. Fold in the zucchini, carrot, raisins, and walnuts. Stir in the dry ingredients until just moistened.

Spread the mixture in the pan and bake until a toothpick inserted in the center of the cake comes out clean but moist, about 30 minutes. Let cool in the pan. Set a couple of wire racks over wax paper. When the cake is completely cool, cut it into 24 squares as follows: Cut the cake into thirds crosswise, then in half lengthwise, then cut each of the six squares into quarters. Place the cake squares on the wire racks (set over wax paper to keep the mess down).

Method for the icing

In a medium saucepan over low heat, melt the butter and stir in the orange marmalade. Gradually sift in the confectioners' sugar, stirring after each addition to integrate the sugar and butter. Stir in the warmed orange juice a little at a time, just until the mixture reaches the consistency of a glaze. Pour the glaze over each tea cake to coat thoroughly and immediately top with an orange wedge, with a tiny mint leaf on each side.

Candy Cane Shortbread in a Bento Christmas Box

MAKES ABOUT 6 DOZEN SHORTBREAD SQUARES

Bento boxes originated in Japan in the twelfth century and were made of lacquerware, a material that predated plastic as a lightweight, easily cleanable dinner- and serveware that was used as a less breakable alternative to porcelain and ceramics. On occasion I have used bento boxes as an elegant way to serve sushi. In recent years the term "bento box" has been adopted by lunchbox manufacturers for plastic or insulated lunch containers with divided compartments. You can still get real lacquerware today, although it can be somewhat expensive, especially because it is typically hand painted. If you wish to give cookies as a gift in a reusable box, Target offers a variety of lacquer boxes in a wide range of sizes and prices. Alternatively you can bake a batch of the shortbread cookies that can then be arranged and stored in a large bento box and brought right to the table for service with after-dinner tea. As another idea, perhaps for gift giving, consider tea boxes made of renewable bamboo grown without fertilizers or pesticides. They have compartments to hold about a dozen shortbread cookies, are easily wiped clean, and can later be used to store tea bags. They cost only about $10 to $20 and are available at Crate and Barrel.

INGREDIENTS FOR THE CANDY CANE SHORTBREAD

1 cup plus 2 tablespoons unsalted butter, very soft, plus some to butter the baking dish

1¾ cups plus 2 tablespoons all-purpose flour

½ cup plus 2 tablespoons cornstarch

½ teaspoon salt

⅓ cup granulated sugar

¼ cup superfine sugar, for topping

6 small candy canes, crushed

EQUIPMENT

7×11-inch clear glass baking dish (glass is necessary in order to view the browning process)

Method

Preheat the oven to 325°F and butter a 7×11-inch glass baking dish.

Sift the flour and cornstarch together in a bowl.

Place the butter in a mixing bowl. (The butter must be very soft—the consistency of mayonnaise or whipped cream.) Add the salt to the butter and mix well, then add the granulated sugar to the butter and mix just until combined. Add the flour mixture and mix just until a smooth dough forms.

Pat the dough evenly into the buttered baking dish. The dough should be no more than ⅔ inch deep. Bake until the top and bottom are lightly browned, about 30 minutes. The middle of the shortbread should remain light.

Place the baking dish on a wire rack. Sprinkle the shortbread with the superfine sugar and crushed candy cane, and when the shortbread has cooled a bit but is still warm to the touch, use a long knife to cut the shortbread into 1-inch squares—make 7 cuts lengthwise and 11 cuts across. Cool the squares thoroughly before removing them from the baking dish.

Presentation

Fill a bento box or boxes with shortbread cookies.

Nut Bread Pudding with Date Compote and Cardamom Ice Cream

SERVES 6 TO 8

Bread pudding originated as a way to use up dry bread and pastry, giving it a second life as a custard by infusing it with milk and eggs. There are hundreds of possible versions, depending on what kind of bread and/or pastry you use, combined with fruits, currants, jams, and jellies. The exotic flavor of cardamom lends itself to both sweet (as in this ice cream) and savory uses in cooking.

The timeline here goes through all the steps from start to finish, but for your own sanity you may wish to make the cardamom ice cream in advance and store it in the freezer. The bread pudding can be served warm, at room temperature, or chilled. The date compote is usually served slightly warm as a counterpoint to the ice cream.

As with most of my recipes contained in this book, each component recipe can stand on its own. If made by itself, the cardamom ice cream takes about 1 hour and 20 minutes, including 30 minutes of downtime for chilling and 25 minutes for the ice cream maker to do the work for you. The bread pudding also takes about 1 hour and 20 minutes, 1 hour of which is baking time, when you can attend to other things. The compote takes only about 14 minutes. Also, if you feel like making only the ice cream or only the bread pudding, go for it! These treats easily stand on their own.

INGREDIENTS FOR THE NUT BREAD PUDDING

6 slices oat-hazelnut bread (such as Arnold or Freihofer's), cut into ½-inch cubes to yield 1½ cups

1 pound cake (such as Entenmann's), cut into ½-inch cubes to yield 1½ cups

1 cup golden raisins

1 cup dried apricots, cut into ¼-inch pieces

4 large eggs

¾ cup sugar

2 cups whole milk

1 cup heavy cream

1½ teaspoons vanilla extract or 2 whole vanilla beans

½ teaspoon salt

One 6-ounce jar mint jelly

INGREDIENTS FOR THE CARDAMOM ICE CREAM

1 tablespoon cardamom pods

1 cup heavy cream

1 cup whole milk

2 egg yolks

½ cup sugar

2 tablespoons vanilla extract

INGREDIENTS FOR THE DATE COMPOTE

½ stick (4 tablespoons) butter

1 cup dates (about 6 ounces), cut into ½-inch pieces

½ cup raisins

1 cup whiskey (such as bourbon)

1 cup apple juice

½ teaspoon allspice

2 tablespoons crushed walnuts

EQUIPMENT

Ice cream maker

Candy thermometer

Method for the bread pudding

Preheat the oven to 325°F. Grease a 1½- to 2-quart glass baking dish, eight 6-ounce individual baking dishes, or six 8-ounce individual baking dishes.

Combine the bread and cake in a large mixing bowl. Fold in the golden raisins and dried apricots.

In a medium bowl, mix the eggs, sugar, milk, cream, vanilla, and salt. Strain this mixture through a conical strainer over the bread mixture and allow to soak together until the baked goods are infused, about 10 minutes. (Meanwhile, grind the cardamom pods, below.)

Spread the pudding mixture into the large baking dish or carefully spoon it into the individual baking dishes.

Prepare a bain marie (water bath) by placing the baking dish or dishes into a larger pan, placing the larger pan into the oven, and pouring enough hot water into the outer dish to go halfway up the side of the baking dish(es) without splashing any into the custard. Bake until the pudding firms up and puffs up and a toothpick inserted in the center comes out clean, about 1 hour. (Meanwhile, begin tempering the cream for the ice cream, below.)

TIMELINE

Ingredient prep:

Cut bread and cake for
    bread pudding .... 3 minutes
Cut apricots and dates for compote .... 4 minutes
Measure ingredients .... 5 minutes
**Subtotal estimated ingredient
    prep time .... 12 minutes**

Grease baking dishes and add bread ..... 2 minutes
Mix eggs, sugar, and milk for bread
    pudding, strain, and pour over
    baked goods .... 5 minutes
Saturation time for custard (10 minutes)
    Overlaps with:
    Grind the cardamom pods and
        sift (5 minutes)
    Begin warming the cream, milk, and
        cardamom for ice cream (5 minutes)
    Overlaps with:
    Beat egg yolk, sugar, and vanilla for
        ice cream (5 minutes) .... 10 minutes
    Prepare bain marie and place
        bread pudding in oven .... 5 minutes
Baking time for bread pudding (60 minutes)
    Overlaps with:
    Temper egg mixture for ice cream
        and cook until thickened (5 minutes)
    Cooling and chilling time for ice cream
        ingredients (30 minutes)
    Process ice cream in ice cream maker
        (25 minutes) and transfer to
        freezer (5 minutes) .... 60 minutes
Allow bread pudding to rest (15 minutes)
    Overlaps with:
    Prepare date compote
        (10 minutes) .... 15 minutes
**Subtotal estimated active
    cooking time .... 97 minutes**

Assembly .... 5 minutes

***Estimated time,
start to finish .... 1 hour and 54 minutes***

Remove the bread pudding from the oven and from the water bath and let rest for 15 minutes. Spread the mint jelly over the top of the pudding. (The jelly can be slightly thinned with a little warm water if you have difficulty spreading it.)

Method for the cardamom ice cream

Grind the cardamom pods in a coffee grinder dedicated to grinding spices and either pick out the pods or sift through a sieve into a small bowl to remove the chaff.

Combine the cream and milk in a medium, heavy-bottomed saucepan over low heat. Stir in the cardamom powder and heat to a simmer (just below boiling). The mixture needs to reach 160°F as measured with a candy thermometer.

In a separate small bowl, beat the egg yolks, sugar, and vanilla until the mixture is completely smooth and light yellow, preferably with an electric mixer.

Temper the ice cream mixture by gradually adding about a quarter of the warmed cream mixture to the egg mixture, stirring constantly to combine. Then gradually add the tempered egg mixture to the rest of the cream, stirring constantly. (This technique, called a liaison, ensures that you don't end up with scrambled eggs.) Continue to cook over low heat until the mixture coats the back of a spoon. Cool to room temperature, then chill in the refrigerator until cold or speed chill for about 30 minutes in the freezer without allowing it to actually freeze.

Process the mixture in an ice cream maker until it is frozen to the consistency of ice cream, about 25 minutes. Serve immediately or store in the freezer until needed.

Method for the date compote

Melt the butter in a small skillet over low heat. Add the dates and raisins, raise the heat to medium-low, and sauté for 3 to 4 minutes. Add the whiskey, increase the heat to medium, and cook until most of the alcohol has evaporated. Add the apple juice, allspice, and walnuts and increase the heat a little to allow the mixture to reduce and thicken and the flavors to integrate, about 5 minutes, but watch it carefully so that it doesn't burn.

Presentation

Serve the bread pudding warm, at room temperature, or chilled. Top with warm date compote and serve with scoops of cardamom ice cream.

CODA

There is a very human and understandable tendency to want to put things into categories, to define people and subjects within easily recognizable parameters. I'm often asked to define my cuisine, by training, by region, by preference for certain methods or ingredients. I generally don't do a very good job of it because that's not the way I think about food. Every time you say, "My cuisine is this or that," you shut yourself off from everything that does not fall under the heading of "this or that." It's like writing an encyclopedia entry on yourself and then putting the book away on a shelf, or worse, like writing your culinary epitaph: *HE ALWAYS DID IT THIS WAY* (REST IN PEACE).

I know I have a cooking style that's unique to me, just as I have a unique fingerprint and personality. Unlike a fingerprint, though, your personality can evolve and change over time, can react to new stimuli, ideas, and influences. When I'm designing dishes, I like to react to the ingredients in front of me and bring my style to them, not my preconceived notions. And every time I learn something new, I like to think that my style changes to accommodate it, not the other way around.

Don't limit yourself. Don't tell yourself or anybody else that you're a good cook or a bad cook or that you can't cook. In the first instance, you may be, but you can always be better; in the second, try again—cooking is a craft you can learn, not a magical inborn gift. And don't tell me you can't cook. If you're a human being, you get hungry, and if you get hungry, cook. Don't always make somebody else do it for you. Expressing yourself with food is as natural an impulse as walking, talking, and breathing.

I have said it before and I will say it again: Cook!

ACKNOWLEDGMENTS

Over the years I have purchased and been given many cookbooks as Christmas and birthday presents, and I am always intrigued by the acknowledgments.

Thanks are often given to the author's family and to the various people who have helped the author's dream become a reality. However, I'm going to give you what I believe is the reality through my eyes and from my heart.

Just as no chef can run a restaurant on his own, the production of this book would not have been possible without the thousands of e-mails, phone calls, Facebook messages, and Twitter followers who over the years have taken time out of their busy lives and schedules to send me words of encouragement and ask questions about my life and cooking experiences. This book was born because of you all, and I thank you dearly.

Hopefully this book will answer many of those questions and give you the encouragement to try new foods and cooking techniques.

Food is an international language that crosses all barriers. I encourage you to continue to learn, to invite friends and family over, and to make cooking a family affair.

Special thanks go to Randall Williams, my business partner and friend. Brian and I would like to extend our thanks to Virginia O'Reilly for her tirelessly creative efforts on this book, and to our wonderful families. And thanks to Cassie Jones, a true professional; Ben Fink, who did an incomparable job on the photography; and chef David Britton, for helping to cook the food for the photo shoot.

Thanks also to the Restaurant School at Walnut Hill College in Philadelphia, for allowing us to invade its beautiful campus and subject the students to an experience of a lifetime. I hope they will never forget it. To Jocelyn Wood, Barbara Portale, Kyle Andrich, Frank Cusack, James Carnes, Jordan Torres, Megan McCoy, Adam Straga, Nick Waldron, and all the wonderful faculty and instructors: Please continue to enlighten and teach the young chefs of the future.

Thank you, thank you, thank you!

INDEX

Note: Recipes in **boldtype** have photos in color inserts.

Marinara sauce, preparing, 42–43

Mascarpone-Chive Dumplings and Candied Walnuts with Champagne Vinaigrette, Salad of Tender Greens with, 30–31

Mashed Potatoes, 140

Mashed Potatoes, Sour Cream, with Tomato Caper Chutney, 222

Meat. *See* Beef; Lamb; Pork; Veal; Venison

Meatballs, Swedish, in a Bag, 84–85

Meat mallets, 21

Melon and Shrimp Gazpacho, 98–99

Mesquite Beef Medallions with Tomato Demi-glace over Cheddar Grits, 51–53

Mint and Champagne Peach Soup, 28

Mirepoix, 40

Mise en place

  description of, 6–9

  examples of, 8–9

  rules for, 8

Mixing bowls, 20

Mornay Sauce, 122

Mornay Sauce, Broccoli with, 123

Mortar and pestle, 21

Mozzarella

  Fresh, Plum Tomato, Basil, and Shaved Prosciutto, Pizza-style Crepes with, 241–42

  Windy City Stovetop Pizza, 244–45

Mushrooms

  Chicken Marsala with Garlic-Scented Red Bliss Potato Salad, 134–35

  Chicken Pot Pie, 238–39

  Cremini, and Golden Raisins, Porcini-Dusted Pork Chops with, over Horseradish-Scented Potatoes, 150–52

  Lamb Tenderloin over Rice with Sauce Robért, 54–55

  Pineapple and Artichoke Pasta with Pine Nuts, 232–33

  Porcini, with Potato Gnocchi, Truffle Olive Oil, and Mushroom Sauce, 208–9

  Portobello, and Ruby Port Reduction, Tuna with, over Citrus Rice, 174–75

  Sprouts, Squash, and 'Shrooms with White Wine and Hoisin Sauce, 230–31

  Veal Blanquette, 104–5

Mussel(s)

  Soup, Saffron, 100–101

  Unbeatable Bouillabaisse, 102–3

Mustard

  Dijon, Sauce, Brussels Sprouts with, 220

  stone-ground, cooking with, 13

N

Noodles

  Chicken Stroganoff with Fried Heirloom Tomatoes, 214–15

Nut(s)

  Almond Rochers, 258–59

  Bread Pudding with Date Compote and Cardamom Ice Cream, 274–76

  Pecan Bourbon Pralines, 263

  Pine, Pineapple and Artichoke Pasta with, 232–33

  Salad of Tender Greens with Mascarpone-Chive Dumplings and Candied Walnuts with Champagne Vinaigrette, 30–31

  Walnut Wontons with Goat Cheese over Apples, 81–83

O

Ocean Perch over Herbed Couscous with Baby Bok Choy and Lemon Horseradish Sauce, 179–81

Oils

  cooking oils, 15

  Curry, 168–69

  Herb-Lemon, 88

Olive oil, about, 15

Olive(s)

  Allium Tossed Salad, 226–27

  Cauliflower Huevos Salad, 219

  and Sun-dried Tomato–Stuffed Black Bass over Braised Potatoes with Tomato Broth, 196–97

  Veal Scaloppine and Lemon Confit over Warm Salade Niçoise with Potato Puree, 130–31

Onion(s)

  Allium Tossed Salad, 226–27

  Beef Carbonnade, 106–7

  Caramelized, –Potato Puree, Honey-Roasted Figs, and Port Wine Sauce, Veal Chops with, 127–29

  Chicken Pot Pie, 238–39

  cooking with, 16

grinding spices, 16
preparing at home, 41
toasting spices, 16
Spinach
Veal Saltimbocca, 44–45
Spirits, cooking with, 17
Squash
Pan-Seared Salmon and Lemon Confit over Sage Ratatouille, 182–84
Sprouts, and 'Shrooms with White Wine and Hoisin Sauce, 230–31
Zucchini and Orange Marmalade Tea Cakes, 270–71
Zucchini and Red Onion Quiche, 248–51
Starters. *See* Appetizers
Steaming, description of, 38
Stews
Beef Carbonnade, 106–7
Duck Confit with Three-Bean Cassoulet, 32–35
foundation ingredients, 86
freezing, 22
making in advance, 42
preparing, 86–87
Unbeatable Bouillabaisse, 102–3
Veal Blanquette, 104–5
Stocks
buying, 41
freezing, 22
preparing, 22, 42
Strainers, 20
Sugars and sweeteners, 18–19
Swedish Meatballs in a Bag, 84–85
Sweet Potato(es)
Cakes and Black Cherry Chutney, Roasted Chicken Thighs with, 154–55
Gnocchi, Roasted Cornish Game Hen with, 144–47
Mashed Potatoes, 140
Swiss cheese
Cheese Fritters with Sauce Tomate, 78–79
Mornay Sauce, 122
Veal Saltimbocca, 44–45

T
Tarts
Artichoke, Savory, Citrus-Braised Chicken Breast with Sweet Roasted Garlic and, 136–39

Lemon Cream Tartes, 268–69
Savory Shrimp and Celery Cream, with Lime Aioli, 62–65
Zucchini and Red Onion Quiche, 248–51
Tequila, Red, Green, and Yellow Bell Peppers, and Sautéed Shrimp, Linguine Serrano with, 206–7
Thickeners, 17–18
Thyme
growing, 16
-Roasted Pork Chops with White Wine Reduction, Crisp BBQ Wontons, and Roasted Root Vegetables, 156–59
-Roasted Sea Bass with Shrimp Fritters, Sweet Corn, and Roasted Garlic Essence, 185–87
Tomato(es)
Allium Tossed Salad, 226–27
Asiago-Stuffed Chicken Cacciatore, 67–69
Caper Chutney, 222
Demi-glace, Mesquite Beef Medallions with, over Cheddar Grits, 51–53
Heirloom, Fried, Chicken Stroganoff with, 214–15
marinara sauce, preparing, 42–43
Plum, Fresh Mozzarella, Basil, and Shaved Prosciutto, Pizza-style Crepes with, 241–42
Plum, Rock Shrimp Sauce, Braised Greens, and Chive Essence, Herb-Steamed Halibut Fillet with, 176–78
Relish and Saffron Broth, Pan-Seared Scallops with, 194–95
Sauce Tomate, 78
Sun-dried, and Olive–Stuffed Black Bass over Braised Potatoes with Tomato Broth, 196–97
Sun-dried, Pesto–Crusted Chicken Breast over Creamy Polenta with Cave-Aged Cheddar and Pineapple-Mango Demi-glace, 142–43
Tortillas
Lobster Brie Quesadilla, 77
Tuna
with Portobello Mushrooms and Ruby Port Reduction over Citrus Rice, 174–75
Seared, with Hummus on Crostini, 75